Christ the Way, the Truth, and the Life

Christ the Way, the Truth, and the Life

John Brown of Wamphray

Soli Deo Gloria Publications
. . . for instruction in righteousness . . .

Christ the Way, the Truth, and the Life
© 2016 by Soli Deo Gloria

Soli Deo Gloria Publications
An imprint of Reformation Heritage Books
2965 Leonard St. NE
Grand Rapids, MI 49525
616-977-0889 / Fax 616-285-3246
orders@heritagebooks.org
www.heritagebooks.org

Printed in the United States of America
16 17 18 19 20 21/10 9 8 7 6 5 4 3 2 1

Library of Congress Cataloging-in-Publication Data

Names: Brown, John, 1610?-1679, author.
Title: Christ the way, the truth, and the life / John Brown of Wamphray.
Description: Grand Rapids, Michigan : Soli Deo Gloria Publications, 2016.
Identifiers: LCCN 2016021327 (print) | LCCN 2016021935 (ebook) | ISBN
    9781601784599 (hardcover : alk. paper) | ISBN 9781601784605 (epub)
Subjects: LCSH: Justification (Christian theology) | Sanctification—
    Christianity. | Bible. John, XIV, 6—Criticism, interpretation, etc. |
    Reformed Church—Doctrines.
Classification: LCC BT764.3 .B76 2016 (print) | LCC BT764.3 (ebook) |
    DDC 234/.7–dc23
LC record available at https://lccn.loc.gov/2016021327

For additional Reformed literature, both new and used, request a free book list from Reformation Heritage Books at the above address.

CONTENTS

Publisher's Preface

John Brown of Wamphray was born in Kirkcudbright-shire in the south of Scotland, probably around the years 1609 or 1610.[1] In 1630, he graduated with an MA from Edinburgh. His mother was a friend of Samuel Rutherford (1600–1661), who served as the minister of Anwoth, Kirkcud-brightshire, from 1627 until his deprivation in 1636. In 1637, Rutherford wrote to Jean (or Jane) Brown about her son, "I had always (as I said often to you) a great love to dear Mr. John Brown, because I thought I saw Christ in him more than in his brethren."[2] Some time afterward, Brown was ordained as a

---

1. Sources on John Brown's life are few. See Thomas Lockerby, *A Sketch of the Life of the Rev. John Brown, Sometime Minister of the Gospel in Wamphray* (Edinburgh: Thornton & Collie, 1839); Ian B. Doyle, "John Brown of Wamphray: A Study of His Life, Work, and Thought" (PhD diss., University of Edinburgh, 1956). Some biographical information on Brown may also be found in William Crookshank, *The History of the State and Sufferings of the Church of Scotland from the Restoration to the Revolution*, 2 vols. (Paisley: George Caldwell, 1789); Samuel Rutherford, *Letters of Samuel Rutherford* (London: Oliphants, [1904]); William Steven, *The History of the Scottish Church, Rotterdam* (Edinburgh: Waugh and Innes, 1833); Robert Wodrow, *History of the Sufferings of the Church of Scotland from the Restoration to the Revolution*, 4 vols. (Glasgow: Blackie & Son, 1835); Hew Scott, *Fasti Ecclesiae Scoticanae: The Succession of Ministers in the Church of Scotland from the Reformation* (Edinburgh: Oliver and Boyd, 1917), 2:224–25. This preface is adapted from Joel R. Beeke, "John Calvin and John Brown of Wamphray on Justification," in *Reformed Orthodoxy in Scotland: Essays on Scottish Theology, 1560–1775*, ed. Aaron C. Denlinger (London: Bloomsbury T&T Clark, 2015), chapter 11.
2. Rutherford, *Letters*, 159.

minister of the Church of Scotland and settled in Wamphray, Dumfriesshire—a village of perhaps a few hundred people near the River Annan.

During Brown's ministry there, Scotland and England entered the Solemn League and Covenant (1643) to unify the kingdoms in Reformed religion. Brown would later write, "These lands did thus enter into covenant with the great God of heaven and earth."[3] The Westminster Assembly put hands and feet on this pact by writing the Directory for the Public Worship of God, the Confession of Faith, and the Larger and Shorter Catechisms.

After the restoration of Charles II to the monarchy, Scottish Covenanters began to suffer for insisting that Britain hold to the Directory, Confession, and Catechisms to which its authorities had bound themselves by covenant.[4] On November 6, 1662, Brown was imprisoned in the Tolbooth for calling some ministers "perjured knaves and villains" because they acknowledged the authority of Andrew Fairfoul, just installed as the first archbishop of Glasgow. William Crookshank writes, "Great were the hardships he underwent in prison, for he was denied even the necessaries of life," even to the point that "he was brought almost to the gates of death."[5] On December 11, the authorities granted Brown's petition for release, but only on condition of banishment from Scotland.

Brown arrived in the Netherlands on March 12, 1663, where he spent the rest of his life. He assisted the minister of the Scottish church in Rotterdam and devoted himself to theological and historical writing for the Covenanters' cause.

---

3. John Brown, *An Apologetical Relation of the Particular Sufferings of the Faithful Ministers and Professours of the Church of Scotland, Since August. 1660* (n.p.: 1665), 63.
4. Brown, *Apologetical Relation*, 74.
5. Crookshank, *History*, 1:159.

His work evidently irritated the Scottish authorities, for in 1676 King Charles II wrote to the States-General of the United Netherlands requesting that they expel him from their territories. Brown, however, remained.

Brown was counted a blessing by many Reformed Christians among both Scots and Dutch. One of his fellow Scottish exiles in Rotterdam, Robert MacWard, said that his sermons had a "pure gospel texture, breathing nothing but faith in Christ and communion with him."[6] He was highly respected by Dutch Further Reformation divines such as Wilhelmus à Brakel and Jacobus Koelman.[7] His writings supported the Covenanter view of church and state,[8] defended the Puritan view of the Sabbath and the moral law, opposed the teachings of the Quakers and Richard Baxter, and promoted experiential, Christ-centered Christianity. Copies of his defense of the Sabbath were in the New England library of Thomas Prince (1687–1758), minister of the Old South Church in Boston, and in the library of Yale in 1808.[9] The work was also cited by the eccentric English theological writer John Hutchinson (1674–1737)[10] and Thomas Bell (1733–1802), minister in Glasgow, in a polemic against "popery."[11]

One of Brown's last public acts was the ordination of Richard Cameron in 1679, who perished back in Scotland a year

6. Lockerby, *Sketch of the Life of the Rev. John Brown*, 177.

7. Steven, *History of the Scottish Church, Rotterdam*, 72.

8. Iain B. Doyle, "The Doctrine of the Church in the Later Covenanting Period," in *Reformation and Revolution*, ed. Duncan Shaw (Edinburgh: St. Andrews Press, 1967), 212–36.

9. *Catalogue of the Library of Rev. Thomas Prince* (Boston: Crocker and Brewster, 1846), 8; *Catalogue of Books in the Library of Yale-College, New-Haven* (New Haven: Oliver Steele, 1808), 52.

10. J[ohn] H[utchinson], *The Covenant in the Cherubim* (London: J. Hodges, 1749), 7:9.

11. Thomas Bell, *The Standard of the Spirit Lifted Up against the Enemy Coming in Like a Flood* (Glasgow: William Smith, 1780), 210.

later. Brown died in September 1679. His will indicated that one hundred guilders from the sale of his books should be donated to the church for the help of the poor.[12] Robert Wodrow (1679–1734) said in retrospect that Brown was "a man of very great learning, warm zeal, and remarkable piety."[13]

John Brown of Wamphray is to be distinguished from several other theological authors named John Brown, including:

- John Brown of Priesthill (c. 1627–1685), a Covenanter victim who had a remarkable ministry among children.

- John Brown of Haddington (1722–1787), associate synod minister and theological writer, best known for his *The Self-Interpreting Bible* and *A Dictionary of the Holy Bible*, but also the able author of twenty-seven additional works.[14]

- John Brown of Whitburn (1754–1832), oldest son of John Brown of Haddington and a well-known devotional author of several books[15] and editor of the *Select Remains* of his father.

---

12. Lockerby, *Sketch of the Life of the Rev. John Brown*, 181.

13. Wodrow, *History*, 1:304.

14. John Brown of Haddington wrote *An Essay towards an Easy… Explication of the Assembly's Shorter Catechism*; *A Compendious View of Natural and Revealed Religion*; *A Compendious History of the British Churches in England, Scotland, Ireland, and America*; *A Concordance to the Holy Scriptures*; *A Harmony of Scripture Prophecies, and History of Their Fulfilment*; *The Christian, the Student, and Pastor*; *Practical Piety Exemplified*; *Sacred Tropology*; *The Christian Journal, or Common Incidents, Spiritual Instructors*; *Six Letters on Gospel Preaching*; *Ten Letters on the Exemplary Behaviour of Ministers*; *The Young Christian, or the Pleasantness of Early Piety*; and two catechisms for children (*Big Brown* and *Little Brown*).

15. John Brown of Whitburn wrote *Gospel Truth*; *Memoirs of James Hervey*; *Memoir of Thomas Bradbury*; *Religious Letters*; *Christian Experience*; *Evangelical Beauties of Hugh Binning*; *Evangelical Beauties of Archbishop of Leighton*; and *Memorials of the Nonconformist Ministers of the Seventeenth Century*.

- John Brown of Edinburgh (1784–1858), son of John Brown of Whitburn and grandson of John Brown of Haddington, minister in the United Presbyterian Church, Professor of Exegetical Theology, and well-known author of expository works on Psalm 18, Isaiah 53, John 17, Romans, 1 Corinthians 15, Galatians, Hebrews, 1 Peter, 2 Peter 1, and the Lord's Prayer, plus other books.[16]

- John Brown of Bedford (1830–1906), an English Congregationalist who pastored the Bunyan Church in Bedford for the last forty years of his active ministry and authored several works,[17] as well as being editor of the works of John Bunyan.

Though John Brown of Wamphray is little known today, he held a prominent place in Scottish theology. James Walker wrote, "Brown of Wamphray was, without doubt, the most important theologian" in Scotland at the time.[18] John Macleod considered Brown to be perhaps "our greatest divine between Rutherford and Halyburton," that is, in the latter part of seventeenth-century Scotland.[19]

Brown's blending of doctrinal truth and Christ-centered piety is most clearly displayed in his *Christ the Way, the Truth, and the Life.* First published in Rotterdam in 1677, this experiential

---

16. John Brown of Edinburgh wrote *Exposition of the Discourses and Sayings of Our Lord; The Christian Pastor's Manual; Discourses Suited to the Administration of the Lord's Supper; Christian Hope; The Mourner's Friend; Religion and the Means of Its Attainment;* and *Forgetfulness of God.*

17. John Brown of Bedford wrote *John Bunyan, His Life, Times, and Work; The Pilgrim Fathers of New England;* and *Puritan Preaching in England; Eras of Nonconformity.*

18. James Walker, *Theology and Theologians of Scotland, Chiefly of the Seventeenth and Eighteenth Centuries,* 2nd rev. ed. (Edinburgh: T&T Clark, 1888), 107.

19. John Macleod, *Scottish Theology in Relation to Church History since the Reformation* (1946; repr., Edinburgh: Banner of Truth Trust, 1974), 148.

series of sermons on John 14:6 has been reprinted several times in Edinburgh from 1740 to 1839. The original subtitle is: *A Short Discourse, Pointing Forth the Way of Making Use of Christ for Justification, and Especially and More Particularly for Sanctification in All Its Parts, From John xiv. verse 6. Wherein Several Cases of Conscience Are Briefly Answered, Chiefly Touching Sanctification.* This volume richly deserves reprinting again. It is an insightful spiritual advisory on living the Christian life as it ought to be lived—centering on Christ, mortifying sin, loving the souls of others, and glorifying God. Here is biblical, Reformed, Puritan spirituality at its best.

Would you learn the art of continually fleeing by faith to Christ for your justification and sanctification? Read and reread this precious volume, filled with experiential truth about how to go to Christ continually for every spiritual need. Use it as a devotional gem and pray for the Holy Spirit to grant you a growing, daily making use of Christ by faith.

—Joel R. Beeke

Dedication

To the right honorable and religious lady, the Lady Strathnaver.

Madam,

Jesus Christ Himself, being the chief cornerstone in whom all the building [is] fitly framed together, grows to a holy temple in the Lord. As it ought to be the principal concern of all who have not [sat] down on this side of Jordan to satisfy their souls (once created for and in their own nature requiring in order to satisfaction, spiritual, immortal, and incorruptible substance) with husks prepared for beasts, to be built in and on this cornerstone for a habitation of God through the Spirit—so it ought to be the main design and work of such as would be approve[d] of God as faithful laborers and coworkers with God to be following the example of him who determined not to know anything among those he wrote to save Jesus Christ and Him crucified. Oh! This noble, heart-ravishing, soul-satisfying, mysterious theme, Jesus Christ crucified, the short compend[ium] of that incontrovertibly great mystery of godliness—God manifest in the flesh, justified in the Spirit, seen of angels, preached to the Gentiles, believed on in the world, received up into glory, in which are things the angels desire to look to or with vehement desire bend, as it were, their necks and bow down their heads to look and peep into (as the word used [in] 1 Peter 1:12 imports)—is a subject for angelical heads to pry into [and] for the most indefatigable and industrious spirits to be occupied about. The searching into and studying of this one truth, in reference to a closing with it as our life, is an infallible mark of a soul divinely enlightened and endued with spiritual and heavenly wisdom. For though it be to the Jews a stumbling block and to the Greeks foolishness, yet to them who are called it is Christ the power of God and the wisdom of God because the foolishness of God is wiser than men, and the weakness of God is stronger than men. Oh what depths of the manifold wisdom of God are there in this mystery! The more it is preached, known, and believed aright, the more it is understood to be beyond understanding and to be what it is—a mystery. Did ever any preacher or believer get a broad look of this boundless ocean in which infinite wisdom; love that passes all understanding; grace without all dimensions; justice that is admirable and tremendous; and God in His glorious properties, condescensions, high and noble designs, and in all His perfections and virtues flow over all banks? Or were they ever admitted to a prospect hereof in the face of Jesus Christ and were not made to cry out, "Oh the depth and height, the breadth and length! Oh the inconceivable and incomprehensible boundlessness of all infinitely transcendent perfections!"? Did ever any with serious diligence, as knowing their life lay in it, study this mysterious theme and were not in full conviction of soul, made to say, the more they promoved[1] in this study and the more they descended in their divings into this depth or soared upward in their mounting speculations in this height, [that] they found it the more an unsearchable mystery? The study of other themes (which, alas, many who think it below them to be happy are too much occupied in), when it has wasted the spirits, wearied the mind, worn the body, and rarified the brain to the next degree

---

1. *Promoved*: to move forward.

to a distraction, what satisfaction can it give as to what is attained or encouragement as to future attainments? And when, as to both these, something is had, and the poor soul puffed up with an airy and fanciful apprehension of having obtained some great thing, but in truth a great nothing, or a nothing pregnant with vanity and vexation of spirit, foolish twins causing no gladness to the father, for "he that increaseth knowledge increaseth sorrow" (Eccl. 1:18)—what peace can all yield to a soul reflecting on posting away time, now near the last point and looking forward to endless eternity? Oh the thoughts of time wasted with and fair opportunities of good lost by the vehement pursuings and huntings after shadows and vanities—[this] will torment the soul by assaulting it with piercing convictions of madness and folly in forsaking all to overtake nothing with dreadful and soul-terrifying discourses of the saddest of disappointments and with the horror of an everlasting and irrecoverable loss. And what has the laborious spirit then reaped of all the travail of his soul when he has lost it? But, on the other hand, oh, [with] what calmness of mind, serenity of soul, and peace of conscience, because of the peace of God which passes all understanding, will that poor soul look back, when standing on the border of eternity, on the bygone days or hours it spent in seeking after, praying, and using all appointed means for some saving acquaintance with and interest in this only soul up-making and soul-satisfying mystery, and on its yielding up itself, through the efficacious operations of the Spirit of grace, wholly, without disputing, to the powerful workings of this mystery within, and in becoming crucified with Christ and living through a crucified Christ living in it by His Spirit and power. And with what rejoicing of heart and glorious singing of soul will it look forward to eternity and its everlasting abode in the prepared mansions, remembering that there its begun study will be everlastingly continued, its capacity to understand that unsearchable mystery will be inconceivably greater, and the spiritual, heavenly, and glorious joy which it will have in that practical reading its divinity without book of ordinances will be its life and felicity forever! And what peace and joy in the Holy Ghost, what inward inexpressible quiet and contentment of mind will the soul enjoy in dwelling on these thoughts when it will have in addition the inward and well-grounded persuasion of its right through Christ to the full possession of that all which now it cannot conceive, let be[2] comprehend? The foretastes of this fills it with joy unspeakable and full of glory and the hope of shortly landing there, where it will see and enjoy and wonder and praise and rest in this endless and felicitating work, making it to sing while passing through the valley and shadow of death. Oh if this were believed! Oh that we were not drunk to a distraction and madness, with the adulterous love of vain and airy speculations, to the postponing, if not utter neglecting, of this main and only up-making work of getting real acquaintance with and a begun possession of this mystery in our souls—Christ, the grand mystery, formed within us, living and working within us by His Spirit and working us up into a conformity to and a heart-closing with God manifested in the flesh, [so] that we may find in experience, or at least in truth and reality, have a true transumpt[3] of that gospel mystery in our souls! Oh, when will we take pleasure in pursuing after this happiness that will not flee from us but is rather pursuing us! When will we receive with joy and triumph this King of glory that is courting us daily and is seeking access and entry into our souls! Oh, why cry we not out in the height of the passion of spiritual longing and desire, "Oh come Lord Jesus,

---

2. *Let be*: let alone.
3. *Transumpt*: copy.

King of glory, with Thine own key, and open the door and enlarge and dilate the chambers of the soul that Thou may enter and be entertained as the King of glory, with all Thy glorious retinue, to the ennobling of my soul and satisfying of all the desires of that immortal spark"? Why do we not covet after this knowledge which has a true and firm con[nect]ion with all the best and truly divine gifts. Oh happy soul that is wasted and worn to a shadow, if that could be, in this study and exercise, which at length will enliven and, as it were, bring in a new heavenly and spiritual soul into the soul, so that it will look no more like a dead, dispirited thing out of its native soil and element but as a free, elevated, and spiritualized spirit, expatiating itself and flying abroad in the open air of its own element and country. Oh happy day, oh happy hour that is really and effectually spent in this employment! What would souls, swimming in this ocean of pleasures and delights, care for? Indeed, with what abhorrency would they look on the bewitching allurements of the purest kind of carnal delights, which flow from the mind's satisfaction in feeding on the poor apprehensions and groundlessly expected comprehensions of objects, suited to its natural genius and capacity? Oh what a more hyperbolical, exceeding, and glorious satisfaction has a soul in its very pursuings after (when it misses and cannot reach) that which is truly desirable! How does the least glimpse through the smallest cranny of this glorious and glorifying knowledge of God in Christ, apprehended by faith, raise up the soul to that pitch of joy and satisfaction which the knowledge of natural things, in its purest perfection, will never be able to cause. And to what a surmounting measure of this joy and contentation[4] will the experiencing and feeling, by spiritual sense, the sweet and relish of this captivating and

---

4. *Contentation*: contentment.

transcendently excellent knowledge raise the soul to? Oh,
must not this be the very suburbs of heaven to the soul! When
the soul thus sees and apprehends God in Christ, and that as
its own God through Christ (for as all saving knowledge draws
out the soul to an embracing and closing with the object, so it
brings in the object to the making up of the reciprocal union
and in-being), it cannot but admire with exultation and exult
with admiration at that condescendence of free grace that has
made it, in any measure, capable of this begun glory and will
further make it meet, by this begun glory, to be a partaker of
the inheritance of the saints in light. And what will a soul that
has tasted of the pure delights of this river of gospel manifestations and has seen, with soul-ravishing delights, in some
measure the manifold wisdom of God wrapped up in it, and
the complete and perfect symmetry of all the parts of that
noble contexture, and also the pure design of that contrivance to abase man and to extol the riches of the free grace of
God, so that the sinner, when possessed of all designed for
him and effectuated in him by this, may know who alone
should wear the crown and have all the glory—what, I say, will
such a soul see in another gospel (calculated to the meridian
of the natural, crooked, and corrupt temper of proud man,
who is soon made vain of nothing, which, instead of bringing
a sinner, fallen from God through pride, back again to the
enjoyment of Him through a mediator, does but foster that
innate plague and rebellion which procured his first excommunication from the favor and banishment out of the paradise
of God) that will attract its heart to it and move it to a compliance with it? When the poor sinner that has been made to
pant after a savior and has been pursued to the very ports of
the city of refuge by the avenger of blood, the justice of God,
has tasted and seen how good God is and felt the sweetness of
free love in a crucified Christ and seen the beauty and glory of

the mystery of His free grace, suitably answering and over-coming the mystery of its sin and misery—oh, what a complacency has he in this and in the way of gospel salvation in which free grace is seen to overflow all banks, to the eternal praise of the God of all grace. How saltless and unsavory will the most cunningly devised and patched-together mode of salvation be, that men, studying the perversion of the gospel and seeking the ruin of souls with all their skill, industry, and learning, are setting off with forced rhetoric and the artifice of words of man's wisdom and with the plausible advantages of a pretended sanctity and of strong grounds and motives to dili-gence and painfulness, to a very denying and renouncing [of] Christian liberty, when once it is observed how it entrenches on and darkens luster or diminishes the glory of free grace and has the least tendency to the setting of the crown on the creature's head, in whole or in part. The least perception that by this the sinner's song (ascribing blessing, honor, glory, and power to Him that was slain and has redeemed them to God by His blood, out of every kindred and tongue and people and nation, and has made them to their God kings and priests) will be marred—[this] will be enough to render that device detest-able and convince the soul that it is not the gospel of the grace of God and of Christ but rather the mystery of iniquity. What a peculiar savoriness does the humbled believer find in the doctrine of the true gospel grace, and the more that he be by this made nothing, and Christ made all; that he in his highest attainments be debased and Christ exalted; that his most lovely peacock feathers be laid, and the crown flourish on Christ's head; that he be laid flat, without one foot to stand on, and Christ the only supporter and carrier of him to glory; that he be as dead without life, and Christ live in him—[then] the more lovely, the more beautiful, the more desirable and acceptable is it to him. Oh what a complacency has the graced soul in that contrivance of infinite wisdom in which the mystery of the grace of God is so displayed that nothing appears from the lowest foundation stone to the uppermost copestone[5] but grace, grace, free grace making up all the materials, and free grace with infinite wisdom cementing all? The gracious soul can be warm under no other covering but what is made of that web, in which grace, and only grace, is both wooft and warp. And the reason [for this] is manifest, for such a one has the clearest sight and discovery of his own condition and sees that nothing suits him and his case but free grace. Nothing can make up his wants but free grace. Nothing can cover his deformities but free grace. Nothing can help his weaknesses, shortcomings, faintings, sins, and miscarriages but free grace. Therefore is free grace all his salvation and all his desire. It is his glory to be free grace's debtor forevermore. The crown of glory will have a far more exceeding and eternal weight and be of a hyperbolically hyperbolic[6] and eternal weight, and yet easily carried and worn, when he sees how free grace and love has lined it, and free grace and free love sets it on and keeps it on forever. This makes the glorified saint wear it with ease by casting it down at the feet of the gracious and loving purchaser and bestower. His exaltation is the saint's glory, and by free grace, the saints receiving and holding all of free grace, is He exalted. Oh, what a glory is it to the saint to set the crown of glorious free grace with his own hands on the head of such a savior and to say, "Not unto me, not unto me, but unto Thee, even unto Thee alone, be the glory forever and ever." With what delight, satisfaction, and complacency will the glorified saint, on this account, sing the redeemed and ransomed their song? And if the result and effect of free grace will give such a

5. *Copestone*: capstone.
6. *Hyperbolically hyperbolic*: probably (roughly), "exceedingly exceeding."

sweet sound there and make the glorified's heaven, in some respects, another thing, or at least, in some respect, a more excellent heaven than Adam's heaven would have been—for Adam could not have sung the song of the redeemed; Adam's heaven would not have been the purchase of the blood of God; nor would Adam have [sat] with Christ Redeemer on His throne; nor would there have been in his heaven such rich hangings of free grace nor such mansions prepared by that gracious and loving husband Christ, who will come and bring His bought bride home with Him. Seeing, I say, heaven, even on the account of free grace, will have such a special, lovely, desirable, and glorious luster, oh how should grace be prized by us now! How should the gospel of the grace of God be prized by us! What an antipathy to glory, as now prepared and dressed up for sinful man, must they show whose whole wits and parts are busied to darken the glory of that grace which God would have shining in the gospel and who are at so much pains and labor to dress up another gospel (though the apostle has told us [Gal. 1:7] that there is not another) in which gospel grace must stand by and law grace take the throne, that so man may sacrifice to his own net and burn incense to his own drag and may, at most, be grace's debtor in part. And yet no way may the saved man account himself more grace's debtor than the man was who willfully destroyed himself in not performing of the conditions, for grace, as the new gospellers, or rather gospel-spillers mean and say, did equally to both frame the conditions, make known to the contrivance, and tender the conditional peace and salvation. But as to the difference between Paul and Judas, it was Paul that made himself to differ, and not the free grace of God determining the heart of Paul by grace to a closing with and accepting of the bargain. It was not grace that wrought in him both to will and to do. It was he, and not the grace of God in him—what is more contradictory to the gospel of the grace of God? And yet vain man will not condescend to the free grace of God. Pelagianism and Arminianism needs not put a man to much study and to the reading of many books to the end it may be learned (though the patrons hereof labor hot in the very fires to make their notions hang together and to give them such a luster of unsanctified and corrupt reason as may be taking with such as know no other conduct in the matters of God), for naturally we all are born Pelagians and Arminians. These tenets are deeply engrave[d] in the heart of every son of fallen Adam. What serious servant of God finds not this in his dealing with souls whom he is laboring to bring into the way of the gospel? Indeed, what Christian is there who has acquaintance with his own heart and is observing its biases and corrupt inclinations that is not made to cry out, "Oh wretched man that I am! Who will deliver me from these dregs of Pelagianism, Arminianism, and Jesuitism, which I find yet within my soul?" Hence, it may seem no wonderful or strange thing (though, after so much clear light, it may be astonishing to think that now in this age so many are so openly and avowedly appearing for this dangerous and deadly error) to us to hear and see this infection spreading and gaining ground so fast, there needs few arguments or motives to work up carnal hearts to an embracing of it and to a cheerful acquiescing in it. Little labor will make a spark of fire work on gunpowder. And, methinks, if nothing else will, this one thing should convince us all of the error of this way that nature so quickly and readily complies with it. For who that has an eye on or regard of such things sees not what a world of carnal reasonings, objections, prejudices, and scruples natural men have in readiness against the gospel of Christ, and with what satisfaction, peace, and delight they reason and plead themselves out of the very reach of free grace, and what work there is to get a poor soul in any measure [a]wakened and convinced of its lost condition, wrought up to a compliance with the gospel way of salvation? How many other designs, projects, and essays does it follow with a piece of natural vehemency and seriousness, without wearying, were it even to the wasting of its body and spirits, let be its substance and riches, before it be brought to a closing with a crucified mediator and to an accounting of all its former workings, attainments, and painful laborings and gain as loss for Christ, and for the excellency of the knowledge of Christ, and as dung that it may win Christ and be found in Him, not having its own righteousness which is of the law but that which is through the faith of Christ, the righteousness which is of God by faith (Phil. 3:7–9). And may it not seem strange that now, after so many have found, through the grace of God, the sweet experience of the gracious workings of the gospel grace of God on their hearts, and so are in case, as having this witness within them, to give verdict against those assertions, indeed, more, and many more than were in several ages before—[that] yet Satan should become so bold as to vent these desperate opinions so diametrically opposite to the grace of God declared in the gospel and engrave[d] in the hearts of many hundreds by the finger of God, confirming, in the most undoubted manner, the truth of the gospel doctrines. This would seem to say that there are such clear sunshine days of the gospel and of the Son of Man a-coming (and who can tell how soon this night will be at an end?) that all these doctrines of nature will receive a more conspicuous and shameful dash than they have received for these many ages. Until this time when Satan raised up and sent forth his qualified instruments for this desperate work, God always prepared carpenters to fright these horns, and thus gospel truth came forth as gold out of a furnace, more clear and shining. And who can tell but there may be a dispensation of the pure grace of God in opposition to these perverting ways of Satan yet to come that, as to the measure of light and power, will excel whatever has been since the apostles' days. Even so, come, Lord Jesus.

However, madam, the grace of God will be what it is to all the chosen and ransomed ones. They will find in it which will make whatever comes in competition with it or would darken it contemptible in their eyes. And happy [are] they of whom in this day in which darkness covers the earth and gross darkness the people it may be said [that] the Lord has arisen on them, and His glory has been seen on them. For whatever others whose understanding is yet darkened and they alienated from the life of God through the ignorance that is in them because of the blindness of their hearts imagine of the gospel grace, and however they discern nothing of the heavenly and spiritual glory of the grace of God, yet they, being delivered or cast into the form and mold of the doctrine of the gospel which they have obeyed from the heart through the powerful and irresistible efficacy of the mighty grace of God, have seen such an alluring excellency in that gracious contrivance of infinite wisdom to set forth the unparallelableness of the pure grace of God and are daily seeing more and more of the graciousness and wisdom of that heavenly invention in its adequate suitableness to all their necessities, that as they cannot but admire and commend the riches of that grace that interlines every sentence of the gospel and the greatness of that love that has made such a completely broad plaster to cover all their sores and wounds. So the longer they live, and the more they drink of this pure fountain of heavenly nectar, and the more their necessities press them to a taking on of new obligations because of new supplies from this ocean of grace, the more they are made to admire the wisdom and goodness of the author. And the more they are made to fall in love with, to delight and lose themselves in the thoughts of this incomprehensible grace of God, indeed, and to long to be there where they will be in better case to contemplate and have more wit to wonder at and better dexterity to prize and a stronger head to muse upon and a more enlarged heart to praise for this boundless and endless treasure of the grace of God, with which they are enriched through Jesus Christ. Sure[ly], if we be not thus enamored and ravished with it, it is because we are yet standing without or, at most, on the threshold and border of this grace. Were we once got within the jurisdiction of grace and had yielded up ourselves to the power thereof and were living and breathing in this air—oh, how sweet a life might we have! What a kindly element would grace be to us! As sin had reigned to death, even so grace should reign through righteousness to eternal life by Jesus Christ our Lord (Rom. 5:21). Grace reigning within us through righteousness would frame and fit our souls for that eternal life that is insured to all who come once under the commanding, enlivening, strengthening, confirming, corroborating, and perfecting power of grace. And seeking grace for grace, and so living and walking and spending on grace's costs and charges— oh how lively and thriving proficients might we be! The more we spend of grace (if it could be spent), the richer should we be in grace. Oh what an enriching trade must it be to trade with free grace, where there is no loss and all is gain, the stock, and gain, and all is insured. Indeed, more, laboring in grace's field would bring us in Isaac's blessing a hundredfold. But, alas, it is one thing to talk of grace, but a far other thing to trade with grace. When we are so great strangers to the life of grace through not breathing in the air of grace, how can the name of the Lord Jesus be glorified in us and we in Him, according to the grace of our God and the Lord Jesus Christ (2 Thess. 1:12)? Consider we what an affront and indignity it is to the Lord dispensator of grace, that we look so lean and

ill-favored, as if there were not enough of the fattening bread
of the grace of God in our Father's house, or as if the great
steward, who is full of grace and truth, were unwilling to
bestow it on us or grudged us of our allowance, when the fault
is in ourselves. We will not follow the course that wise grace
and gracious wisdom has prescribed. We will not open our
mouth wide that He might fill us nor go to Him with our
narrowed or closed mouths that grace might make way for
grace and widen the mouth for receiving of more grace, but
[rather we] lie by in our leanness and weakness. And, alas, we
love too well to be so. Oh, but grace be ill-wared[7] on us who
carry so unworthily with it as we do. Yet it is well with the
gracious soul that he is under grace's tutory and care, for grace
will care for him when he cares not much for it nor yet sees
well to his own welfare. Grace can and will prevent—indeed,
must prevent afterward as well as at the first—that grace may
be grace and appear to be grace and continue unchangeably
to be grace, and so free grace. Well is it with the believer whom
grace has once taken by the heart and brought within the
bond of the covenant of grace. Its deadliest condition is not
desperate. When corruption prevails to such a height that the
man is given over for dead, there being no sense, no motion,
no warmth, no breath almost to be observed; yet grace, when
violently constrained by that strong distemper to retire to a
secret corner of the soul and there to lurk and lie quiet, will
yet at length, through the receiving influences of grace promised in the covenant and granted in the Lord's good time,
come out of its prison, take the fields, and recover the empire
of the soul. And then the dry and withered stocks, when the
God of all grace will be as dew to Israel, will blossom and grow
as the lily and cast forth his roots as Lebanon. His branches

---

7. *Ill-wared*: poorly laid out.

will spread, and his beauty will be as the olive tree, and his smell, as Lebanon. It is a happy thing either for church or particular soul to be planted in grace's sappy soil. They lie open to the warm beams of the Sun of Righteousness, and the winter blasts may be sharp and long. Clouds may intercept the heat, and nipping frosts may cause a sad decay, and all the sap may return and lie, as it were, dormant in the root. Yet the winter will pass, the rain will be over and gone, and the flowers will appear on the earth. The time of singing of birds will come, and the voice of the turtle will be heard in the land. Then will even the wilderness and solitary place be glad, and the desert will rejoice and blossom as the rose. It will blossom abundantly and rejoice even with joy and singing. The glory of Lebanon will be given to it, the excellency of Carmel and Sharon. They will see the glory of the Lord and the excellency of our God. We wonder that 'tis not always hot summer days, a flourishing and fruitful season, with souls and with churches. But know we the thoughts of the Lord? See we to the bottom of the deep contrivance of infinite wisdom? Know we the usefulness, indeed, necessity of long winter nights, stormy blasts, rain, hail, snow, and frost? Consider we that our state and condition, while here, calls for those vicissitudes and requires the blowing of the north as well as of the south winds? If we considered how grace had ordered all things for our best and most for the glory and exaltation of grace, we would sit down and sing under the saddest of dispensations; and, living by faith and hope, we would rejoice in the confident expectation of a gracious outgate.[8] For as long as grace predominates (and that will be until glory take the empire), all will run in the channel of grace. And though now sense (which is often faith's unfaithful friend) will be always suggesting false tales of

8. *Outgate:* escape.

God and of His grace to unbelief and raising by this discontents, doubts, fears, jealousies, and many distempers in the soul to its prejudice and hurt, yet in [the] end, grace will be seen to be grace. And the faithful will get such a full sight of this manifold grace, as ordering, tempering, timing, shortening, or continuing of all the sad and dismal days and seasons that have passed over their own or their mother's head, that they will see that grace did order all, indeed, every circumstance of all the various tossings, changes, ups and downs that they did meet with. And oh, what a satisfying sight will that be when the general assembly and church of the firstborn, which are in-rolled in heaven, and every individual saint will come together and take a view of all their experience, the result of which will be grace began; grace carried on; and grace has perfected all. Grace was at the bottom of all. What shoutings, grace, grace to it, will be there, when the headstone will be brought forth? What soul-satisfying complacency in and admiration at all that is past will a back-look at this yield, when everyone will be made to say, "Grace has done all well. Not a pin of all the work of grace in and about me might have been wanted. Now I see that the work of God is perfect. Grace was glorious grace, and wise grace, whatever I thought of it then. Oh what a fool have I been in quarrelling at and in not being fully satisfied with all that grace was doing with me?" Oh, how little is this believed now!

In conscience, madam, that your ladyship (to me no ways known but by a savory report) will accept of this bold address, I recommend your ladyship, my very noble lord your husband, and offspring, to the word of His grace and subscribe myself, madam,

> Your and their servant in the gospel
> and the grace of God,
> John Brown

The Author to the Reader

Christian reader,

After the foregoing address, I need not put you to much more trouble. Only I will say that he must needs be a great stranger in our Israel or sadly smitten with that epidemic plague of indifferency, which has infected many of this generation to a benumbing of them and rendering them insensible and unconcerned in the matters of God and of their own souls and sunk deep in the gulf of dreadful inconsideration, who sees not or takes no notice of nor is troubled at the manifest and terrible appearances of the inexpressibly great hazard [that] our all, as Christians in this life, is this day exposed into. I mean the mystery of the gospel of the grace of God in which the exceeding riches of His grace in His kindness toward us through Christ Jesus has been shown. We have enjoyed for a considerable time a clear and powerful dispensation of this in great purity and plenty. But, alas, is it not manifest to all that will not willfully shut their eyes that this mercy and goodness of God has been wickedly abused and the pure administration of His grace and love perfidiously sinned away by this apostate generation? Are our spots this day the spots of His children? Are their fruits answerable to the Lord's pains and labor about us to be seen even among the greatest of professors? Is there that gospel holiness, tenderness, watchfulness, growing in grace and in the knowledge of Jesus Christ, that growing up in

Christ, in all things that heavenly-mindedness, that fellowship with the Father and with His Son Christ Jesus, and that conversation in heaven, that the dispensation of grace we have been favored with beyond many and have been long living under did call for at our hands? Alas! Our grapes are but wild and stinking. Wherefore (and who can think it strange, if it be so?) the Lord seems to be about to contend with us by covering our horizon with Egyptian darkness—many who would not receive the love of the truth, that they might be saved, being already given up to strong delusion, that they should believe a lie, and many more in hazard to be drawn aside to crooked paths by men of corrupt minds, who have been and are still busy to vent and spread abroad, with no little petulancy and confidence, damnable doctrines, to the perverting of the doctrine of the gospel of Jesus Christ and to the subverting and overturning of the very foundations of our hope and assurance, and that in such a way and by such means and stratagems as seem to have wrath written on them in legible letters. For the more plausible and taking a corrupt doctrine be, it is the more dangerous and judgment-like, and more are by this in hazard to be deluded and drawn away.

Indeed (which is yet more terrible and dreadful), it is to be feared that the jealous God, in His holy and righteous judgment, has given a providential commission (to speak so)[1] to the seducing spirit to persuade and prevail. For is not this the clear language of the present holy and righteous dispensations of God and of the stupendously indifferent frame and disposition of the generality of men called Christians, not only provoking God to spew them out of His mouth but disposing them also to a receiving of whatever men, lying in wait to deceive, will propose and obtrude?

---

1. *To speak so:* so to speak.

Alas! The clouds are not now a-gathering, but our horizon is covered over with blackness, and great drops are a-falling that presage[2] a terrible overflowing deluge of error and apostacy from the truth and profession of the gospel of Jesus Christ to be at hand, if the Lord wonderfully prevent it not. And behold (oh wonderful!) the generality of professors are sleeping in security, apprehending no danger. Satan is more cunning now than to drive men to popery by rage and cruelty (and yet what he may be permitted to do after this manner, who can tell?) or by openly pleading in his emissaries for this abomination (and yet even thus is he already prevailing with not a few) or to send forth his agents for Arminianism and Socinianism (though even this way too he is too much prevailing). But his main work now seems to be to bring in another gospel (and yet there is not another) or rather an anti-evangelic and anti-Christian delusory dream, overturning at once the whole gospel of our Lord and Savior Jesus Christ. And for this end he employs the Quakers, on the one hand, men of desperate and anti-evangelic principles, the very sink of all abominations, old and late (as I will show, if the Lord will continue health and strength, in an examination of their doctrine and principles, lately emitted by one Robert Barcley), and, on the other hand, men (or moralists, if you will call them so) pleading for and crying up an anti-evangelic holiness, a mere shadow without substance or reality, and that in place of Christ Himself. And in order to the carrying on of this desperate design, the old dragon is employing men of seeming different principles and ways, whom, though their faces seem to look to contrary airths,[3] yet he holds despite this fast tied by their tails (as Samson's foxes were), that by this, if the Lord permit it, he may, by the

---

2. *Presage*: to foreshadow.
3. *Airths*: directions.

fire of enmity to the pure gospel of the grace of God burning in their tails, cause a conflagration of that truth, in which lies all our hope. For this new model of religion that many are so busied about is such as Pelagians, Arminians, Papists, Socinians, Quakers, indeed Turks, and moral heathens—indeed, and all who are enemies to and not reconcilable with the true grace of God held forth in the gospel—will willingly admit of and harmoniously agree in. [It is] a way which complies so well with proud self and with the corrupt nature of man that it is little wonder, if it have many abettors and admirers. I will say no more of this, but only infer:

That sure the consideration of this should move all in whom is anything of the zeal of God and love to souls, their own and others', to appear in the defense of the gospel of our salvation by all means incumbent to them and possible for them. For if this citadel and stronghold in which our all and the all of pure and true religion lies be blown up, [then] we are gone. And indeed, no less is intended by this anti-Christian and anti-evangelic enemy than the utter subversion of true Christian religion. Who would not then be by this alarmed and on their guard when matters are at this pass? Should not all who have any love to their own souls; any zeal for the glory of Christ, anointed of the Father to be our prophet, priest, and king; any desire to see the crown flourishing on His head and to have the gospel preserved pure and uncorrupted be pleading with God by prayer in the behalf of His Son's kingdom, crown, and glory? And [should they not be] wrestling with Him till He were pleased to dispel these clouds and prevent this black day? Especially should they not be laboring to be acquainted, in truth and reality, with the gospel of Jesus Christ, that, having the mysterious truths of it imprinted on their souls and their hearts cast into its mold, they may be preserved from the hurt of this deadly poison? For this, with a constant dependence on and use-making of Christ in all His offices, will prove the best preservative against this infection.

The persuasion of this did induce me to publish the following heads of some sermons, after they have been translated into Dutch and published here, knowing that they might be of no less use to the people of God in Britain and Ireland. I know not a more effectual mean[s] to unstable souls from siding with and embracing every new notion and from being carried about with every wind of doctrine by the sleight of men and cunning craftiness by which they lie in wait to deceive than to put them on the real exercise of gospel godliness and to the daily practice of the main and fundamental gospel work of living by faith in Jesus Christ and of growing up into Him in all things, who is the head from whom the whole body fitly joined together and compacted, by that which every joint supplies according to the effectual working in the measure of every part, makes increase of the body, to the edifying of itself in love. Such, I am sure, as have thus learned the truth as it is in Jesus and are practicing the same accordingly will have an antidote within them against the strongest poison of these seducers and a real answer to and confutation of all their subtile sophisms.[4] The soul exercising itself into gospel godliness will find work enough to take it wholly up and find such a solid ground to stand on and see such a satisfying fullness, answering all its necessities and wants, and such a sure heart-quieting ground of peace, hope, and consolation in Jesus Christ as that it will have no leisure and small temptation to listen to seducing perverters and no inclination to seek after empty cisterns.

---

4. *Sophisms*: deceitful or fallacious arguments.

I know much may be desiderated[5] in this following treatise, and many may have exceptions not without ground against it. Some may think it arrogancy and too great confidence in me to attempt the handling of such a mysterious and necessary part of Christian practice, in which few (if any, so far as I know) have gone before in direct handling of this matter, at least in this method and order—I mean that part which is about sanctification. Others may be displeased with the mean and low style: with my multiplying particulars, which might have been better and more handsomely couched under fewer heads, and with my unnecessary contracting of the whole into such a narrow bound, and other things of that kind. For which and many other failings of the like nature and import, which may without any diligent search be found in it, even by ordinary and unprejudiced readers, I will not industriously labor to apologize, knowing that my very apology in this case will need an apology. Only I will say this: that considering how the snare which the vigilant and active enemy of our salvation, the devil, was laying by an unholy morality did nearly concern all, and especially the meanest (for parts and experience) and less fixed Christians, I thought a discourse on such a subject as I judged most necessary at all times and especially in such a day of hazard should be framed to the capacity of one as well as another. The most understanding can receive benefit by that which is calculated to the capacity of children, when these can reap little edification by what is suited to the palate of those. And the less experienced or such as are of lower understanding will be less able to draw a general to a particular or to improve and so fully to comprehend one particular touched as to be able by this to understand and take in a like particular not mentioned, than such as have their senses more exer-

---

5. *Desiderated*: desired.

cised and are by this in case to make a better improvement of what is but compendiously declared, when those must have the bread broken to their hand, or they will receive but small edification by it. And yet, I suppose, the judicious will observe some variety, smaller or greater, even where particulars seem to be, at the first view, most unnecessarily multiplied. I know and willingly grant (for it is obvious enough) that a discourse of this subject and matter might have required a far larger volume; but then how should such have profited by it, whom poverty might possibly have scared from buying, or the necessary affairs of their ordinary callings would have kept from a diligent perusal of it? And I thought that neither of these should have been overlooked in this special or general design which I had before my eyes.

One thing, as my answer to all, I will but add: If by this others whom the Lord has more enabled with all necessaries for such a work will be by this either instigated or encouraged to write on this subject (I mean mainly the last part of it, touching the use-making of Christ in sanctification, for, blessed be the Lord, many have been employed of the Lord to speak soundly and edifyingly to the use-making of Christ as to righteousness and justification) a full, plain, edifying, and satisfying discovery of this necessary and important truth (namely, Christ made of God to us wisdom, righteousness, sanctification, and redemption) and, in addition, point out plainly and particularly the way how believers in all their particular and various exigencies may and should so make use of and apply that all fullness which is treasured up in the head for the benefit and advantage of the members of the mystical body—as they may not only theoretically see but practically also experience this truth that in Him they are complete, and so they may be helped to understand how through the necessary and constant use-making of Him as all in all they may grow up in Him in all things—if this be, I say, done by any to better purpose, I will think this my adventure not altogether fruitless and in part at least excusable.

As for you, O Christian, whose instruction, edification, and confirmation in the faith of our Lord Jesus Christ, the faith which was once delivered to the saints, I mainly intended in this undertaking, I have a few things to add:

Know then that there are certain men (as the apostle Jude speaks) crept in unawares, who were of old ordained to this condemnation, ungodly men, turning the grace of our God into lasciviousness and denying the only Lord God and our Lord Jesus Christ. For in these last days we see that these perilous times are come (of which Paul advertised Timothy, 2 Tim. 3:1, etc.), in which men will be lovers of their own selves, covetous, boasters, proud, blasphemers, disobedient to parents, unthankful, unholy, without natural affection, truce breakers, false accusers (or make bates[6]), incontinent, fierce, despisers of those that are good, traitors, heady,[7] high-minded, lovers of pleasure more than lovers of God, having the form of godliness but denying the power of it—for of this sort are they which creep into houses and lead captive silly women, laden with sins, led away with diverse lusts, ever learning and never able to come to the knowledge of the truth. And because it is so, he exhorts to give diligence to make your calling and election sure by giving all diligence to add to faith, virtue; to virtue, knowledge; and to knowledge, temperance; and to temperance, patience; and to patience, godliness; and to godliness, brotherly kindness; and to brotherly kindness, charity. For if you do these things, you will never fall, as the apostle Peter assures us (2 Peter 1:5–10). For it is the elect who

6. *Make bates*: someone who stirs up strife.
7. *Heady*: rash or violent.

are secured from full and final defection and apostasy (Matt. 24:24, 31; Mark 12:22; 13:27; Rom. 8:33; 9:11; 11:5–6). And the promise of salvation is made to such as will endure to the end. The crown is for the overcomers and such as are faithful to the death (Matt. 10:22; 24:13; Mark 13:13; Rev. 2:10–11, 17, 26–28; 3:5, 12, 21). All which, and the like, are set down that by this His people might be rationally moved to a constant seriousness in the working out of their own salvation in fear and trembling. And the forewarnings [are] given of the great difficulty of the reaching the end of our faith, the salvation of our souls, because of the many active, vigilant, indefatigable, subtile, and insinuating adversaries, who by good words and fair speeches will readily deceive the hearts of the simple. And [they are] to awaken the more His people to be sober and vigilant, because their adversary the devil (who acts and moves his under agents[8] in their several modes, methods, and motions, so as he may best, according to the various tempers, present dispositions, advantages, or disadvantages of such as he intends to seduce—which he carefully studies and plies for this end—obtain his designed end: their ruin and destruction) as a roaring lion, walking about seeking whom he may devour. And this calls them to haste[n] out [of] their slumber and security who will be loath to miss his opportunity, surprise them to their great loss and disadvantage.

It is, beloved, high time now to awake, to look about us, to consider where we are, on what ground we stand, whether the enemy or we have the advantage, how and in what posture we are to rencounter[9] with deceivers that seek to cheat us out of all our souls and of the Lord our righteousness and draw us off the paths of life, that when we come to die (beside[s] the

8. *Under agents:* secret agents.
9. *Rencounter:* to meet by chance.

unspeakably great loss we would by this be at, even here, in missing the comfortable accesses to God through Jesus Christ the inflowings of grace and strength for spiritual duty through the Lord our strength, the sweet communications of peace and joy in the Holy Ghost, the shedding abroad of the love of God in our hearts by the Holy Ghost which is given to us, and the full assurance of hope through the Lord Jesus our hope), we might be frustrated of all our expectations and find that all that which men made us grip to, lay hold on, and lean to instead of Christ was but a mere shadow and a lie in our right hand to the unexpressible grief, vexation, and sorrow of soul when all should end in a dreadful and horrible disappointment.

But let us not think that our purposes, firm-like resolutions to adhere to the truth, and our present abhorrence at and detestation of errors now broached to the overturning the very foundations of true Christianity will sufficiently guard us from and make us proof against the shots and assaults of these crafty seducers. Nor think that our learning and knowledge in the theory of the truth nor our abilities to rencounter sophisters will secure us from a fall. Let us not think that the enemies are contemptible, and therefore we need be the less anxious. Nor yet [let us] think that former experiences and through-bearings,[10] in the like cases, will be a pillow by which we may now lay ourselves down to sleep. If we do, we will certainly deceive ourselves if all our strength and standing be in ourselves and through ourselves. And if this be the ground of our hope, the righteous Lord in His holy justice may give us up to be a prey. Peter's instance should never be forgotten by us. And such as tempt the Lord have no ground to expect His last issue.

---

10. *Through-bearings*: a word for "perseverance."

Our strength must be in Christ. To the Rock of Ages must we fly. To our chambers in Him must we retire, and there must we hide ourselves. On Christ's lee-side[11] can we only ride safe[ly] and be free of the hazard of the storm. To Him therefore must our recourse be daily by new and fresh acts of faith in and through Him and His influences, communicated according to the tenor of the covenant of grace. Through faith, eyeing the promiser, the promise, with the price purchasing, and so drawing and sucking light, direction, strength, stability, and what our present exigent calls for must we think to stand. And happy [are] they who, conscious to themselves of their own weakness and convinced of the insufficiency of all things within them, in godly fear hide themselves under the wings of the Almighty and get into this stronghold, resolving there to abide and there to be secured from all their adversaries within or without. These humble fearers may expect a safe and noble outgate, when more strong-like and more confident adventurers will (being left to themselves, because trusting in themselves) shamefully fall and be triumphed over by the enemy, to the grief of the godly and for a snare to others.

The best way then to keep the faith of Christ, which many are now seeking to shake and to loose us from, is to be exercising the faith of Christ. The serious and upright practicing of the gospel is the only best mean[s] to keep you firm in the profession of the gospel, when the gospel with you is not a few fine notions in the brain but is heavenly and necessary truth sunk into the heart and living and acting there. It will keep you, and you will own it more firmly and steadfastly in a day of trial. Your walking in Christ and working and living by Him living in you will so root you in the gospel truth that enemies will pull in vain when seeking to overthrow you. The gospel

---

11. *Lee-side*: the side of shelter.

of the grace of God received and entertained in your soul in love and constant suitable improvement will fortify you and secure itself in you so that vehement blasts will but contribute to its more fixed abode and more fruitful actings in you. Live up then to the gospel, and so be sure of it, and be safe in it. I mean, let Christ live in you as your all and cast all your care and cumber[12] on Him. Lay all your difficulties before Him. Lean all your weight on Him. Draw all your necessities out of Him, and undertake all your duties in Him. Be strong in Him and in the power of His might. Let Him be your counsellor, conductor, leader, teacher, captain, commander, light, life, strength, and all, [and] so will you stand and have cause to glory, even in your infirmities, for you will find the power of Christ resting on you, and you will have cause to say, "Therefore I take pleasure in infirmities, in reproaches, in necessities, in persecutions, in distresses for Christ's sake; for when I am weak, then am I strong" [2 Cor. 12:10]. Remember that great word: "I can do all things through Christ which strengtheneth me" (Phil. 4:13).

It has been the usual and ordinary question of believers: How will we make use of Christ for sanctification? To this great and important question, I (though the meanest and most unfit for such a work of all that God has sent to feed His flock) have adventured, or endeavored at least, to give such as truly desire to cleanse themselves from all filthiness of the flesh and spirit, perfecting holiness in the fear of God, some satisfaction in this, laying before them some plain directions framed to their capacities and suited to some of their most ordinary and usual causes. Some of which are more comprehensive, and others more particular, [which] may be looked on as exemplary instances, serving for other cases of the like

---

12. *Cumber*: hindrance.

nature. For hardly could every particular circumstantiate case be particularly spoken to, and some might judge that to be superfluous. If you, in the light and strength of Christ, will really practice what is here pointed forth, I may be confident to say [that] your labor will not be in vain in the Lord, and you will attain to another sort of holiness than that which proud pretenders boast of and will be far without the reach of that snare, which unstable souls are too readily entangled with—I mean, the plausible pretension of more than ordinary sanctity which yet is but forced, feigned, constrained, mostly external, and framed to cause admiration in beholders, whom they intend to make a prey of. This will be no temptation to you who by experience find a more safe, satisfying, full, free, easy, pleasant, and heartsome[13] way of mortifying lusts, growing in grace and in the knowledge of Jesus Christ, and so perfecting holiness by running immediately to Christ and by living in and on Him, who is made of God to us wisdom, righteousness, sanctification, and redemption. That the Lord may bless the same to you for this end will be and is the desire and prayer of him who is,

Your servant in the work of the gospel,
John Brown

---

13. *Heartsome*: to give heart.

Recommendation

Christian reader,

If you answer this designation and are really a partaker of the unction, which is the high import of that blessed and glorious name called upon you, [then] your eye must affect your heart, and a soul swelled with godly sorrow must at last burst and bleed forth at a weeping eye while you look on most of this licentious and loathsome generation arrived at that height of prodigious profanity as to glory in their shame and boast of bearing the badge and black mark of damnation. But, besides this swarm who savage it to hell and make such haste hither as they foam themselves into everlasting flames, carrying under the shape and visage of men, as devils in disguise, the face of the church is covered with a scum of such who are so immersed in the concerns of this life and are so intense in the pursuit of the pleasures, gain, and honors of it as their way does manifestly witness them to be sunk into the deep oblivion of God and desperate inconsideration of their precious and immortal souls. But, in the third place, besides these who are hurried into such a distraction with the cares of this life that they, as natural brute beasts made to be destroyed, are never at leisure to consider either the nature and necessity of their noble souls or to converse with the notion of a deity. You may perceive a company of self-deceiving speculatists, who make broad the phylacteries of their garments and boast of some high attainments in religion, indeed, [and] would have others look on them as arrived at the very porch of heaven and advanced to a high pitch of proficiency in the ways of God because they can discourse a little of the mysteries of salvation; and, without ever diving farther into the depth and true nature of religion, [they] dream themselves into a consideration of being saints and conclude themselves candidates for glory.

This is that heart-moving object which presents itself to your eye and observation this day. This is that deplorable posture in which you may perceive most men at the very point of perishing eternally, who are within the pale of the visible church, some dancing themselves headlong in all haste into the lake of fire and brimstone, some so much concerned in things which have no connection with their happiness as to drop unconcernedly into the pit, out of which there is no redemption. And others [are] dreaming themselves into endless perdition. And all of them unite in a deriding at or despising the means used and essays[1] made in order to their recovery.

But if His servants, in following their work closely, seem to have gained a little ground on men and almost persuaded them to be Christians, Satan, to the end he may make all miscarry and counterwork these workers together with God and poison poor souls by a perversion of the gospel beyond the power of an antidote, has raised up, instigated, and set on work a race of proud rationalists, for they are wiser than to class themselves among those poor fools, those base things, those nothings, to whom Christ is made all things, to whom Christ is made wisdom that He may be righteousness, sanctification, and redemption to them—indeed, they must be wise men after the flesh, wise above what is written. A crucified Christ is really to them foolishness and weakness, though the

---

1. *Essays:* attempts.

power of God and the wisdom of God. They will needs go to work another way. They will needs glory in His presence and have a heaven of their own band-wind.[2] Oh, my soul, enter not into their secrets! And, oh, sweet Jesus, let Thy name be to me, "The Lord my righteousness." Thou hast won it—wear it. And gather not my soul with such who make mention of any other righteousness but of Thine only to bring in another gospel among us than the gospel of the grace of God. As they determine to know some other thing than Christ and Him crucified, so with the enticing words of man's wisdom they bewitch men into a disobedience to the truth, setting somewhat else before them than a crucified Christ. And this they do that they may remove men from those who call them into the grace of Christ to another gospel. A christ, it is true, they speak of. But it is not the Christ of God, for all they drive at (Oh, cursed and truly anti-Christian design!) is that He may profit them nothing, while they model all religion according to this novel project of their magnified morality. This is that which gives both life and luster to that image which they adore, to the Dagon after whom they would have the world wonder and worship.

That there is such a moralizing or muddizing (if I may be for once admitted to coin a new word to give these men their due) of Christianity now introduced and coming in fashion, many of the late pieces in request do evince. Now that Christianity should moralize men above all things, I both give and grant; for he who is partaker of the divine nature and has obtained precious faith must add virtue to his faith. But that it should be only conceived and conceited as an elevation of nature to a more clear light, in the matter of morality, in which our Lord is only respected as a heavenly teacher and perfect pattern proposed for imitation, is but a proud, pleasing fancy

---

2. *Band-wind*: effort or making.

of self-conceited, darkened, and deluded dreamers, robbing God of the glory of His mercy and goodness; our Lord Jesus Christ of the glory of His grace and merit; the Spirit of the efficacy of His glorious and mighty operations; and themselves and their pilgrimages, who give them the hand as guides, of the comfort and fruit of all.

It cannot escape your observation how busy Satan is this day, on the one hand, to keep men, [who are] under the call of the gospel to give all diligence to make their calling and election sure, idle all the day, so that no persuasion can induce them to engage seriously to fall about a working out their own salvation in fear and trembling; and, on the other, equally diligent and industrious to divert men from trusting in the name of the Lord and staying on their God. [Instead, he is] setting them on work to go and gather fuel and kindle a fire and compass themselves about with sparks, that they may walk in the light of their own fire and in the sparks that they have kindled, knowing well that they will this way most certainly lose their toil and travail and have no other reward at His hand of all their labor but to lie down in everlasting sorrow, while the stouthearted and far from righteousness and salvation will get their soul for a prey and be made to rejoice in His salvation and bless Him who has made them meet to be partakers of the inheritance of the saints in light.

I am neither the fit person for so great an undertaking, nor do these limits within which I must bound myself permit me to expatiate in many notions about the nature of this excellent and precious thing [of] true gospel holiness. Oh! If, in the entry, I could on my own behalf and others sob out my "alas!" from the bottom of my soul, because, be what it will, it is some other thing than men take it to be. Few habituate themselves to a thinking on it, in its high nature and soul-enriching advantages, till their hearts receive suitable impressions of it, and their lives be the very transumpt of the law of God written in their heart. The thing, alas, is lost in a noise of words and heap of notions about it. Neither is it a wonder that men fall into mistakes about it, since it is only the heart possessed of it that is capable to understand and perceive its true excellency. But if it be asked what it is, we say [that] it may be shortly taken up as the elevation and raising up of a poor mortal to a conformity with God. As a participation of the divine nature or as the very image of God stamped on the soul, impressed on the thoughts and affections, and expressed in the life and conversation, so that the man in whom Christ is formed and in whom He dwells, lives, and walks has while on the earth a conversation in heaven—not only in opposition to those many whose end is destruction, whose god is their belly, whose glory is in their shame, who mind earthly things, but also to those pretenders to and [im]personators of religion, who have confidence in the flesh and worship God with their own spirit, which in the matters of God is flesh and not spirit, and have somewhat else to rejoice in than in Christ Jesus, and a being found in Him, not having their own righteousness.

True gospel holiness, then, consists in some similitude and likeness to God and fellowship with Him founded on that likeness. There is such an impression of God, His glorious attributes, His infinite power, majesty, mercy, justice, wisdom, holiness, and grace, etc., as sets Him up all alone in the soul without any competition and produces those real apprehensions of Him that He is alone excellent and matchless. Oh, how preferable does He appear, when indeed seen, to all things! And how does this light of His infinite gloriousness, shining into the soul, darken and obscure to an invisibleness all other excellencies, even as the rising of the sun makes all the lesser lights to disappear. Alas! How is God unknown in His glorious being and attributes! When once the Lord enters the soul and shines into the heart, it is like the rising of the sun at midnight. All these things which formerly pretended to some loveliness and did dazzle with their luster are eternally darkened. Now, all natural perfections and moral virtues in their flower and perfections are at best looked on as *aliquid nihil*.[3] What things were formerly accounted gain and godliness are now counted loss for the excellency of the knowledge of Christ Jesus the Lord, and the soul cannot only suffer the loss of them all without a sob, but be satisfied to throw them away as dung, that it may win Him and be found in Him. Now, the wonder of a deity, in His greatness, power, and grace, swallows up the soul in sweet admiration. Oh, how does it love to lose itself in finding here what it cannot fathom! And then it begins truly to see the greatness and evil of sin. Then it is looked on without the covering of pleasure or profit and loathed as the leprosy of hell. Now the man is truly like God in the knowledge of good and evil, in the knowledge of that one infinite good, God, and in the knowledge of that one almost infinite evil, sin. This is the first point of likeness to Him: to be conformed to Him in our understanding, that as He knows Himself to be the only self-being and fountain-good, and all created things in their flower and perfection with all their real or fancied conveniences being compared with Him but as the drop of a bucket, or nothing, indeed, less than nothing, vanity (which is nothing blown up, by the force or forgery of a vainly working imagination, to the consistence of an appearance), so for a soul to know indeed and believe in the heart that there is nothing [that] deserves the name of good besides God, to have the same superlative and transcendent thoughts of that great and glorious self-being God and the same diminishing and debasing thoughts of all things and beings besides Him.

---

3. *Aliquid nihil*: to deem someone nothing.

And that as the Lord sees no evil in the creation but sin and hates that with a perfect hatred, as contrary to His holy will, so for a soul to aggravate sin in its own sight to an infiniteness of evil, at least till it see it only short of infiniteness in this respect, that it can be swallowed up of infinite mercy. But from where has the soul all this light? It owes all this and owns itself as debtor for it to Him who opens the eyes of the blind. It is He who commands the light to shine out of darkness who has made these blessed discoveries and has given the poor benighted[4] soul the light of the knowledge of the glory of God in the face of Jesus Christ. These irradiations are from the Spirit's illumination. 'Tis the Spirit of wisdom and revelation that has made daylight in the darkened soul. The man who had the heart of a beast as to any saving or solid knowledge of God or himself has now got an understanding to know Him that is true. Now is Christ become the poor man's wisdom. He is now renewed in knowledge after the image of Him that created him. He might well babble of spiritual things, but till now he understood nothing of the beauty and excellency of God and His ways. Indeed, he knew not what he knew. He was ignorant as a beast of the life and luster of those things which he knew in the letter. Nothing seemed more despicable to him in the world than true godliness. But now he judges otherwise, because he has the mind of Christ. The things which in his darkness he did undervalue as trifles to be mocked at, he now can only mind and admire since he became a child of light. Now being delivered from that blindness and brutishness of spirit, which possesses the world (and possessed himself till he was transformed by the renewing of his mind), who esteem basely of spiritual things and set them at nought—[these] he prizes as alone precious. The world wonders what pleasure or

---

4. *Benighted*: overtaken by darkness.

content can be in the service of God, because they see not by tasting how good He is. To be prying into and poring on invisible things is to them visible madness. But to the enlightened mind, the things that are not seen are only worth seeing, and while they appear not to be, they only are, whereas the things that are seen appear but to be, and are not. Though the surpassing sweetness of spiritual things should be spoke[n] of to them, who cannot favor the things of God, in such a manner as the glorious light of them did surround men, yet they can perceive no such thing. All is to them cunningly devised fables. Let be spoke what will, they see no form, no comeliness, no beauty in this glorious object—God in Christ reconciling sinners to Himself. Alas! The mind is blinded; the dungeon is within; and till Christ open the eyes as well as reveal His light, the soul abides in its blindness and is buried in midnight darkness. But when the Spirit of God opens the man's eyes, and he is translated by an act of omnipotency out of the kingdom of darkness into the kingdom of His dear Son, which is a kingdom of marvelous light—oh what matchless beauty does he now see in these things, which appeared despicable and dark nothings to him till he got the unction, the eye salve, which teaches all things. Now he sees (what none without the Spirit can see) the things which God has prepared for them that love Him and are freely given them of God. And these, though seen at a distance, reflect such rays of beauty into his soul that he beholds and is ravished. He sees and is swallowed up in wonder.

But then, in the next place, this is not a spiritless inefficacious speculation about these things, to know no evil but sin and separation from God and no blessedness but in the fruition of Him. It is not such a knowledge of them as does not principle motion to pursue after them. This I grant is part of the image of God, when the Sun of Righteousness by arising on the man has made daylight in his soul and by these divine discoveries has taught him to make the true parallel between things that differ and to put a just value on them according to their intrinsic worth. But this divine illumination does not consist in a mere notion of such things in the head, nor does it subsist in enlightening the mind, but in such an impression of God on the soul as transforms and changes the heart into His likeness by love. Knowledge is but one line, one draught or lineament of the soul's likeness to Him. That alone does not make up the image, but knowledge rooted in the heart and engraven on the soul, shining and showing itself forth in a gospel-adorning conversation, that makes a comely proportion. When the same hand that touched the eye and turned the man from darkness to light and gave a heart to know Him that He is the Lord, [then] that does also circumcise the man's heart to love the Lord his God with all his heart and with all his soul and with all his mind, and this love, manifesting its liveliness in its constraining power to live to Him and for Him. Light without heat is but wildfire; but light in the mind, begetting heat in the heart, making it burn Godward, Christward, and heavenward, light in the understanding, setting on fire and inflaming the affections, and these shining out in a heavenly conversation—[this] makes up the lively image of God, both in feature and stature, both in proportion and color. Faith begins this image and draws the lineaments. And love bringing forth obedience finishes and gives it the lively luster. The burnings of love in obedience to God is that which illuminates the whole and makes a man look indeed like Him to whose image he is predestinate[d] to be conform[ed]. And then [it] makes him who is ravished with the charms of that beauty say, as in a manner overcome by this, "How fair is your love, my sister, my spouse? How much better is your love than wine, and the smell of your ointments than all spices?" But consider that as these beams which irradiate the soul are from the Spirit of Christ, so that spiritual heat and warmth come out of the same airth and proceed from the same author. For our fire burns as He blows. Our lamp shines as He snuffs and furnishes oil. Men therefore should not indulge themselves in this delusion to think that that which will pass for pure religion and undefiled before God consists either in an outward blameless conversation or in putting on and wearing an external garb of profession. No, as the top of it reaches higher, so the root of it lies deeper. It is rooted in the heart. This seed being sown in an honest heart (or making the heart honest in which it is sown) takes root downward and brings forth fruit upward. As trees that grow as far underground as above, so these trees of righteousness, the planting of the Lord that He may be glorified, grow as far and as fast underground as above. Godliness grows as far downward in self-emptying, self-denial, and self-abasing, in hungering and thirsting after more of righteousness, in the secret engagements of the heart to God in Christ, in these burstings of heart and bleeding of soul, to which God alone is witness, because of shortcoming in holiness, because of a body of death within, and because of that law in the members warring against the law of the mind, and bringing often into captivity to the law of sin, as it grows upward in a profession. And this is that pure religion and undefiled before God, which is both most pleasant to Him and profitable to the soul.

But to make the difference between dead morality, in its best dress, and true godliness more clear and obvious [so] that loveliness of the one may engage men into a loathing of the other, this dead carion and stinking carcase of rotten morality, which still stinks in the nostrils of God, even when embalmed with the most costly ointments of its miserably misled patrons, we say that true godliness, which in quality and kind differs

from this much pleaded for and applauded morality, a black
heathen by a mongrel kind of Christians baptized of late with
the name of Christianity and brought into the temple of the
Lord, concerning which He has commanded that it should
never in that shape and for that end it is introduced enter into
His congregation. And the bringers for their pains are like
to seclude themselves forever from His presence. It respects
Jesus Christ, first, as its principle; second, as its pattern; third,
as its altar; and, fourth, as its end.

I. I say, true holiness in its being and operation respects Jesus
Christ as its principle. "I live," said that shining saint, "yet not
I, but Christ lives in me." As that which gives religion its first
being is the religation of the soul to God, so that which gives it
motion and draws forth that life into action is the same God's
working all their works in them and for them, so that in all
they do they are workers together with God. Every act of holiness is an act of the soul made alive to God through Jesus
Christ and quickened to each action by the supervenience[5]
of new life and influence. "Therefore," says Christ, "without
Me you can do nothing." It is not, "Being out of Me you can
do nothing," for He spoke it to those who were in Him, but,
"If you leave Me out in doing, all you do will be nothing." 'Tis
Jesus Christ who gives life and legs, so that our runnings are
according to His drawings. "My soul follows hard after Thee,"
said that holy man. But from where is all this life and vigor?
"Thy right hand upholds me." Oh! It is the upholdings and
helpings of this right hand, enlarging the man's heart, that
makes a running in the ways of His commandments. It is He
who, while the saints work out the work of their own salvation,
works in them both to will and to do. It is He who gives power

_____

5. *Supervenience*: to follow after.

to the faint and who, to them that have no might, increases strength, so that the poor, lifeless, languishing lie-by is made to mount up with eagle's wings and surmount all these difficulties with a holy facility, which were simply insuperable and pure impossibilities. Now the man runs and does not weary, because Christ draws; and he walks and does not faint, because Christ, in whom dwells the fullness of the Godhead bodily, dwells in him and walks in him, and dwells in him for that very end that he may have a completeness and competency of strength for duty. All grace is made to abound to him, that he, always having all sufficiency in all things, may abound unto every good work. He is able of himself to do nothing, no, not to think anything as he ought. But he has a sufficiency of God by which he is thoroughly furnished unto every good work, so that he may say, "I am able for all things." It is more than "I am able to do all things," as we read it. Its just import is, "I am able to do all things and to endure all things." And that which keeps it from vain boasting is what is added: "through Christ which strengthened me," or, "putting power in me," or rather, "empowering me," which is by a supervenient act drawing forth life into a liveliness of exercise, according to the present exigent. There is a power in a saint, because Christ is in him, that overpowers all the powers of darkness without and all the power of indwelling corruption within, so that when the poor weak creature is ready to despond within sight of his duty and say, because of difficulty, "What is my strength that I should hope?"—[then] Christ says, "Despond not. My grace is sufficient for you, and My power will rest on you." [And this will be] to a reviving you and raising you up and putting you in case to say, "When I am weak, then I am strong. His strength, who empowers me, is made perfect in my weakness, so that I will glory in my infirmities and be glad in being grace's debtor." But what power is that which raises the dead sinner and carries the soul in its actings so far without the line and above the sphere of all natural activity, when stretched to its utmost? Oh, it is an exceeding[ly] great power which is to them-ward who believe, that must make all things, however difficult, easy, when He works in them to will and to do according to the working of His mighty power (or, as it is on the margin, and more emphatic, "of the might of His power"), which He wrought in Christ when He raised Him from the dead and set Him at His own right hand, etc. He that raised up the Lord Jesus from the dead raises up believers also by Jesus. And being raised and revived by Him to walk in newness of life, the life of Jesus, in its communications of strength, is manifest in their mortal flesh, according to that of the same apostle: "The life that I live in the flesh," says he, "I live by the faith of the Son of God. Faith brings in Christ in my soul; and Christ, being my life, carries out my soul in all the acts of obedience in which, though I be the formal agent, yet the efficiency and the power by which I operate is from Him, so that I can give no better account of it than this: I, [and] not I." But who then, if not you? "The grace of God," says he, "which was with me." But this mystery to our bold (because blind) moralists of an indwelling Christ working mightily in the soul is plain madness and melancholy. However, we understand his knowledge in the mystery of Christ who said, "The life I live in the flesh, etc." And from what we understand of his knowledge in that mystery which he had by revelation, we understand our moralists to be men of corrupt minds, who concerning the faith have made shipwreck. But what is that, "The life I live in the flesh, etc."? The import of it seems to be this, if not more: While I have in me a soul animating my body as the principle of all my vital and natural actions, I have Jesus Christ animating my soul. And by the impulse and communicate[d] virtue and strength of an indwelling Christ, I am made to run the ways of

His commandments, in which I take so great delight, that I am found of no duty as of my enemy.

II. The gospel holiness respects Jesus Christ as its pattern. It proposes no lower pattern for imitation than to be conform[ed] to His image (he that is begotten again into a lively hope, by the resurrection of Christ from the dead, girds up the loins of his mind, which are the affections of his soul, lest by falling flat on the earth he be hindered in running the race set before him, as looking to the forerunner, his pattern) in this girdle of hope, that he may be "holy in all manner of conversation," keeping his eye on the precept and pattern, that his practice may be conform[able]. "It is written," says he, "be ye holy, for I am holy." The hope of seeing God and being ever with Him imposes a necessity on him who has it to look no lower than at Him who is glorious in holiness. And therefore he is said to purify himself even as He is pure. And knowing that this is the end of their being quickened together with Christ, that they may walk even as He walked, they in their working and walking aim at no less than to be like Him. And therefore [they] never sit down on any attained measure, as if they were already perfect. The spotless purity of God, expressed in His laws, is that to which they study assimilation. Therefore, they are still in motion toward this mark and are changed from one of glorious grace into another, into the same image, even as by the Spirit of the Lord, who never gives over His putting them to cleanse from all filthiness of the flesh and of the spirit, till that be true in the truest sense: "You are all fair, my love; there is no spot in you." And knowing that perfect fruition of him cannot be without the perfect conformity to Him, in this do they exercise themselves to grow in grace and to be still advancing toward some more likeness to His image, forgetting all their attainments as things that are behind, and by

their teachings forth to that which is before, make it evident
that they make every begun degree of grace and conformity
to God a prevenient capacity for a new degree which yet they
have not attained. I know our moralists look on themselves as
matchless, in talking of following His steps as He has left us an
example. In this they make a flourishing with flaunting effron-
tery, but for all their boasting of wisdom, such a poor simple
man as I am made to wonder at their folly, who proposing,
as they say, the purity of Christ as their pattern, are not even
thence convinced that in order to a conformity to this there
is a simple and absolute necessity of the mighty operations
of that Spirit of God, by which this end can be reached. But
while they flout at the Spirit's working as a melancholy fancy,
by which the soul is garnished with the beauty of holiness and
made a habitation for God, I doubt not to say of these great
sayers that they understand neither what they say nor of what
they affirm. Indeed, does not the talking of the one, not only
without seeing the necessity of the other but speaking against
it, say in the heart of everyone who has not the heart of a
beast that they have never yet got a sight of the holiness of that
pattern nor of their own pollutions and impotency? For if they
had, they would give themselves up to Jesus Christ to be washed
by Him, without which they can have no part with Him. Oh
there will be a vast difference at the latter day between them
who have given their black souls to Jesus to bleach, when He
will present them without spot, not only clothed with wrought
gold but all glorious within, and those who have never dipped,
indeed, who have despised to dip their defiled souls in any
other fountain, save in the impure puddle of their own performances. This will make them loathsome in His sight and cause
His soul [to] abhor those who have done this despite to the
Spirit of grace as to slight that blessed fountain opened for
sin and for uncleanness, let them pretend as high as they will

to look to Him as a pattern; while, because the plague-sore is gone up in their eye, they look not to Him as a price nor to the grace of Jesus Christ as that which can only principle any acceptable performance of duty, He will plunge them in the ditch, and it will cost them their souls for rejecting the counsel of God against themselves in not making use of Him who came by water as well as by blood.

III. This gospel holiness respects Christ as the altar. It is in Him and for Him, that His soul is well pleased with our performance—this is the altar on which you must lay your gift and leave it, without which your labor is lost, and whatever you do is loathed as a corrupt thing. As believers draw all their strength from Him, so they expect acceptance only through Him, and for Him. They do not look for it, but in the beloved. They dare not draw near to God in duty, but by Him. This is the new and living way which is consecrate[d] for them. And if such who offer to come to God do not enter in here, instead of being admitted to a familiar converse with God, they will find Him a consuming fire. When the saints have greatest liberty in prayer, and so of all other performances, when their hearts are most lifted up in the ways of the Lord, they abhor at thinking their prayer can any otherways be set forth before Him as incense or the lifting up of their hands as the evening sacrifice, but as presented by the great intercessor and perfumed by the merit of His oblation. If they could weep out the marrow of their bones and the moisture of their body in mourning over sin, yet they durst[6] not think of having what comes from so impure a spring and runs through so polluted a channel presented to God, but by Jesus Christ, in order to acceptance. For as they look to the exalted Savior to get their

---

6. *Durst*: to dare.

repentance from Him, so when by the pourings out on them of the Spirit of grace and supplication, He has made them [to] pour out their hearts before Him and has melted them into true tenderness so that their mourning is a great mourning, they carry back these tears to be washe[d] and bathed in His blood, as knowing without this of how little worth and value with God their salt water is. But when they are thus washed, He puts them in His bottle and then pours them out again to them in the wine of strong consolation. Thus are they made glad in His house of prayer, and their sighs and groans come up with acceptance on His altar. Oh blessed altar that sanctifies the gold! This is that altar to which the mocking moralist has no right. It is by Him that the poor believer offers up his sacrifice to God continually. Whatever he does in word or deed, he desires to do all in the name of the Lord Jesus. As he knows He lives to make intercession and to appear in the presence of God for His poor people, both to procure influences for duty and plead for acceptation, so he depends on Him for both, as knowing he can never otherways hear nor have it said to him, "Well done thou good and faithful servant." It may be he can do little. He has but a mite to offer. But he puts it in the mediator's hand to be presented to God. He has not gold nor silver nor purple to bring. He can do no great things. He has but goats' hair or rams' skins, but he gives them the right tincture. He makes them red in the blood of Christ, and so they are a beautiful incarnation.

But let us, on the other hand, take a short view of what our moralists substitute in its place, as in their account both more beautiful in the eye and more beneficial to the souls of men, in which I intend to be brief. I might comprehend the account to be given shortly and give it most exactly, yet truly in these few words. As the most undoubted deviation from and perfect opposition to the whole contrivance of salvation and the conveyance of it into the souls of men, as revealed in this gospel which brings life and immortality to light, that fighters against the grace of God in its value and virtue can forge, stretching their blind reason to the over-throw of true religion and ruin of the souls of men. For to this height these masters of reason have in their blind rage risen up against the Lord and against His anointed. This is the dreadful period of that path, in which we are persuaded to walk, indeed hectored, if we would not forfeit the repute of men by these grand sophies, who arrogate to themselves the name and thing of knowledge, as if wisdom were to die with them. The deep mysteries of salvation, which angels desire to look into and only satisfy themselves with admiration at, must appear as respondents at their bar. And if they decline the judge and court as incompetent, they flee out and flout at subjecting this blind mole, man's reason, to the revelation of faith in a mystery. The manifold wisdom of God and the mani-fold grace of God must either condescend to their unfoldings and be content to speak in their dialect, or else these wits, these Athenian dictators, will give the deep things of God, because beyond their divings, the same entertainment which that great gospel preacher Paul met with from men of the same mold, kidney, and comple[x]ion, because he preached to them Jesus. "What would the babbler say," said they. The Spirit of wisdom and revelation they know not, they have not, they acknowledge not. Indeed, they despise Him in His saving and soul-ascertaining illuminations. And the workings of that mighty power to them-ward who believe is, to the men of this new mold (because they have not found it), an insufferable fancy to be exploded with a disdain and indignation, which discovers what spirit actuates them in this opposition.

But I would recommend to you who can neither purchase nor peruse what is more voluminous (however worthy) the serious perusal, as of the whole of that savory and grace-breathing peace, the fulfilling of the Scriptures; so in this that short but sweet digression against black-mouthed Parker, in which the gracious author takes out his own soul and sets before your eye the image of God impressed on it. For while he deals with that desperado by clear and convincing reason, flowing natively from the pure fountain of divine revelation, he has the advantage of most men, and writers too, in silencing that proud blasphemer of the good ways of God with arguments taken from what he has found acted on his own soul. And likewise I would recommend as a sovereign antidote against this poison the diligent perusing and pondering of what is shortly hinted against the hellish belchings of the same unhallowed author (in the preface to that piece of great Mr. Durham on the commands) by a disciple, who, besides his natural acuteness and subactness[7] of judgment in the depth of the gospel mysteries, is known by all who know him (and for myself, I know none now alive his equal) to have most frequent access to lean his head on his master's bosom, and so in best case to tell his fellow disciples and brethren what is breathed into his own soul, while he lives in these embraces and under the sheddings abroad of that love of God in his soul, which drew and did dictate these lines against that flouter at all such fruitions. Nor can I here omit to observe how, when the devil raised up Parker, that monster, to bark and blaspheme, the Lord raised up a Merveil to fight him at his own weapon, who did so cudgel and quell that boasting bravo as I know not if he be dead of his wound, but for anything I know, he has laid his speech.

It was not the author's design in this piece (leveled only at this mark to teach you how to make use of the strength and grace that is in Christ Jesus and find the promised ease

---

7. *Subactness*: the quality of being subdued.

in performance of duties, in handling of which argument he
has been remarkably assisted. And you cannot read with atten-
tion, but you must bear him witness and bless the Lord on his
behalf that he has hit the mark at which he aimed) to engage
in a formal debate with these audacious moralists who would
boast and bogle us out of the good old way in which, if men
walk, they must find rest to their souls. Yet if by the doctrine
he has here explained and pressed as the only way of life they
do not find what a mortal wound he has given their morality,
all the lovers of the truth will see it. And it may be, the Lord
sparing life and continuing the same gracious and great assistance he has had in engaging with many and great adversaries
to the truth at home and abroad, they may see somewhat from
his pen which may make the lovers of our Lord Jesus Christ
in sincerity and of the operations of His Spirit sing over these
successors to Sisera, who with their jumping chariots and
rattling wheels assault the truth. At his feet they bowed, they
fell, they lay down at his feet, they bowed, they fell where they
bowed, there they fell down dead; so let all the enemies of Thy
truth perish, O Lord!

How to make the whole more useful for you, for whose
advantage 'tis mainly intended, I leave to the author's own
direction. Only this I must say: his method and mold in which
he casts his sweet matter and his way of handling this so
seasonable a subject is so accommodate[d] to each case and
brought home to the conscience and down to the capacity of
the meanest Christian, which was his aim—that the feeble, in
this day, might be as David. That even though many worthy
men have not only hinted but enlarged upon the same matter,
yet you cannot but see some heart-endearing singularity in
his way of improving and handling this great gospel truth.
Next, I must tell you that as I myself read it with much satisfaction (though, alas, I dare not say, I have by reading reaped

the designed advantage), so that you may be blushed into a perusal of it and profiting by it, I must likewise tell you, I say, it has been turned into Dutch. And that it has not only met with great acceptation among all the serious and godly in these parts who have seen it, but is much sought after. And they profess themselves singularly by this edified and set a-going after God by its efficacious persuasiveness, with a singing alacrity. And if it have not the same effect on you and me, they and it will arise up against us in judgment.

Up, therefore, Christians, and be doing. Listen to such a teacher, who, lest you tire in your race or turn back, teaches you a certain and sweet way of singular proficiency and progress in the ways of God. It may be it is not your work nor mine to write both against these soul-murdering, however magnified, methods of taking men off Jesus Christ. But our penury of parts for that should first put us to seek plenty of tears that we may weep to see our master so wounded by the piercing pens of those who, to patronize their mock religion, wrest the Scriptures and with wicked hands wring the Word of the Lord till it weep blood. This, I say, should provoke you and me to weep on Him till He appear and beat the pens of such deceivers out of their hand by a blow of His. Second, it should provoke us to know the truth that we may contend earnestly for the faith delivered to the saints, and to have these contradicted truths so impressed in their life on our souls that the pen of the most subtle pleader for this perversion of the gospel may neither delete these nor be able to stagger us, but we may, from the efficacious working of these, have the witness in ourselves and know the men who teach otherways not to be of God. Third, it should be our ambition, when the all of religion is cried down and a painted shadow, a putrid, however perfumed, nothing put in its place, to make it appear by our practice that religion is an elevation of the soul above the sphere and activity of dead morality, and that it is no less or lower principle that acts us than Christ dwelling in us and walking in us. How can the love of God and of Christ and of the Spirit be in us, if these perverse praters against the power of godliness provoke us not to emit a practical declaration to the world and extort a testimony to His grace by our way from the enemies of it? Improve, therefore, this His special help to that purpose, which in a most seasonable time is brought to your hand.

But to sum up all shortly, there are but three things which make religion a heavy burden. First, the blindness of the mind, and here you are taught to make use of that eye salve by which the eyes of the blind see out of obscurity and out of darkness. He who formerly erred in spirit, by the light held forth in these lines, may see a surpassing beauty in the ways of God. Second, that aversion and unwillingness which is in the mind by which the sweet and easy yoke of His commands is spurned at as heavy. In order to the removing of it, and that you may be among His willing people, here you have Christ held forth in His conquering beauty, displaying His banner of love over souls, so that you cannot look on Him as held forth, but faith will bow your neck to take on His yoke, because it sees it is lined with the love of Christ. And then this love that lines the yoke, shed abroad in the heart, will constrain to a bearing of it. But, third, when the spirit is willing, there remains yet much weakness. Love kindled in the heart conquers the mind into a compliance with His will and a complacency in His commands. But its greatest strength is often to weep over a withered hand. Now that your hands which fall down may be made strong for labor, and you may be girded with strength and have grace for grace, indeed, all grace to make you abound unto every good word and work, the author leads you up to the full fountain of all gospel furniture and strength and teaches you how to make use of Christ as your sufficiency for working all your works in

you and for you. I say, therefore, again to you: Take heart; let
not your hands fall down; essay nothing you would have well
done or easily done in your own strength, but yet however
difficult the duty be, approach it as having no confidence in
the flesh but with an eye to your stock, that rich storehouse of
all furniture. And it will be with you as it was with the priests,
before whom Jordan recoiled, so soon as their foot entered
within the brink. God will make your difficulties vanish and,
by the illapses of the Spirit of power and might from Jesus
Christ depended on, will so strengthen you that your duty
is made easy to admiration and becomes the delight of your
soul. Pray for the continuance of the life of the author, who,
by his assiduous working for Christ, has been often near unto
death, not regarding his own life to supply the lack of other
men's service to the interest and church of God. And let him
be comforted for this piece of travel undertaken for your
soul's interest by hearing you do improve it to your advantage,
for which it is so exactly calculate[d]. And with all I beg your
fervent and earnest intercessions for grace and more grace,
to him who is your poor yet soul's well-wisher and servant for
Christ's sake,

—R. M. W.

CHAPTER 1

The Introduction with Some General Observations from the Cohesion

Jesus saith unto him, I am the way, the truth, and the life: no man cometh unto the Father, but by me. —JOHN 14:6

Doubtless it is always useful, indeed, necessary for the children of God to know the right way of making use of Christ, who is made all things to them which they need, even "wisdom, and righteousness, and sanctification, and redemption" (1 Cor. 1:30). But it is never more necessary for believers to be clear and distinct in this matter than when Satan by all means is seeking to pervert the right ways of the Lord and, one way or other, to lead souls away and draw them off Christ, knowing that, if he prevail here, he has gained his point. And therefore he endeavors not only to darken it by error, either more gross or more subtle, but also to darken it by mistakes and prejudices. From this, it comes to pass that not only strangers are made to wander out of the way, but oftentimes many of His own people are walking in darkness of ignorance and mistakes and remain lean through want of the real exercise of the life of faith, which would make them fat and flourishing, because it would make them "strong in the Lord, and in the power of his might" [Eph. 6:10] and to grow up in Christ in all things.

The clearing up then of this truth cannot but be most seasonable now, when Satan is prevailing with many whom he cannot get tempted to looseness and profanity to sit down on something which is not Christ and to rest on something with themselves distinct from Him, both in the matter of justification and sanctification. This subtle adversary is now setting some to work to cry up[1] by preaching, speaking, and printing a way to heaven which is not Christ—a kind of morality, civility, and outward holiness on which the soul is to rest. And this holiness, not wrought and effectuated through the strength of Jesus [nor] by faith sucking life and furniture[2] from Him, but through our own art and skill, which in effect is nothing but an extract of refined popery, Socinianism, and Arminianism, devised and broached of purpose to draw the soul off Christ that he may stand on his own legs and walk by his own power and thank himself, at least in part, for the crown at length.

Further, through the great goodness of God, the true way of a soul's justification is admirably cleared up, and many are, at least theoretically, acquainted with it, and many also practically, to the quieting of their wakened consciences and stopping the mouth of their accusers and obtaining of peace, joy, and the lively hope of the everlasting crown. Yet many gracious souls profess their unacquaintedness with the solid and thriving way of use-making of Christ for growth in grace and true sanctification. Therefore, some discovery of the truth here cannot but be useful, seasonable, indeed, and acceptable to them. If He who is the truth would give grace to understand and to unfold this so necessary and always advantageous a truth and would help to write of and explain this truth by faith in Him who is here said to be the truth, then should we

---

1. *To cry up*: to create.
2. *Furniture*: necessary equipment, help, or sustenance.

have cause to bless and magnify His name. But if He, because of sin, will hide Himself and not let out these beams of light by which we might discover light, we will but darken counsel with words without our knowledge and leave the matter as unclear as ever. Therefore is it necessary there be both in him that writes and in such as read a single dependence on Him who is for a leader (Isa. 55:5) and has promised to "bring the blind by a way that they knew not" and to "lead them in paths that they have not known" and to "make darkness light before them, and crooked things straight" (Isa. 42:16), that thus by acting faith on Him we may find insofar the truth of this verified—namely, that He is the way, the truth, and the life.

Now, for clearing up of this matter, we would know that our Lord Jesus from the beginning of this chapter is laying down some grounds of consolation, sufficient to comfort His disciples against the sad news of His departure and death and to encourage them against the fears they had of much evil to befall them when their Lord and Master should be taken from them, which is a sufficient proof of the tender heart of Jesus, who allows all His followers strong consolation against all fears, hazards, troubles, and perplexities which they can meet with in their way. He will not leave them comfortless, and therefore He lays down strong grounds of consolation to support their drooping and fainting hearts, as loving to see His followers always rejoicing in the Lord and singing in the ways of Zion—that the world may see and be convinced of a reality in Christianity and of the preferableness of that life, despite all the troubles that attend it to any other, however sweet and desirable it may appear to flesh and blood.

In prosecution of which design, He told them that they knew where He went and the way also which He was to take and by which He was to bring them to the Father (v. 4) to the mansion spoken of, and so to life eternal. But Thomas rashly and incredulously (as too usually he did, [John] 11:16; 20:25) vents himself and little less than contradicts his Master, saying, "We know not whither thou goest; and how can we know the way?" (v. 5), in which we have an emblem of many a believer who may have more grace and knowledge of God and of Christ than they will be able to see or acknowledge that they have, what through temptations, inward distempers, sense of their many defects and great ignorance, strong desires of high measures, clearer discoveries of the vastness of the object, mistakes about the true nature of grace, despising the day of small things, and indistinctness as to the actings of grace, or want of understanding and right uptaking of grace in its various outgoings and actings under various notions, and the like.

On which, Christ, after His usual manner, takes occasion to clear up that ground of consolation further to them and to let them see the true way of coming to the Father, that by this they might be helped to see that they were not such strangers to the way as they supposed. And, in addition, He amplifies and lays out the properties and excellencies of this way as being the only true and living way, and that in such a manner as they might both see the way to be perfect, full, safe, saving, and satisfying and also learn their duty of improving this way always and in all things until they come home at length to the Father, saying, "I am the way, the truth, the life; no man cometh unto the Father, but by me."

Christ, [by] then saying that He not only is the way to the Father—even the true way—but that He is so the true way as that He is also truth itself in the abstract; and so the living way, that He is life itself in the abstract—[this] gives us ground to consider after what manner it is that He is the truth and the life, as well as the way, and that for clearing up and discovering of Him being an absolutely perfect, transcendently excellent, incomparably preferable, and fully satisfying way, useful to believers in all cases, all exigents, all distresses, all difficulties, all trials, all temptations, all doubts, all perplexities, and in all causes or occasions of distempers, fears, faintings, discouragements, etc., which they may meet with in their way to heaven. And this will lead us to clear up the duty of believers, on the other hand, and to show how they should in all their various cases and difficulties make use of Christ as the only all-sufficient way to the Father and as truth and life in the way—and so we will be led to speak of Christ being to His people all that is requisite for them here in the way, whether for justification or sanctification, and how people are to make use of Him as being all, or, as being made of "God…unto us wisdom, and righteousness, and sanctification, and redemption" (1 Cor. 1:30).

Before we come to the words in particular, we would look on them as having relation to Thomas's words in the preceding verse, in which he did little less than contradict what Christ had said in verse 4 and learn several very comfortable points of doctrine, as:

I. That Jesus Christ is very tender of His followers and will not cast them off nor upbraid them for every escape by which they may provoke Him to anger and grieve His Spirit. But [He] gently passes by many of their failings when He finds they are not obstinate in their mistake nor perverse in their way. For how gently and meekly does He here pass over Thomas's unhandsome expression, finding that Thomas spoke here not out of obstinacy and pertinaciousness but out of ignorance and a mistake. And the reason is because (1) Christ knows our infirmity and weakness and is of a tender heart, and therefore [He] will not break the bruised reed (Isa. 42[:3]). Well knows He that rough and untender handling would crush us and break us all in pieces. And (2) He is full of bowels of mercy and can have compassion on them that are out of the way and can be touched with the feeling of our infirmities (Heb. 4:15; 5:2).

Which truth, as on the one hand, should encourage all to choose Him for their leader and give up themselves to Him who is so tender of His followers. So, on the other hand, it should rebuke such as are ready to entertain evil and hard thoughts of Him, as if He were a hard master and ill to be followed, and put all from entertaining the least thought of His untenderness and want of compassion.

II. But, moreover, we see that weaknesses and corruptions breaking out in believers when they are honestly and ingenuously laid open before the Lord will not fear Him away but rather engage Him the more to help and succor. Much of Thomas's weakness and corruption appeared in what he said, yet the same being honestly and ingenuously laid open to Christ not out of a spirit of contradiction but out of a desire to learn, Christ is so far from thrusting him away that He rather condescends the more out of love and tenderness to instruct him better and clear the way more fully. And that because (1) He knows our mold and fashion, how feckless[3] and frail we are, and that if He should deal with us according to our folly, we should quickly be destroyed. (2) He is not as a man, hasty, rash, proud; but gentle, loving, tender, and full of compassion. (3) It is His office and proper work to be an instructor to the ignorant and a helper of our infirmities and weaknesses, a physician to bind up and cure our sores and wounds.

Who would not then willingly give up themselves to such a teacher that will not thrust them to the door nor give them up to themselves always when their corruptions would provoke Him to it? And what a madness is this in many to stand back

---

3. *Feckless*: weak or useless.

from Christ because of their infirmities and to scar[4] at Him because of their weakness, when the more corruption we find, the more we should run to Him? And it is soon enough to depart from Christ when He thrusts us away and says He will have no more to do with us. Indeed, He will allow us to stay after we are thrice thrust away. Only let us take heed that we approve not ourselves in our evils, that we hide them not as unwilling to part with them, that we obstinately maintain them not nor ourselves in them, but that we lie open before Him and deal with Him with honesty, ingenuousness, and plainness.

III. We see, further, that ignorance ingenuously acknowledged and laid open before Christ puts the soul in a fair way to get more instruction. Thomas having candidly according as he thought in the simplicity of his heart professed his ignorance is in a fair way now to get instruction. For this is Christ's work: to instruct the ignorant, to open the eyes of the blind.

Why then are we so foolish as to conceal our ignorance from Him and to hide our case and condition from Him, and why does not this commend Christ's school to us so much the more? Why do we not carry as ingenious scholars,[5] really desirous to learn?

IV. But we may learn that our ill condition and distempers put into Christ's hand will have remarkable out-gates[6] and an advantageous issue, seeing Christ takes occasion here from Thomas laying open his condition, not without some mixture of corruption, to clear up the truth more fully and plainly than it was before. For by this (1) Christ gives an open declaration of the glory of His power, mercy, goodness, wisdom,

---

4. *Scar*: glare at or be disgusted by.
5. *Scholars*: students.
6. *Out-gates*: escapes.

etc. (2) He has occasion to give a proof of His divine art and glorious skill of healing diseased souls and of making broken bones stronger than ever they were. (3) Thus He effectually accomplished His noble designs and perfects His work in a way tending to abase man by discovering his infirmities and failings and to glorify Himself in His goodness and love. (4) Thus He triumphs more over Satan and in a more remarkable and glorious manner destroys his works. (5) Thus He declares how wonderfully He can make all things work together for good to His chosen ones that love Him and follow Him. (6) Indeed, thus He engages souls to wonder more at His divine wisdom and power; to despair less in time coming when cases would seem hard; to acknowledge His great and wonderful grace and His infinite power and wisdom that can bring life out of death; and also to be more sensible of the mercy and thankful for it.

Oh, believer, what manner of joy is here! How happy you are that has given up yourself to Him! Your worst condition can turn to your advantage. He can make your ignorance, vented with a mixture of corruption, turn to the increase of your knowledge. Bless Him for this and with joy and satisfaction abide under His tutory[7] and at His school. And in addition, be not discouraged, be your case of ignorance and corruption what it will. Lay it before Him with sincerity and singleness of heart and then you may glory in your infirmities, "that the power of Christ may rest upon [you]" (2 Cor. 12:9), for you will see in due time what advantage infinite love and wisdom can bring to your soul by this.

May not this be a strong motive to induce strangers to give up themselves to Him who will sweetly take occasion at their failings and shortcomings to help them forward in the way?

---

7. *Tutory*: teaching or instruction.

And what excuse can they have who sit [under] the call of the gospel and say, in effect, they will not go to Christ because their case is not good? And, oh, that believers were not sometimes led away with this error of scaring at Christ because of infirmities seen and discovered!

V. It is remarkable that as the disciples did oftentimes vent much of their carnal conceptions of the kingdom of Christ as apprehending it to be some carnal, outward, pompous, stately, and, on that account, desirable condition, so there might be much of this carnal apprehension lurking under this acknowledgment and question of Thomas. And the Lord, who knew their thoughts, does here wisely draw them off those notions and sets them about another study to tell us that it is best and most useful and profitable for us to be much taken up in the study and search of necessary fundamental truths and, particularly, of the way to the Father. For (1) here is the substantial food of the soul. Other notions are but vain, and oftentimes they make the case of the soul worse; but the study of this is always edifying. (2) The right understanding of this and other fundamental truths will not puff up but keep the soul humble and will make the soul active and diligent in duty. (3) The fruit of this study is profitable and lasting. (4) And the right uptaking of these truths will discover the vanity of other sciences, falsely so called, and the folly of spending our time about other things. (5) The right understanding of this fundamental will help us to understand other truths the better. (6) A mistake in this and such like fundamentals or the ignorance of them is more dangerous than the ignorance of or mistake in other things.

Oh! If this were teaching us all in humility to be much in the study of such fundamental necessary truths as this is and to guard against a piece of vanity in affecting knowledge, the effect of which is nothing but a puffing of us up with pride and conceit!

VI. We may here take notice of what may serve to discover Thomas's mistake, and what is the ground of Christ's assertion (v. 4), which Thomas does little less than contradict (v. 5)—namely, that such as had any acquaintance with Christ did according to the measure of their knowledge of Him both know heaven and the way to it. From this we see these truths:

1. Persons may have some real acquaintance with Christ and yet be for a time very indistinct in their notions about Him and apprehensions of Him. They may know Christ in some measure and yet look on themselves as great strangers to the knowledge of heaven and be often complaining of their ignorance of the right way to heaven.

2. Where there is the least measure of true acquaintance with Christ, with love to Him and a desire to know more of Him, Christ will take notice of it, though it be covered over with a heap of mistakes and accompanied with much ignorance, weakness, and indistinctness. He sees not as man sees, which is good news to some that are weak in knowledge and unable to give any good account of any knowledge they have—yet one thing they can say: that He who knows all things knows that they love Him.

3. Various are the dispensations of God's grace to His own. To some, He gives a greater [and] to others a lesser measure of knowledge of the mysteries of the kingdom of heaven—and to one and the same person, more at one time than at another. Various are His manifestations and out-lettings of grace and love. Small beginnings may come to much at length. Thomas and

the rest of the disciples had but little clear and distinct apprehensions of the way of salvation through Jesus Christ. And yet, before all was done, they attained to such a measure of understanding in the mysteries of God as that we are said to be "built upon the foundation of the apostles…Jesus Christ himself being the chief corner stone" (Eph. 2:20). This should teach the best much sobriety and not to judge of all by themselves or to think that God's way with them must be a standard or a rule by which to judge of all the rest, as if His way of dealing were one and the same with all.

4. The knowledge of Christ is all. Know Him, and we know heaven and the way to it; for on this ground does Christ make good what He said touching their knowing where He went and the way, and [He] answers the objection that Thomas did propose—namely, because He was the way, etc., and they, being acquaint[ed] with Him (which here is presupposed), were not ignorant of the place where He was going nor of the way leading there. The knowledge then of Jesus Christ is a true and full compend[ium] of all saving knowledge. Hence it is life eternal to know Him (John 17:3). They that know Him know the Father (8:19; 14:9). They that see Him see the Father also (14:9). He is in the Father, and the Father, in Him (10:38; 14:10–11; 17:21). And so, knowing Him, they know heaven, for what is heaven else but the presence and glorious manifestations of the Father? For when Christ speaks of Him going to heaven, He says He was going to the Father. So, knowing Him, they know the way—both how Christ was to go to heaven as

our cautioner,[8] head, and attorney, and how we must follow.

Let then a man have never so much knowledge and be acquainted with the mysteries of all arts and sciences and with the depths of nature and intrigues of states and all the theory of religion. If he be unacquainted with Jesus, he knows nothing as he ought to know.

And, on the other hand, let a poor soul that is honest and has some knowledge of and acquaintance with Him be satisfied, though he cannot discourse nor dispute nor speak to cases of conscience as some others. If we know Him, it matters not though we be ignorant of many things and by this become less esteemed of by others. Here is the true test by which we may take a right estimate of our own or of others' knowledge. The true rule to try knowledge by is not fine notions, clear and distinct expressions, but heart-acquaintance with Him "in whom are hid all the treasures of wisdom and knowledge" (Col. 2:3).

Oh, sad! That we are not more taken up in this study which would be a compendious way for us to know all. Why spend we our money for that which is not bread and our labor for that which will not profit us? Why waste we our time and spirits in learning this science and that art, when, alas, after we with much labor and toil have attained to the yondmost pitch there, we are never one whit the nearer heaven and happiness? Indeed, it were well if we were not further off! Oh! If we were wise at length and could think more of this one thing necessary and could be stirred up to learn more of Him and to make this the subject of all our study and labor.

---

8. *Cautioner:* surety.

CHAPTER 2

Of the Words Themselves in General

We come now to the words themselves in which Christ asserts that He is (1) "the way"; (2) "the truth"; (3) "the life"; and (4) "that no man cometh to the Father, but by him."

In them we learn these two things in general:

The Misery of Man by Nature

First, the misery of wretched man by nature. This cannot be in a few words expressed.

These words will point out those particulars of it, which we will but mention:

1. That he is born an enemy to and living at a distance from God by virtue of the curse of the broken covenant of life made with Adam.

2. That he neither can nor will return to God of himself. His way is not in himself. He has need of another to be his way.

3. That he is a blind, wandering creature, ready to by-ways and to wander. Indeed, he loves to wander. He goes astray as soon as he is born, speaking lies.

4. He cannot discern the true way but is blinded with prejudice on account of it and full of mistakes. He is nothing but a lump of error.

5. He is dead legally and really. How can he then come home? How can he walk in the way, though it were pointed out to him?

6. He, even when he enters into the way, is subject to so many faintings, swoonings, upsittings, etc., that except he get new quickening, he must lie by the way and perish.

In a word, his misery is such as cannot be expressed, for as little as it is believed and laid to heart or seen and mourned for and lamented.

Now, for a ground to our following discourse, I would press the solid, thorough, and sensible apprehension of this, without which there will be no use-making or application of Christ—for the "whole need not a physician, but... [the] sick," and Christ is not come to "call the righteous, but sinners to repentance" (Matt. 9:12; Mark 2:17). Indeed, believers themselves would live within the sight of this and not forget their frailty, for though there be a change wrought in them, yet they are not perfect but will have need of Christ as the way, the truth, and the life till He bring them in and set them down on the throne and crown them with the crown of life. And, oh, happy [are] they who must not walk on foot without this guide leading them by the hand, or rather carrying them in His arms. Let all they who would make use of Christ remember what they were and what they are and keep the sense of their frailty and misery fresh, [so] that seeing their need of Him, they may be in better case to look out to Him for help and supply and be more distinct in their application of Him.

The Complete Mediator, Christ
The second general is that Christ is a complete mediator, thoroughly furnished for all our necessities. Are we at a distance from the Father? He is a way to bring us together. Are we

wandered out of the way? He is the way to us. Are we blind and ignorant? He is the truth. Are we dead? He is the life. Concerning this fullness and completeness of His, we would mark these things:

I. He is thoroughly furnished with all things we stand in need of: the way, the truth, and the life. He has eye salve, clothing, gold tried in the fire, etc.—for the Spirit of the Lord is on Him and "hath anointed [him]" (Isa. 61:1).

II. He is suitably qualified, not only having a fullness and an all-fullness so that whatever we need is to be had in Him but also a suitable fullness answering our case to the life. Are we out of the way? He is the way. Are we dead? He is life. Etc.

III. He is richly qualified with this suitable good. He has not only "wisdom and knowledge" but "treasures" of it, indeed, "all the treasures" of it (Col. 2:3). There is fullness in Him. Indeed, it has pleased the Father "that in him should all fulness dwell" (1:19). Indeed, the fullness of the Godhead dwells in Him bodily (2:9).

IV. Hence, this is an up-making completeness and fullness, for we are said to be "complete in him" (2:10). And He is said to be all in all. He "filleth all in all" (Eph. 1:23).

V. It is also a satisfying completeness. The eye is not satisfied with seeing, nor the ear with hearing. The avaricious man is not satisfied with gold, nor the ambitious man with honor. But still they are crying with the loch leech,[1] "Give, Give!" But the man who gets Christ is full. He sits down and cries, "Enough, enough!" And no wonder, for he has all. He can desire no

---

1. *Loch leech*: medicinal leech used for bloodletting.

more. He can seek no more, for what can the man want that is complete in Him?

VI. There is here that which will answer all the objections of a soul, and these sometimes are not few. If they say they cannot know the way to the Father, then He is the truth to instruct and teach them that and so to enter them into it. And if they say they cannot walk in that way nor advance in it one step but will faint and sit up, succumb and fall by, [then] He answers that He is the life to put life and keep life in them and to cause them to walk by putting a new principle of life in them and breathing of new on that principle.

Oh thrice happy [are] they who have fled to Him for refuge! It is easy for them to answer all objections and cavils of Satan and of a false heart. It is easy for them to put Christ to answer all. And, on the other hand, who can tell the misery of such as are strangers to Jesus? How will their wants be made up? How will they answer challenges, accusations, temptations, doubts, fears, objections, and discouragements cast up in their way?

Oh! Should not this endear the way of the gospel to us and make Christ precious to us! Is it not a wonder that such an all-sufficient mediator who is able to save to the uttermost all that come to God through Him should be so little regarded and sought, and that there should be so few that embrace Him and take Him as He is offered in the gospel?

How can this be answered in the day of accounts? What excuse can unbelievers now have? Is not all to be found in Christ that their case calls for? Is He not a complete mediator, thoroughly furnished with all necessaries? Are not the riches of His fullness written on all His dispensations? The mouths, then, of unbelievers must be forever stopped.

CHAPTER 3

How Christ Is the Way in General:
"I Am the Way"

_W_e come now to speak more particularly to the words and, first, of Him being a way. Our design being to point at the way of use-making of Christ in all our necessities, straits, and difficulties which are in our way to heaven and particularly to point out the way how believers should make use of Christ in all their particular exigencies and so live by faith in Him, walk in Him, grow up in Him, advance and march forward toward glory in Him. It will not be amiss to speak of this fullness of Christ in reference to unbelievers, as occasion offers, because this will help to clear the other.

Before we can clear up how any can make use of Christ, we must speak something of their necessity of Him and of Him being furnished fitly, fully, richly, and satisfyingly for their case. And this will make the way of use-making of Christ more plain.

Man Is Lost
While Christ then says, "I am the way," He points out these things to us: (1) That man is now estranged from the Lord and in a wandering condition. He has departed from God. He is revolted and gone. "They are all gone out of the way" (Rom. 3:12). "They go astray as soon as they be born, speaking lies" (Ps. 58:3). (2) No, not only so, but we love naturally to wander

and to run away from God, as Jeremiah complains of that wicked people (Jer. 14:10). Naturally, with "the dromedary," we traverse our ways (2:23) and run hither and thither but never look toward Him. No, we are like those spoken of (Job 21:14). We desire not the knowledge of His ways, [and] we will have none of Him (Ps. 81:11) nor of His reproofs (Prov. 1:30).

Oh, how sad is this! And yet how is it sadder that this is not believed nor once considered. And that it is not believed is manifest, for:

I. How rare is it to meet with persons that are not very well pleased and satisfied with themselves and their condition? They thank the Lord it was aye[1] well with them. They have no complaints. They see no wants nor necessities. They wonder what makes folk complain of their condition, of their evil heart, or of their hazard and danger. They understand not these matters.

II. Do we not find people very quiet and at rest, though they remain in the congregation of the dead (Prov. 21:16). They sleep in a sound skin, because they see no hazard. The thoughts of their condition never bereave them of one night's rest. No challenges have they. All is at peace with them, for the strong man keeps the house.

III. How rare is it to find people exercised about this matter and busied with it in their thoughts either while alone or while in company with others, or, once seriously thinking and considering of it, indeed, or so much as suspecting the matter?

IV. How rare is it to see any soul broken in heart and humbled because of this who is walking under this as under a load,

---

1. *Aye*: always.

whose soul is bleeding under the consideration of this! Is there any mourning for this?

V. Where is that to be heard: "Men and brethren, what shall we do to be saved?" How will we enter into the right way? Where is that good old way, that we may walk in it? Few such questions and cases troubling consciences, and no wonder, for a deep sleep is on them.

VI. How comes it, then, that the pointing forth of the way is so little hearkened to? Surely were this natural condition perceived [then] a report of the sure and safe way would be much more welcome than it is. Christ by His messengers would not be put to cry so often in vain, "This is the way; turn in hither."

Here is enough to convince of this ignorance and insensibleness. But it is His Spirit which convinces the world of sin (John 16) that must bear home this conviction.

Man Is Hopelessly Lost

Secondly, it points out to us this: that "the way of man is not in himself" (Jer. 10:23)—that is, that nothing he can do can or will prove a way to him to the Father, for Christ is the way, as excluding all other means and ways. And that man can do nothing to help himself into the way is clear, for:

1. His way is darkness (Prov. 4:19). He knows no better; he is satisfied with it. There he sleeps and rests.

2. He cannot nor does not desire to return. He hates to be reformed.

3. Indeed, he thinks himself safe. No man can convince him of the contrary. The way he is in seems right to him, though the end of it be death (Prov. 14:12; 16:25).

4. Every man has his own particular way to which he turns (Isa. 53:6), some one thing or other that he is pleased with and that he thinks will abundantly carry him through. And there he rests. And what these ordinarily are, we will hear presently.

5. In this his way, which yet is a false way, he trusts (Hos. 10:13). He leans on it, little knowing that it will fail him at length and that he and his hope and confidence will perish.

Is it not strange then to see men and women "gadd[ing]… about" to seek their way, as it is said (Jer. 2:36), as if they could find it out, or as if they could of themselves fall on the way. What a lamentable sight is it to see people wearying themselves with very lies (Ezek. 24:12) and wearied in the multitude of their own counsels (Isa. 47:15).

But what are those false and lying ways which men weary themselves in and all in vain, and which they choose and trust and yet are not the way which will prove safe and sure?

Answer. It will not be easy to reckon them all up. We will name some that are principal and most ordinary, such as:

I. Good purposes and resolutions with which many deceive themselves, supposing that to be all which is required. And, alas, all their purposes are like to Ephraim's goodness—like the early cloud and morning dew that soon vanishes. Their purposes are soon broken off and soon disappointed because [they are] made without counsel (Prov. 15:22). Many foolishly rest here: that they have a good mind to do better and to amend their ways, and they purpose after such a time or such time [when] they will begin a new manner of life. But their purposes never come to any effect, and so at length they and their purposes both perish.

II. Some convictions and inward challenges. The Word now and then pierces them so far, and sore and sharp dispensations from the Lord so far affect their heart that they see it is not well with them. And they are made with Saul to cry out, "I have sinned" (1 Sam. 15:24). And they advance no further. Those convictions either die out again or work no further change. And, poor souls, they think because at such a sermon or such a communion they had some such convictions and sharp challenges, therefore they imagine all is well with them—when a Judas may have convictions sharper than ever they had, and a Felix (Acts 24:25).

III. Convictions followed with some sort of amendment. Some may dreadfully deceive themselves with this and conclude that all is right with them and that the way they are in is safe and sure because they have had convictions which have been so effectual as to cause them to amend many things and become, as to many things, changed men and women, when, alas, their way is but a way of darkness still. It is not Christ. They have never come to Him. Herod, hearing John Baptist, had his own convictions and amendments, for he did many things (Mark 6:20).

IV. Many rest on their outward civility and morality or negative holiness. They cannot be challenged for gross faults, and that is all the way they have to rest in. Alas! Could not a wicked Pharisee say as much as they—namely, that he was no extortioner, unjust person, or an adulterer, nor such as the publican was (Luke 18:11)? How many heathens as to this will outstrip such as profess themselves Christians? And yet they lived and died strangers to the right way to happiness. See what that poor young man said (Luke 18:21).

V. Some may win to more than civility and attain to a kind of outward holiness and outward performance of the duties of religion, such as hearing, reading, prayer, communicating, and rest there and yet perish. For that is but their own way. It is not the right way. Had not the foolish virgins lamps? And did they not wait with the rest (Matthew 25). And will not many say in that day, "We have eaten and drunk in thy presence, and thou hast taught in our streets," to whom Christ will answer, "I know not whence ye are; depart from me, all ye workers of iniquity" (Luke 13:26–27)? Were not the Jews much in duties and outward ordinances? And yet see how the Lord rejected them all (Isa. 1:11–15; 66:3).

VI. Much knowledge deceives many. They think because they can talk of religion, speak to cases of conscience, handle places of Scripture, and the like that therefore all is right with them, when, alas, that is but a slippery ground to stand on. The Pharisees sat in Moses' seat and taught sometimes sound doctrine and yet were heart-enemies to Jesus (Matthew 23). And will not many think to plead themselves into heaven by saying that they have prophesied in His name (7:22)? There is a knowledge that puffs up (1 Cor. [8:1]). Some there are whose knowledge seems to be operative and practical and not merely speculative. Some may escape the pollutions of the world through the knowledge of the Lord and Savior Jesus Christ and yet again become entangled in them and overcome, so that "their latter end is worse…than the beginning" (see 2 Peter 2:20–22). Knowledge, I grant, is good, but it is not Christ. And so it is not the way to the Father, and many, alas, lean to it and are deceived at last.

VII. A kind of seeming seriousness in the performance of duties and in seeking of God deceives many. They think because they are not conscious to their own dissembling but they look on themselves as earnest in what they do—that therefore, all is well. Says not Christ that "not every one that saith…Lord, Lord, shall enter into the kingdom of heaven" (Matt. 7:21)? That is, not everyone that renews their suits and ingeminates[2] their desires, cry, and cry over again, and, as it were, will not give it over, and yet they come short of their expectation. Did not the foolish virgins seem earnest and serious when they continued waiting with the rest and at length cried, "Lord, Lord, open unto us"—and yet they are kept at the door. Many consider not that there is a secret and close hypocrisy that some may be under and not know it, as well as a gross hypocrisy and dissimulation which may be easily observed. Will not many seek to enter in that will not be able (Matt. 7:13; Luke 13:24)?

VIII. Many deceive themselves with this: that they are looked on by other godly, discerning persons and ministers as good, serious Christians, and that they carry so handsomely and so fair that no man can judge otherwise of them than that they are good, serious seekers of God. But, alas, the day is coming which will discover many things, and many ones will be deceived both of themselves and of others. "Not he that commendeth himself is approved, but whom the Lord commendeth" (2 Cor. 10:18). Therefore, Paul exhorts Timothy to study to show himself "approved unto God" (2 Tim. 2:15). Men look only on the outside and cannot see into the heart, but God searches the heart. And it is an easy matter to deceive men, but God will not be deceived.

---

2. *Ingeminates*: repeat or reiterate.

IX. Some may suppose themselves in a safe and sure way if they outstrip others in religious duties and be much in extraordinary duties, when, alas, for all that, the heart may be rotten. The Pharisee fasted twice [each] week (Luke 18:12) and yet was but an enemy to Christ. Oh, how deceitful is the heart of man!

X. Inward peace and quietness of conscience may deceive some, and they may suppose that all is right with them because they do nothing over the belly of their conscience. Their heart does not accuse them of falsehood and dissimulation in their way with God or man, but they do all things according to their light. No doubt that young man spoke according to his judgment and light when he said, "All these have I kept from my youth" (Luke 18:21). And Paul says of himself that he had lived "in all good conscience before God until this day" (Acts 23:1), meaning that even while he was a Pharisee unconverted he had not tortured his conscience nor done anything directly against it but had always walked according to his light (see Acts 26:9).

XI. A way of zeal may deceive many who may think their case unquestionable, because they are zealous for their way, and, as they think, their zeal is pure for God. Was not Paul, while a Pharisee, very zealous when out of zeal to his way he persecuted the church (Phil. 3:6)? "See my zeal for the LORD," could I thus say (2 Kings 10:16). And the Jews had a zeal of God, but not according to knowledge (Rom. 10:2). And Christ tells us that such as should persecute the apostles to death would think they did God good service (John 16:2).

XII. Some also may put it beyond question that they are in the right way because they are more strict in all their ways than others and will not so much as keep fellowship or company with them, saying, with those, "Stand by yourself, for I am holier than you. Come not near to me" (cf. Isa. 65:5), who yet are but a smoke in God's nose and a fire that burns all the day. XIII. Some may rest on and deceive themselves with their great attainments and more than ordinary experiences, when, alas, we see to what a height some may come and yet prove nothing. Let such souls read with trembling that word of Paul (Heb. 6:4–5), where we see some may come to be enlightened, to taste of the heavenly gift, to be made partakers of the Holy Ghost, to taste the good word of God and the powers of the world to come, and yet prove castaways—taking these expressions as pointing forth something distinct from real grace.

Many such false ways in which men please themselves might be mentioned. By these, everyone may see cause of searching and trying over and over again. It is a dreadful thing to be deceived here, and it is best to put it to a trial when there is a possibility of getting the matter helped. And many may fear and tremble when they see they are not yet come the length of many such as sit down without Christ and lose all their labor. Oh, if this could put people to a serious examination and trial of themselves and of the nature of that way in which they are and rest at present!

There Is Only One Way for All
Thirdly, we might here observe that this true and living way is but one for all. There is but "one mediator between God and men" (1 Tim. 2:5), one mediator for both Old and New Testaments, the seed of the woman. Even though the Lord's dispensations with His people in that one way may be various, as His way with His people under the law is different from His way with His people under the gospel, and His dispensations with individual believers, whether under the law or under the gospel, is not the same in all things.

And this should teach us to relinquish our own ways and to enter into this one only way. And it should move such as are in this way to study unity and agreement among themselves and yet not infer or suppose that God's way with them must be in all things alike. Indeed, though the Lord's way with them be different from His way with others and more dark, disconsolate, and bitter, yet let them be quiet and silent before the Lord and acknowledge His goodness that has brought them into the one only way, Jesus Christ, and keeps them there.

Jesus Christ Is the Way to the Father
But, fourthly, the main thing here and which is obvious is this: that Jesus Christ is the way to the Father, the one and only way, the sovereign and excellent way, and He alone is the way. There is not another. "Neither is there salvation in any other: for there is none other name under heaven given among men, whereby we must be saved" (Acts 4:12).

For clearing of this, we will speak a little to these four things and show:

1. What is our case and what need we have of a way.

2. How Christ answers this our case and necessity and is a fit way for us.

3. How He alone is the way and answers this our case.

4. What are the rare advantages and specialities of this way.

And this will make way for our clearing up how Christ is made use of as a way by poor sinners.

What Is Our Case and What Need We Have of a Way
For the first of these, our present case and necessity, something was spoken to it before. We will reduce all these to two heads. The first is our state of guilt and separation from God

because of sin and guilt. The next is our state of wickedness and enmity against God.

As to the first, we may take notice of these things: (1) That sin [both] original and actual has separated us from God and cast us out of His favor and out of that station of favor and friendship which once we were advanced to in Adam; (2) that we are under God's curse and wrath and excommunicated from the presence of the Lord by a sad yet just sentence according to law, and so [we] are under death.

As to the next thing, we may take notice of these particulars:

1. That we are impure and polluted with sin and daily iniquity.

2. That we are ignorant of the right way of returning into favor with God, seeking out to ourselves many inventions.

3. That we are impotent for any good work or commanded duty.

4. That not only so, but we are unwilling to do anything that is good or to enter into the way when pointed out to us. Indeed, we are enemies to God by wicked works and have an innate hatred to all His ways.

5. We desire not to be out of the condition in which we are. There we love to lie and sleep and desire not to be roused up or awakened.

6. We are under the power and command of Satan, who leads us out of the way, indeed, and drives us forward in the wrong way to our perdition.

These things are plain and undeniable and need no further confirmation—though, alas, it is little believed or laid to heart by many.

How Christ Answers This Our Case and
Necessity and Is a Fit Way for Us
For the second, how Christ answers this our case and necessity, He is a way to us to help us out of both [of] these—both
out of our state of guilt and separation and out of our state of
wickedness and enmity.

And, first, He helps us out of our state of guilt and separation:

I. By taking away our guilt and sin, being made sin for us, "who
knew no sin; that we might be made the righteousness of God
in him" (2 Cor. 5:21). He has filled the great gap between God
and us with His body and has made of it, as it were, a bridge by
which they may go over to the Father. We enter now into the
holiest by the blood of Jesus "by a new and living way, which
he hath consecrated for us, through the veil, that is to say,
his flesh" (Heb. 10:19–20). We are now brought near by His
blood (Eph. 2:13), so that through Him we are restored again
to friendship with God and made one with Him; for Christ the
mediator has made both one, reconciling Jews and Gentiles
"both unto God in one body by the cross, having slain the
enmity thereby" (2:16).

II. By taking away the curse and wrath that was due to us, being
"made a curse for us" (Gal 3:13). So that He is become our
peace and "through him we both have access by one Spirit unto
the Father...[and] are no more strangers and foreigners, but
fellowcitizens with the saints, and of the household of God"
(Eph. 2:18–19; cf. v. 14). He is set forth to be a propitiation
through faith in His blood (Rom. 3:25; 1 John 2:2; 4:10). By
Him have we "now received the atonement" (Rom. 5:11).

Next, He helps us out of our state of wickedness and enmity:

I. By taking away our impurity and uncleanness by washing us and cleansing us in His blood (Ezek. 16:6–9; Col. 1:22); having purchased grace for us (Eph. 5:1, 3), we are blessed with all spiritual blessings in Him. He applies His merits and lays the foundation of grace and holiness in the soul and carries on the work of mortification and vivification. And so, killing the old man by His Spirit both meritoriously and efficiently, He cleanses and washes. Hence we are said to be baptized with Him in His death and buried with Him by baptism into death that we should walk in newness of life. And so our old man is crucified with Him that the body of sin might be destroyed, that henceforth we should not serve sin (Rom. 4:3–4, 6). And for our daily infirmities and escapes by which we pollute ourselves, His blood is a "fountain opened to the house of David and to the inhabitants of Jerusalem for sin and for uncleanness" (Zech. 13:1), and to this fountain He brings by the Spirit of repentance, which He, as an exalted prince, bestows (Acts 5:31), and by faith. So 1 John 2:1: "If any man sin, we have an advocate with the Father, etc."

II. As for our ignorance and blindness, He takes that away, being given for a light to the Gentiles (Isa. 42:6; 49:6; Luke 2:32). He is sent to open the blind eyes (Isa. 42:7), to bring out the prisoners from their dark prisons (v. 7; 61:1). Indeed, He is anointed for this end so that such as walk in darkness see a great light. And they that dwell in the land of the shadow of death—on them the light has shined (Isa. 9:2; Matt. 4:15). And He has eye salve to give (Rev. 3:18).

III. He is qualified for taking away our impotency so that through Him we can do all things (Phil. 4:13). When we are weak, we are strong in Him who is our strength and lives in us

(2 Cor. 12:10; Gal. 2:20). Hence, He "worketh in [us] both to will and to do of his good pleasure" (Phil. 2:13).

IV. He also takes away our natural averseness, unwillingness, wickedness, and hatred of His ways, making His people willing in the day of His power (Ps. 110[:3]). So He takes away the enmity that is in us (Col. 2:20) and reconciles us to God and to His ways [so] that our hearts do sweetly comply with them, and we become most willing and glad to walk in them, indeed, and to run the way of His commandments through Him enlarging of our hearts (Ps. 119:[3]2).

V. He likewise takes away that desire and willingness which we have to lie still in our natural condition by convincing us of the dreadful hazard thereof through the Spirit of conviction, by which He convinces the world of it (John 16:8) and circumcises their ears to hear and makes them willing to hearken to the counsel of God.

VI. As for the power and dominion of Satan, He breaks that by "[leading] captivity captive" (Ps. 68:18; Eph. 4:8) and spoiling the strong man's house, for He is come to "destroy the works of the devil" (1 John 3:8). And He "spoiled principalities and powers" (Col. 2:15). Thus, as a captain of salvation, He leads them out as a conqueror. Having paid the price, He delivers also by power and authority from the hand of this jailor.

And thus we see how He answers our case and necessity and is a fit way for us. And though this be not questioned, yet little is it believed and considered and less put in practice.

How He Alone Is the Way and Answers This Our Case
And as for the third particular, that He alone is this way and answers our case by it, it needs not be much spoken to since it is

clear and manifest, confirmed by the experience of all generations and the disappointments of fools who have been seeking other ways. Angels in heaven cannot do our business. They cannot satisfy justice for us, nor have they any power over our heart to turn it as they will. Indeed, they are not acquainted with our secret thoughts. That cabinet is kept close[d] from them and reserved as the peculiar privilege of God alone. The blood of bulls and of goats cannot do it, for the apostle tells us that it is impossible for that to take away sin (Heb. 10:4). That blood shed according to the law did cleanse ceremonially, but it is only the blood of Jesus, typified by that, which cleanses really, so that we are sanctified through the offering of the body of Jesus Christ once for all (v. 10). No pains or labor of ours can avail here. The Lord will not be pleased with thousands of rams or with ten thousands of rivers of oil. He will not take our firstborn for our transgression, nor the son of our body for the sin of our soul (Mic. 6:7). Ordinance and means will not do it, nor any invention of our own. "None of them can by any means redeem his brother, nor give to God a ransom for him: (for the redemption of the soul is precious, and it ceaseth for ever)" (Ps. 49:7–8). He alone has laid down the price. All our sufferings, prayers, tears, labors, penances, and the like signify nothing here. They cannot satisfy justice for one sin.

What Are the Rare Advantages and Specialties of This Way
As to the fourth particular—namely, the singularity of this way—these things make it manifest and apparent:

I. This is such a way as can discover itself and make itself known to the erring traveler. Christ Jesus is such a way as can say to the wandering soul, "This is the way, walk ye in it" (Isa. 30:2[1]). No way can do this. This is comfortable.

II. This way cannot only discover itself to the wandering traveler, but also it can bring folk into it. Christ can bring souls to
Himself when they are running on in their wandering condition. He can move their hearts to turn into the right way, put
grace in their soul for this end, begin resolutions in them, and
sow the seed of faith, and so stay their course which they were
violently pursuing and make them look about and consider
what they are doing. As the former was good news to poor,
blind, and witless creatures that were wandering and knew not
where they were going, so this is good news to poor souls that
find their heart inclining to wander and loving to go astray.

III. This way can cause us [to] walk in it. If we be rebellious
and obstinate, He can command with authority, for He is
given for a leader and commander (55:4). How sweet should
this be to the soul that is weighed with a stubborn, untrac-
table, and unpersuadable heart: that He as a king, governor,
and commander can with authority draw or drive and cause us
[to] follow and run.

IV. This way is truth as well as the way, so that the soul that
once enters in here is safe forever—no wandering here. "The
wayfaring men, though fools, shall not err therein" (35:8). He
will bring "the blind by a way that they knew not…[and] lead
them in paths that they have not known." He will "make darkness light before them, and crooked things straight." Those
things will He do "unto them, and not forsake them" (42:16).

V. This way is also life and so can revive the faint and weary
traveler. "He giveth power to the faint; and to them that have
no might he increaseth strength." Indeed, He renews "their
strength" and makes them "mount up with wings as eagles…
[and] run and not be weary; and…walk, and not faint"

(40:29, 31). And so He gives legs to the traveler; indeed, He carries "the lambs...in his bosom" (v. 11). Oh! Who would not walk in this way? What can discourage the man that walks here? What can he fear? No [other] way can quicken and refresh the weary man. This way can do it. Indeed, it can quicken one that is as dead and cause him [to] march on with fresh alacrity and vigor.

VI. From all these it follows that this way is a most pleasant, heartsome, desirable, and comfortable way. The man is safe here, and he may sing in the ways of the Lord (Ps. 138:5). For "[wisdom's ways] are ways of pleasantness, and all her paths are peace" (Prov. 3:17). He is a way that is food, physic,[3] cordials, and all that the poor traveler stands in need of till He come hence.

Application
From all which, before we come to particulars, we will in general point out those duties which natively result from this by way of use:

I. Oh what cause is there here for all of us to fall wondering— both that God should ever have condescended to have appointed a way how sinners and rebels that had wickedly departed from Him and deserved to be cast out of His presence and favor forever might come back again and enjoy happiness and felicity in the friendship and favor of that God that could have received the glory of His justice in our destruction and stood in no need of us or of anything we could do; as also, that He appointed such a way that Jesus Christ, His only Son, should, to speak so, lie as a bridge between God and

---

3. *Physic:* medicine.

sinful rebels and as a highway that they might return to the great God on Him. Let all the creation of God wonder at this wonderful condescending love of God that appointed such a way, and of Christ that was content to lout so low as to become this way to us, this new and living way, and that for this end He should have taken on flesh and become Immanuel, God with us, and tabernacled with us, that through this veil of His flesh He might consecrate a way to us. Let angels wonder at this condescension.

II. Hence we may see ground of being convinced of these things:

1. That naturally we are out of the way to peace and favor with God and in a way that leads to death, and so that our misery and wretchedness, so long as it is so, cannot be expressed.

2. That we can do nothing for ourselves. Set all our wits at work, we cannot fall on a way that will bring us home.

3. That it is madness for us to seek out another way and to vex ourselves in vain, to run to this and to that means or invention of our own and be found fools in the end.

4. That our madness is so much the greater in this that we will turn to our own ways that will fail us, when there is such a noble and excellent and [in] every way satisfying way prepared to our hand.

5. That our wickedness is so desperate that the way which is pointed out to us does not please us, and that we will not enter into it nor walk in it.

6. That this way, which is also the truth and the life, is only worth the embracing and is only safe and sure. We should be convinced and persuaded of the worth, sufficiency, and desirableness of this way. Reason, with

ordinary light from the Word, may teach these things, but grace can only carry them into the heart and make them take root there.

III. We may read here our obligation to these particulars:

1. To turn our back on all other false and deceitful ways and not rest there.

2. To enter into this way—though the gate be narrow and strait (Matt. 7:13; Luke 13:24), yet to strive to enter in.

3. To resolve to abide in that way as acquiescing in it, resting satisfied with it, and thus to be rooted in Him (Col. 2:7) and to dwell in Him (1 John 3:24) and to live in Him or through Him (1 John 4:9).

4. To walk in this way (Col. 2:6); that is, to make constant use of Him and to make progress in the way in and through Him—to go from strength to strength in Him, drawing all our furniture from Him by faith according to the covenant. And that the soul should guard against (1) stepping aside out of this good and pleasant way; (2) backsliding; and (3) sitting up and fainting by the way.

In a word, this points out our duty to make use of Christ as our way to the Father, and only of Christ.

Particulars

And this leads us to the particulars we will speak a little to.

There are two main things which stand in our way and hinder us from approaching to the Father: (1) unrighteousness and guilt by which we are legally banished because of the broken covenant and the righteous sentence of God according to that covenant; and, (2) wickedness, impurity, and unholiness which is as a physical bar lying in our way, because nothing that is unclean can dwell and abide with Him who is of purer eyes than He can behold iniquity, and nothing that is unclean can enter in there where He is. So then there must be a use-making of Christ as a way through both these impediments. We need justification and pardon for the one, and sanctification and cleansing for the other. Now Christ being the way to the Father both as to justification in taking away the enmity, in changing our state, and removing our unrighteousness and guilt by which we were lying under the sentence of the law, adjudging such sinners as we are to hell, and as to sanctification in cleansing us from all our pollutions, renewing our souls, washing away our spots and defilements, etc.—He must be made use of in reference to both.

In speaking to the first, we will be the shorter, because through God's great mercy, the gospel's pure way of justification by faith in Christ is richly and abundantly cleared up by many worthy authors of late, both as concerning the theoretical and practical part.

CHAPTER 4

How Christ Is Made Use of for Justification as a Way

What Christ has done to purchase, procure, and bring about our justification before God is mentioned already—namely, that He stood in the room of sinners, engaging for them as their cautioner, undertaking and at length paying down the ransom, becoming sin or a sacrifice for sin and a curse for them, and so laying down His life a ransom to satisfy divine justice. And this He has made known in the gospel, calling sinners to an accepting of Him as their only mediator and to a resting on Him for life and salvation, and, in addition, working up such as belong to the election of grace to an actual closing with Him on the conditions of the covenant and to an accepting of Him, believing in Him, and resting on Him as satisfied with and acquiescing in that sovereign way of salvation and justification through a crucified mediator.

Things Required to Be Known

Now, for such as would make use of Christ as the way to the Father in the point of justification, these things are requisite, to which we will only premise this word of caution: that we judge not the want of these requisites a ground to exempt any that hears the gospel from the obligation to believe and rest on Christ as He is offered in the gospel.

I. There must be a conviction of sin and misery. A conviction
of original guilt by which we are banished out of God's presence and favor and are in a state of enmity and death, are
come short of the glory of God (Rom. 3:23), becoming dead
or under the sentence of death through the offense of one
(5:15), being made sinners by one man's disobedience (v. 19),
and therefore under the reigning power of death (v. 17) and
under that judgment that came on all men to condemnation
(v. 18). And of original innate wickedness by which the heart is
filled with enmity against God and is a hater of Him and all His
ways, standing in full opposition to Him and to His holy laws,
loving to contradict and resist Him in all His actings, despising
and undervaluing all His condescensions of love, obstinately
refusing His goodness and offers of mercy, and peremptorily
persisting in rebellion and heart-opposition—not only not
accepting His kindness and offers of mercy but contemning[1]
them, trampling them underfoot as embittered against Him.
As also, there must be a conviction of our actual transgressions
by which we have corrupted our ways yet more, run farther away
from God, brought on more wrath on our souls—according to
that sentence of the law: cursed is everyone that abides not in
all things that are written in the law to do them (Deut. 26:26;
Gal. 3:10). What way this conviction is begun and carried on in
the soul and to what measure it must come I cannot now stand
to explain. Only, in short, know that on whatever occasion it
be begun, whether by a word carried home to the heart by
the finger of God or by some sharp and crossing dispensation,
fear of approaching death, some heinous out-breaking, or the
like, it is a real thing, a heart-reaching conviction, not general
and notional but particular, plain, and pinching, affecting the
heart with fear and terror, making the soul seriously and really

---

1. *Contemning*: disrespecting or viewing with contempt.

to mind this matter, to be taken up with the thoughts of it, and anxiously and earnestly to cry out, "What shall I do to be saved?" and, finally, will make the soul willing to hearken and hear what hopes of mercy there is in the gospel and to embrace the way of salvation which is there laid down. And the reason of this is because Christ Himself tells us [that] the whole needs not the physician, but the sick (Matt. 9:12). He is not come to call the righteous (that is, such as are righteous in their own eyes) but sinners—that is, such as are now no more whole at the heart, as seeing no evil, no hazard or danger, but pricked and pierced with the sense of their lost condition, being under the heavy wrath and vengeance of the great God because of sin and seeing their own vileness, cursedness, wickedness, and desperate madness. Because naturally we hate God and Christ (John 15:23–25) and have a strong and natural antipathy at the way of salvation through Jesus, therefore nothing but strong and inevitable necessity will drive us to a compliance with this gospel device of love.

II. There must be some measure of humiliation. Under this conviction the man is bowed down and made mute before God, no more boasting of his goodness and of his happy condition, no high or great thoughts of his righteousness— for all are looked on now as filthy rags (Isa. 65:6). What things were as gain before to the soul must now be counted loss, indeed, and as dung (Phil. 3:7–8). The man must be cast down in himself and far from high and conceit[ed] thoughts of himself or of anything he ever did or can do. For the Lord "resisteth the proud, but giveth grace unto the humble" (James 4:6; 1 Peter 5:5). He revives the spirit of the humble (Isa. 57:15). He that humbles himself will be exalted (Matt. 18:4; 23:12; Luke 14:11; 18:14).

III. There must be a despairing of getting help or relief out of this condition by ourselves or anything we can do—a conviction of the unprofitableness of all things under the sun for our relief. No expectation of help from our supposed[ly] good heart, good purposes, good deeds, works of charity, many prayers, commendations of others, sober and harmless walking, or anything else within us or without us that is not Christ. For, so long as we have the least hope or expectation of doing our own business without Christ, we will not come to Him. Our heart hangs so after the old way of salvation through works that we cannot endure to hear of any other, nor can we yield to any other. Could we but have heaven by the way of works, we would spare no pains, no cost, no labor, no expenses—indeed, we would put ourselves to much pain and torment by whippings, cuttings, fastings, watchings, and the like. We would [not] spare our firstborn. Indeed, we would dig our graves in a rock with our nails and cut our own days[2] could we but get heaven by this means. Such is our antipathy at the way of salvation through a crucified Christ that we would choose any way but that, cost what it would. Therefore, before we can heartily close with Christ and accept Him, we must be put from those refuges of lies and see that there is nothing but a disappointment written on them all—that all our prayers, fastings, cries, duties, reformations, sufferings, good wishes, good deeds, etc., are nothing in His eyes but so many provocations to the eyes of His jealousy and so further causes of our misery.

IV. There must be a rational, deliberate, and resolute relinquishing of all those things in ourselves on which our heart is ready to dote. The man being convinced of the vanity of all things by which he has been hoping for salvation must now

---

2. *Cut our own days*: lessen our lives.

purpose to loose his grips of them, to turn his back on them, to quit them with purpose of heart, and to say to them, "Get thee hence," as Isaiah 30:22. This is to deny ourselves, which we must do before we become His disciples (Matt. 16:24). This is to forsake our father's house (Ps. 45:10) and to pluck out our right eye and to cut off our right arm (Matt. 5:29–30). This abandoning of all our false props and subterfuges must be resolute, over the belly of much opposition within from the carnal and natural inclinations of the heart and of much opposition without from Satan's ensnaring suggestions and deceitful temptations. It must be a real, rational act of the soul on solid and thorough conviction of their unprofitableness, indeed, of their dangerousness and destructiveness.

V. There must be some knowledge of the nature of the gospel covenant and of the way which now God has chosen by which to glorify His grace in the salvation of poor sinners. That God—Father, Son, and Holy Ghost—thought good for the glory of free grace and wisdom in a way of justice and mercy to send Jesus Christ to assume man's nature and so become God and man in two distinct natures and one person forever and to become under the law, to undergo the curse of it, and to die the cursed death of the cross to satisfy justice and pay the ransom for the redemption of the elect. In which undertaking our Lord was a servant (Isa. 42:1; 49:6; 52:13; 53:11; Zech. 3:8; Matt. 12:18) and had furniture from God for all His undertaking (Isa. 42:1; 61:1–2; Matt. 12:18) and had a promise of seeing His seed and of prolonging His days, etc. (Isa. [43]:10–11). Thus there was a covenant of redemption between God and the mediator, and the mediator undertaking was obliged to perform all that He undertook, and accordingly did so. For, as the Lord laid on Him or caused to meet together on Him "the iniquity of us all" (53:6), so in due time He bare our griefs and carried our sorrows. He was wounded for our transgressions. He was bruised for our iniquities. The chastisement of our peace was on Him. He was cut off out of the land of the living. He was stricken for the transgression of His people. He made His soul an offering for sin and bare the iniquities of His people. Pouring out His soul unto death, He bare the sin of many and made intercession for the transgressors (Isa. 53:4–5, 10–12). So that "what the law could not do, in that it was weak through the flesh, God sending his own Son in the likeness of sinful flesh, and for sin [or by a sacrifice for sin], condemned sin in the flesh" (Rom. 8:3), "that the righteousness of the law might be fulfilled in us" (v. 4). Thus He made Him sin, or a sacrifice for sin, that we might become righteous (2 Cor. 5:2[1]). And He "was once offered to bear the sins of many" (Heb. 9:28). And He "through the eternal Spirit offered himself without spot to God" (v. 14), and "his own self bare our sins in his own body on the tree" (1 Peter 2:24). There must, I say, be some knowledge of and acquaintance with this great mystery of the gospel in which is declared "the manifold wisdom of God" (Eph. 3:10), and with the noble design of God in sending His Son after this manner to die the death that condemned sinners might live and return to the bosom of God, as redeemed not with gold or silver or corruptible things, "but with the precious blood of Christ, as of a lamb without blemish and without spot" (1 Peter 1:18[–19])—and being so redeemed by blood to become kings and priests to God (1 Peter 2:2; Rev. 5:9–10). The man must not be ignorant of this, else all will be in vain. I do not determine how distinct and full this knowledge must be, but sure[ly] there must be so much knowledge of it as will give the soul ground of hope and, in expectation of salvation by this way, cause it [to] turn its back on all other ways and account itself happy if it could once win here.

VI. There must be a persuasion of the sufficiency, completeness, and satisfactoriness of the way of salvation through this crucified mediator, else the soul will not be induced to leave its other courses and betake itself to this alone. He must be sure that salvation is only to be had this way and that undoubtedly it will be had this way, that so with confidence he may cast himself over on this way and sweetly sing of a noble outgate. And therefore he must believe that Christ is really God as well as man and a true man as well as God; that He is fully furnished for the work of redemption, having the Spirit given to Him without measure and endued fully and richly with all qualifications fitting for all our necessities and enabling Him to "save them to the uttermost that come unto God by him" (Heb. 7:25); that he is made of God to us "wisdom, and righteousness, and sanctification" (1 Cor. 1:30); that all power in heaven and in earth is given unto him (Matt. 28:18); that all things are put under His feet and that He is given to be "head over all things to the church" (Eph. 1:22); that in Him dwells all fullness (Col. 1:19); that in Him "are hid all the treasures of wisdom and knowledge" (2:3); indeed, that "in him dwelleth all the fulness of the Godhead bodily" so that we are "complete in him, which is the head of all principality and power" (vv. 9–10).

VII. The soul must know that He is not only an able and all-sufficient mediator but that also He is willing and ready to redeem and save all that will come. For all the preceding particulars will but increase his sorrow and torment him more so long as he supposes through ignorance and the suggestion of Satan that he has no part in that redemption, no access to it, no ground of hope of salvation by it. Therefore, it is necessary that the soul conceive not only a possibility but also a probability of help this way, and that the dispensation of the gospel of grace and the promulgation and offer of these good news to him speak out so much, that the patience of God waiting long and His goodness renewing the offers confirms this—that His serious pressing, His strong motives, on the one hand, and His sharp threatenings, on the other; His reiterated commands, His ingeminated obtestations; His expressed sorrow and grief over such as would not come to Him; His upbraiding and objurations of such as do obstinately refuse; and the like—[all] put His willingness to save such as will come to Him out of all question. Indeed, His obviating of objections and taking all excuses out of their mouth make the case plain and manifest so that such as will not come are left without excuse and have no impediment lying in the way but their own unwillingness.

VIII. The man must know on what terms and conditions Christ offers Himself in the gospel—namely, on condition of accepting of Him, believing in Him, and resting on Him; and that no other way we can be made partakers of the good things purchased by Christ but by accepting of Him as He is offered in the gospel—that is to say, freely, without price or money (Isa. 55:1), absolutely without reservation, wholly, and for all ends, etc. For, till this be known, there will be no closing with Christ; and till there be a closing with Christ, there is no advantage to be had by Him. The soul must be married to Him as a husband, fixed to Him as the branches to the tree, united to Him as the members to the head, become one with Him, "one spirit" (1 Cor. 6:17; see John 15:5; Eph. 5:30). The soul must close with Him for all things, adhere to Him on all hazards, take Him and the sharpest cross that follows Him. Now, I say, the soul must be acquainted with these conditions, for it must act deliberately and rationally here. Covenanting with Christ is a grave business and requires deliberation, posedness of soul, rational resolution, full purpose of heart, and satisfaction of soul. And therefore the man must be acquainted with the conditions of the new covenant.

IX. There must be a satisfaction with the terms of the gospel, and the heart must actually close with Christ as He is offered in the gospel. The heart must open to Him and take Him in (Rev. 3:20). The soul must embrace and receive Him (John 1:12). The man must take Him as his Lord and master, king, priest, and prophet. [He] must give up himself to Him as his leader and commander and resolve to follow Him in all things and thus close a bargain with Him, for, till this be done, there is no union with Christ. And till there be a union with Christ, there is no partaking of the fruits of His redemption as to justification—no pardon, no acceptance, no access to the favor of God, nor peace nor joy in the Holy Ghost, no getting of the conscience sprinkled, nor no intimation of love or favor from God, etc.

X. There must be a leaning to and resting on Him and on His perfect sacrifice. The soul must sit down here as satisfied and acquiesce in this complete mediation of His. This is to believe on Him, to rest on Him (John 3:18; 1 Peter 2:6) as an all-sufficient help. This is to cast the burden of a broken covenant, of a guilty conscience, of deserved wrath, of the curse of the law, etc., on Him that He may bear away those evils from us. This is to put on the Lord Jesus, in part (Rom. 13:14), to cover ourselves with His righteousness from the face of justice, to stand in this armor of proof against the accusations of law, Satan, and an evil conscience. This is to flee to Him as our city of refuge that we may be safe from the avenger of blood. This is to make Him our refuge from the storm of God's anger and a shadow from the heat of His wrath (Isa. 25:4) and our hiding place from the wind, and a covert from the tempest, and as the shadow of a great rock in a weary land (32:2). When we hide ourselves in Him as the complete cautioner that has fully satisfied justice and desire to be found in Him alone, "not having [our] own righteousness, which is of the law, but that which is through the faith of Christ, the righteousness which is of God by faith" (Phil. 3:9)—this is to lay our hand on the head of the sacrifice when we rest on this sacrifice and expect salvation through it alone. This is to cast ourselves in Christ's arms as peremptorily resolving to go no other way to the Father and to plead no other righteousness before God's bar but Christ's. That is faith, indeed, the lively acting of justifying faith.

The Act of Faith
Thus then is Christ made use of as the way to the Father in the point of justification, when the poor awakened sinner, convinced of his sin and misery, of his own inability to help himself, of the insufficiency of all means beside[s] Christ, of Christ's all-sufficiency, readiness, and willingness to help, of the equity and reasonableness of the conditions on which He is offered, and life through Him, is now content and fully satisfied with this way, actually renouncing all other ways whatever, and does with heart and hand embrace Jesus Christ and take Him as He is offered in the gospel to make use of Him for all things, to lean to Him and rest on Him in all hazards, and particularly to refuge itself under His wings and to rest there with complacency, satisfaction, and delight, and hide itself from the wrath of God and all accusations.

Yet it should be known that this act of faith by which the soul goes out to Christ and accepts of and leans to Him is not alike in all [people].

I. In some it may be more lively, strong, and active, like the centurion's faith that could argue syllogistically (Matt. 8:8, etc.), which Christ looked on as a great faith, a greater of which He had not found, no not in Israel (8:10), and like the faith of the woman of Canaan (15:21, etc.) that would take no naysay[3] but of seeming refusals did make arguments which Christ commends as a great faith (8:28). But in others it may be more weak and fainting, not able to reason rightly for its own comfort and strength (as 6:30) but is mixed with much fear (as 8:26)—indeed, and with much faithfulness so that the soul must cry, "Lord, help my unbelief!" ([see] Mark 9:24).

II. In some, the acts and actings of this faith may be more clear and discernible, both by themselves and by spiritual onlookers. In others, so covered over with a heap of doubts, unbelief, jealousy, and other corruption that the actings of it can hardly or not at all be perceived by themselves or others, so that nothing will be heard but complaints, fears, doubtings, and objections.

III. In some, this faith may have strong and perceptible actings, wrestling through much discouragement and opposition and many difficulties, as in the woman of Canaan (Matthew 15), running through with peremptory resoluteness, saying, with Job, "Though he slay me, yet will I trust in him" (Job 13:15), and thus taking the kingdom of heaven with violence. In others, it may be so weak that the least opposition or discouragement may be sufficient to make the soul give over hope and almost despair of overcoming and winning through and be as a bruised reed or a smoking flax.

---

3. *Naysay:* saying no.

IV. In some, though it appear not strong and violent or willful (in a manner) in its actings, yet it may be firm, fixed, and resolute in staying on Him (Isa. 26:3–4) and trusting in Him (Ps. 125:1), resolving to hang there, and, if it perish, it perishes. In others, weak and bashful.

V. In some, it may be yet weaker, going out in strong and vehement hungerings (Matt. 5:6). The man dare not say that he does believe or that he does adhere to Christ and stay on Him. Yet he dare says he longs for Him and pants after Him. As ever the hart does "after the water brooks" (Ps. 42:1–2), he hungers and thirsts for Him and cannot be satisfied with anything without Him.

VI. In some, it may be so weak that the soul can only perceive the heart looking out after Him. On little more ground than a maybe it will be helped (Isa. 45:22). They look to Him for salvation, being convinced that there is no other way. And resolved to follow no other way, they resolve to lie at His door, waiting and looking for a sight of the king's face and to lie waiting till they die, if no better may be.

VII. In some, it may be so weak that nothing more can be perceived but a satisfaction with the terms of the covenant, a willingness to accept of the bargain, and a heart consenting to it, though they dare not say that they actually close with it, indeed, nor dare say that they will be welcome (Rev. 22:17).

VIII. In some, it may be so weak and low that they cannot say that they have any right hunger or desire after Him, nor that their heart does rightly and really consent to the covenant of grace. Yet they would fain[4] be at it and cry out, "Oh for a willing heart! Oh for ardent desires! Oh for a right hunger!" And they are dissatisfied and cannot be reconciled with their hearts for not desiring more, hungering more, consenting more, so that, if they had this, they would think themselves happy and up-made. And thus we see their faith is so low that it appears in nothing more manifestly than in their complainings of the want of it.

So then, the poor, weak believer needs not to be so far discouraged as to despair and give over the matter as hopeless and lost. Let him hang on, depend, and wait. A weak faith today may become stronger within a short time. He that laid the foundation can and will finish the building, for all His works are perfect. And a weak faith, when true, will prove saving and lay hold on a saving, strong mediator.

Moreover, as to the acting of faith on Christ's death and sacrifice for the stopping the mouth of conscience, law, Satan, and for the opposing to the pursuing justice of God because of sin, it may sometimes be strong, distinct, clear, and resolute. At other times again, [it may] be weak, mixed, or accompanied with much fear, perplexity, doubting, and distrust because of their own seen unworthiness, many failings, doubtings of the sincerity of their repentance, and the like.

Those Who Deceive Themselves
This is a main business and of great concernment, yet many are not much troubled about it nor exercised at the heart about it as they ought, deceiving themselves with foolish imaginations—for:

---

4. *Fain*: deny.

I. They think they were believers all their days. They never doubted of God's grace and goodwill. They had always a good heart for God, though they never knew what awakened conscience or sense of the wrath of God meant.

II. Or they think, because God is merciful, He will not be so severe as to stand on all those things that ministers require—forgetting that He is a just God and a God of truth that will do according to what He has said.

III. Or they suppose it is an easy matter to believe and not such a difficult thing as it is called—not considering or believing that no less power than that which raised Christ from the dead will work up the heart to faith.

IV. Or they resolve that they will do it afterward at some more convenient season—not perceiving the cunning slight of Satan in this nor considering that faith is not in their power but the gift of God, and that, if they footnote lay not hold on the call of God but harden their heart in their day, God may judicially blind them so that these things will be hid from their eyes, and so that occasion they pretend to wait for never come.

Oh! If such whom this mainly concerns could be induced to enter into this way, considering:

1. That except they enter into this way, they cannot be safe. The wrath of God will pursue them. The avenger of blood will overtake them. No salvation but here.

2. That in this way is certain salvation. This way will infallibly lead to the Father, for He keeps in the way and brings safe home (Ex. 23:20).

3. 'Tis the old path and the good way (Jer. 6:16). All the saints have the experience of this who are already come to glory.

4. And it is a highway and a way of righteousness in which, if very fools walk, they will not wander (Isa. 35:8–9), and if the weak walk in it, they will not faint (40:31).

5. That except this be done, there is no advantage to be had by Him. His death and all His sufferings as to those persons that will not believe and enter into Him as the way to the Father are in vain.

6. Indeed, such as will not believe in Him say in effect either that Christ has not died nor consecrated a way through the veil of His flesh, or that all that He has done and suffered is not sufficient to bring a soul home to God, or that they can do their own business without Him and that it was a foolish and vain thing for Christ to die the death for that end, or, lastly, that they care not for salvation—they are indifferent whether they perish or be saved.

7. That, as to them, the whole gospel is in vain. All the ordinances, all the administration of ordinances, all the pains of ministers are in vain.

8. That, as to them, all Christ's [e]ntreaties, motives, allurements, patience, and longsuffering, His standing at the door and knocking till His locks be wet with the dew, etc., are in vain. Indeed, they are contemptuously rejected, despised, slighted, and undervalued.

9. That all the great promises are by such rejected as untrue or as not worth the seeking or having, and that all the threatenings, on the other hand, are not to be regarded or feared.

10. In a word, that heaven and the fellowship of God is not worth the seeking, and that hell and the fellowship of devils is not worth the fearing, or, that there is neither a heaven nor a hell and that all are but fictions, and

that there is no such thing as the wrath of God against
sinners, or that it is not much to be feared.

The Warrant to Come to Christ

Warrant to Believe?

If it be asked, What warrant have poor sinners to lay hold on
Christ and grip to Him, as made of God righteousness?—I
answer:

I. Our absolute necessity of Him is a ground to press us to go
and seek help and relief. We see we are gone in ourselves, and
therefore are we allowed to seek out for help elsewhere.

II. Christ's all-sufficient furniture by which He is a qualified
mediator, fitted with all necessaries for our case and condition, having laid down a price to the satisfaction of justice, is a
sufficient invitation for us to look toward Him for help and to
wait at that door.

III. His being appointed of the Father to be mediator of the
covenant and particularly to lay down His life a ransom for sin,
and Christ's undertaking all His offices and performing all the
duties thereof conform[ing] to the covenant of redemption
is a strong encouragement to poor sinners to come to Him—
because He cannot deny Himself, and He will be true to
His trust.

IV. The Father's offering of Him to us in the gospel and Christ's
inviting us who are weary and heavy laden—indeed, calling
and commanding such to come to Him in His own and in His
Father's name under the pain of His and His Father's wrath
and everlasting displeasure, exhorting further and requesting
on terms of love, pressing earnestly by many motives, sending

out His ambassadors to beseech in His stead poor sinners to be reconciled and to turn in to Him for life and salvation, indeed, upbraiding such as will not come to Him—all these are a sufficient warrant for a poor necessitous sinner to lay hold on His offer.

And, further, to encourage poor souls to come to Him, all things are so well ordered in the gospel as that nothing occurs that can in the least prove a stumbling block or a just ground of excuse for their forbearing to believe and to accept of His offers. All objections possible are obviated to such as are but willing. The way is cast up, and all stones of stumbling cast out of it, so that such as will not come can pretend no excuse. They cannot object the greatness of their sins—for the greater their sins be, they have the greater need of one who is sent to take away sin and whose blood purges from all sin (1 John 1:7). What great sinner did He ever refuse that came to Him and was willing to be saved by Him? Is there any clause in all the gospel excluding great sinners? Nor need they object their great unworthiness, for He does all freely for the glory of His free grace. None ever got any good of Him for their worth, for no man ever had any worth. Nor need they object their long refusing and resisting many calls, for He will make such as are willing welcome at the eleventh hour. Him that comes He will in no case put away (John 6:37). Nor can they object their changeableness, that they will not stand to the bargain but break and return with the dog to the vomit; for Christ has engaged to bring all through that come to Him. He will raise them up at the last day (v. 40). He will present them to Himself holy and without spot or wrinkle or any such thing (Ephesians 5). The covenant is fully provided with promises to stop the mouth of that objection. Nor can they object the difficulty or impossibility of believing, for that is Christ's work also. He is the author and finisher of faith (Heb. 12:1). Can

they not with confidence cast themselves on Him, yet if they
can hunger and thirst for Him and look to Him, He will accept
of that. "Look to Me," He says, "and be saved" (cf. Isa. 45:22).
If they cannot look to Him nor hunger and thirst for Him, yet
if they be willing, all is well. Are they willing that Christ save
them in His way and therefore willingly give themselves over
to Him and are willing and content that Christ by His Spirit
work more hunger in them and a more lively faith and work
both to will and to do according to His own good pleasure?
[Then] it is well.

Difficult Conditions?

But it will be said that the terms and conditions on which He
offers Himself are hard.

Answer. I grant the terms are hard to flesh and blood and
to proud, unmortified nature, but to such as are willing to be
saved, so as God may be most glorified, the terms are easy,
most rational, and satisfying, for:

I. We are required to take Him only for our mediator and to
join none with Him and to mix nothing with Him. Corrupt
nature is averse from this and would at least mix something
of self with Him and not rest on Christ only. Corrupt nature
would not have the man wholly denying himself and following
Christ only. And hence many lose themselves and lose all,
because, with the Galatians, they would mix the law and the
gospel together, do something themselves for satisfaction of
justice, and take Christ for the rest that remains. Now, the Lord
will have all the glory, as good reason is, and will have none to
share with Him. He will give of His glory to none. And is not
this rational and easy? What can be objected against this?

II. We are required to take Him wholly that He may be a complete mediator to us—as a prophet to teach, as a king to subdue our lusts [and] to cause us to walk in His ways, as well as a priest to satisfy justice for us [and] to die and intercede for us. Is it not reason[able] that we take Him, as God has made Him for us? Is there anything in Him to be refused? And is there anything in Him which we have no need of? Is there not all the reason then in the world for this—that we take Him wholly? And what stumbling block is here?

III. We are required to take Him freely, without money and without price (Isa. 55:1), for He will not be bought any manner of way. That free grace may be free grace, therefore He will give all freely. True enough it is: corruption would be at buying, though it have nothing to lay out. Pride will not stoop to a free gift. But can any say the terms are hard when all is offered freely?

IV. We are required to take them absolutely, without any reversion of mental reservation. Some would willingly quit all but one or two lusts they cannot think to twin with.[5] And they would deny themselves in many things, but they would still most willingly keep a back door open to some beloved lust or other. And who sees not what double dealing is here? And what reason can plead for this double dealing? Corruption, it is true, will think this hard, but no man can rationally say that this is a just ground of discouragement to any or a sufficient ground to warrant them to stay away from Christ, seeing they cannot be supposed sincerely to desire redemption from any sin who would not desire redemption from every sin. He who loves any known lust and would not willingly be delivered

---

5. *Twin with*: to part with.

from it has no real hatred at any lust as such nor desire to be saved—for one such lust would be his death.

V. It is required that we accept of Him really and cordially, with our heart and soul, and not by a mere external verbal profession. And is there not all the reason in the world for this? He offers Himself really to us, and will we not be real in accepting of Him? What, I pray, can be justly excepted against this? Or, what real discouragement can any gather from this?

VI. We are to take Him for all necessaries—that is, with a resolution to make use of Him as our all-sufficient mediator. And is not this most reasonable? Ought we not to take Him for all the ends and purposes for which God has appointed Him and set Him forth and offered Him to us? What then can any suppose to lie here which should scar a soul from laying hold on Him? Indeed, should not this be looked on as a very great encouragement? And should we not bless the Lord that has provided such a complete and all-sufficient mediator?

VII. We are to take Him and all the crosses that may attend our taking or following of Him. We must take up our cross, be it what it will that He thinks good to appoint to us, and follow Him (Matt. 16:24; Mark 8:34). For he that takes not his cross and follows not after Him is not worthy of Him (Matt. 10:38). I know flesh and blood will take this for a hard saying, but they that consider that Christ will bear the heaviest end of the cross—indeed, all of it—and so support them by His Spirit while they are under it that they will have no just cause to complain; and how He will suffer none to go His errand on their own charges but will be with them when they go through the fire and water (Isa. 43:2) so that they will suffer no loss, neither will the waters overflow them, nor the fire kindle on them, and that he who loses his life for Christ's sake and the gospel's will save it (Mark 8:35); indeed, that they will receive a hundredfold for all their losses (Matt. 19:29), and that even with persecution (Mark 10:30) and in the world to come eternal life. They, I say, who consider this will see no discouragement here nor ground of complaint. Indeed, they will account it their glory to suffer any loss for Christ's sake.

VIII. Hence it follows that we are to take Him so as to avouch[6] Him and His cause and interest on all hazards, stand to His truth, and not be ashamed of Him in a day of trial. Confession of Him must be made with the mouth, as with the heart we must believe (Rom. 10:9). Let corruption speak against this what it will, because it is always desirous to keep the skin whole. Yet reason cannot but say that it is equitable, especially seeing He has said that whoever confesses Him before men, He will confess them before His "Father which is in heaven" (Matt. 10:32). And that "if we suffer [with him], we shall also reign with him" (2 Tim. 2:12). Is He our Lord and master, and should we not own and avouch Him? Should we be ashamed of Him for anything that can befall us on that account? What master would not take that ill at his servant's hands?

Hence, then, we see that there is nothing in all the conditions on which He offers Himself to us that can give the least ground in reason why a poor soul should draw back and be unwilling to accept of this noble offer or think that the conditions are hard.

Cannot Believe?

But there is one main objection which may trouble some, and that is [that] they cannot believe. Faith being the gift of God,

---

6. *Avouch*: affirm.

it must be wrought in them. How then can they go to God for this and make use of Christ for this end, that their souls may be wrought up to a believing and consenting to the bargain and hearty accepting of the offer?

To this I would say these things:

I. It is true that faith is the gift of God (Eph. 2:8), and that it is He alone who works in us, "both to will and to do" (Phil. [2:13]), and [that] none comes to the Son but whom the Father draws (John 6:44). And it is a great matter and no small advancement to win to the real faith and th[o]rough conviction of this our impotency. For by this the soul will be brought to a greater measure of humiliation and of despairing of salvation in itself, which is no small advantage to a poor soul that would be saved.

II. Though faith be not in our power, yet it is our duty. Our impotency to perform our duty does not loose our obligation to the duty, so that our not believing is our sin. And for this God may justly condemn us. His wrath abides on all who believe not in His Son Jesus and will not accept of the offer of salvation through the crucified mediator. And though faith, as all other acts of grace, be efficiently the work of the Spirit, yet it is formally our work. We do believe, but it is the Spirit that works faith in us.

III. The ordinary way of the Spirit working faith in us is by pressing home the duty on us by which we are brought to a despairing in ourselves and to a looking out to Him whose grace alone it is that can work it in the soul for that necessary help and breathing, without which the soul will not come.

IV. Christ Jesus has purchased this grace of faith to all the elect, as other graces necessary to their salvation. And it is promised and covenanted to Him that He will see His seed and will see of the travail of His soul (Isa. 53:10), and that by the knowledge of Him—that is, the rational and understanding act of the soul gripping to and laying hold on Him as He is offered in the gospel—many will be justified (v. 1[1]). Hence He says that all the Father has given to Him will come to Him (John 6:37). And the apostle tells us that we are blessed "with all spiritual blessings...in Christ" (Eph. 1:3).

V. Not only has Christ purchased this grace of faith and all other graces necessary for the salvation of the elect, but God has committed to Him the administration and actual dispensation and out-giving of all those graces which the redeemed stand in need of. Hence He is a prince exalted "to give repentance...and forgiveness of sins" (Acts 5:31). All power in heaven and earth is committed unto Him (Matt. 28:18–19). Hence He is called the author and finisher of faith (Heb. 12:2). And He tells His disciples (John 14:13–14) that whatever they will ask in His name, He will do it. He is made a prince and a savior, having all judgment committed to Him (John 5:22). And He is Lord of all (Acts 10:36; Rom. 14:9).

VI. On this, the sinner, being convinced of his lost condition through sin and misery of an utter impossibility of helping himself out of that state of death, of Christ's all-sufficiency and willingness to save all that will come to Him, and of its own inability to believe or come to Him for life and salvation or to lay hold on and lean to His merits and satisfaction, and so despairing in himself, is to look out to Jesus, the author of eternal salvation, the foundation and chief cornerstone, the author and finisher of faith. I say, the sinner, being thus convinced, is thus to look out to Jesus. Not that that conviction is any proper qualification prerequisite as necessary either to prepare, dispose, and fit for faith or far less to merit any manner of way or bring on faith, but because this is Christ's method to bring a soul to faith by this conviction to the glory of His grace. The soul naturally being averse from Christ and utterly unwilling to accept of that way of salvation must be redacted to that strait [so] that it will see that it must either accept of this offer or die. As the whole needs not a physician, so Christ is come to save only that which is lost. And His method is to convince the world of sin in the first place and then of righteousness (John 16:8–9).

VII. This looking out to Jesus for faith comprehends these things:

1. The soul's acknowledgment of the necessity of faith to the end it may partake of Christ and of His merits.

2. The soul's satisfaction with that way of partaking of Christ by a closing with Him and a resting on Him by faith.

3. A sense and conviction of the unbelief and stubbornness of the heart or a seeing of its own impotency, indeed, and unwillingness to believe.

4. A persuasion that Christ can over-master the infidelity and wickedness of the heart and work up the soul to a willing consent to the bargain.

5. A hope or a half-hope (to speak so) that Christ, who is willing to save all poor sinners that come to Him for salvation and has said that He will put none away in any case that comes, will have pity on him at length.

6. A resolution to lie at His door till He come with life, till He quicken, till He unite the soul to Himself.

7. A lying open to the breathings of His Spirit by guarding against everything (so far as they can) that may grieve or provoke Him and waiting on Him in all the ordinances He has appointed for begetting faith—such as reading the Scriptures, hearing the word, conference with godly persons, and prayer, etc.

8. A waiting with patience on Him who never said to the house of Jacob, "Seek...me in vain" (Isa. 45:19), still crying and looking to Him who has commanded the ends of the earth to look to Him and waiting for Him who waits to be gracious (30:18), remembering that they are all blessed that wait for Him and that there is much good prepared for them that wait for Him (64:4).

9. The sinner would essay this believing and closing with Christ and set about it as he can, seriously, heartily, and willingly, indeed, and resolutely over the belly of much opposition and many discouragements, looking to Him who must help, indeed, and work the whole work—for God works in and with man as a rational creature. The soul then would set the willingness it finds on work and wait for more, and, as the Lord is pleased to commend by His Spirit the way of grace more to the soul and to warm the heart with love to it and a desire after it, [he would] strike the iron while it is hot and, looking to Him for help, grip to Christ in the covenant. And so [he would] set to its seal, though with a trembling hand, and subscribe its name, though with much fear and doubting, remembering that He who works to will must work the deed also (Phil. 2:13), and "he which hath begun a good work...will perform it" (1:6).

10. The soul essaying thus to believe in Christ's strength and to creep when it cannot walk or run would hold fast what it has attained and resolve never to recall any consent or half-consent it has given to the bargain, but still look forward, hold on, wrestle against unbelief and unwillingness, entertain every good motion of the Spirit for this end, and never admit of anything that may quench its lodgings, desires, or expectation.

11. Indeed, if the sinner be come this length, that, with the bit [of] willingness he has, he consents to the bargain and is not satisfied with anything in himself that draws back or consents not, and with the little skill or strength he has is writing down his name and saying, "Even so I take Him," and is holding at this, peremptorily resolving never to go back or unsay what he has said. But, on the contrary, [he] is firmly purposed to adhere, and, as he grows in strength, to grip more firmly and adhere to Him, [then] he may conclude that the bargain is closed already and that he has faith already—for here there is an accepting of Christ on His own terms, a real consenting to the covenant of grace, though weak and not so discernible as the soul would wish. The soul dare not say but it loves the bargain and is satisfied with it and longs for it and desires nothing more than that it might partake of it and enjoy Him whom it loves, hungers for, pants after, or breathes, as it is able, that it may live in Him and be saved through Him.

No Evidence?

But some will say, "If I had any evidence of God's approbation of this act of my soul, any testimony of His Spirit, I could then with confidence say that I had believed and accepted of the covenant and of Christ offered in it. But so long as I perceive nothing of this, how can I suppose that any motion of this kind in my soul is real faith?" For answer:

I. We would know that our believing and God's sealing to our sense are two distinct acts and separable, and often separated. Our believing is one thing, and God's sealing with the Holy Spirit of promise to our sense[s] is another thing. And this follows, though not inseparably, the other. "In whom also after that ye believed, ye were sealed with that holy Spirit of promise" (Eph. 1:13).

II. And so we would know that many a man may believe and yet not know that he does believe. He may set to his seal that God is true in His offer of life through Jesus and accept of that offer as a truth and close with it and yet live under darkness and doubtings of his faith, long and many a day—partly through not discerning the true nature of faith; partly through the great sense and feeling of his own corruption and unbelief; partly through a mistake of the Spirit's operations within or the want of a clear and distinct uptaking of the motions of his own soul; partly because he finds so much doubting and fear, as if there could be no faith where there was doubting or fear, contrary to Matthew 8:26; 14:31; and Mark 9:24; partly because he has not that persuasion that others have had, as if there were not various degrees of faith as there is of other graces, and the like.

III. Therefore, we would know that many may really believe and yet miss this sensible sealing of the Spirit which they would be at. God may think it not yet seasonable to grant them that, lest they forget themselves and become too proud, and to train them up more to the life of faith by which He may be glorified. And for other holy ends, He may suspend the giving of this for a time.

IV. Yet we would know that all that believe have the seal within them: "He that believeth on the Son of God hath the witness in himself" (1 John 5:10), that is, he has that which really is a seal, though he see it not nor perceive it not—even the work of God's Spirit in his soul, inclining and determining him to the accepting of this bargain and to a liking of and endeavoring after holiness, and the whole gospel clearing up what faith is is a seal and confirmation of the business. So that the matter is sealed and confirmed by the Word, though the soul want those sensible breathings of the Spirit, shedding abroad His love in the heart and filling the soul with a full assurance by hushing all doubts and fears to the door—indeed, though they should be a stranger to the Spirit's witnessing thus with their spirits that they are the children of God—and clearing up distinctly the real work of grace within their soul, and so saying in effect that they have in truth believed.

But enough of this, seeing all this and much more is abundantly held forth and explained in that excellent and useful treatise of Mr. Guthrie's entitled "The Christian's Great Interest."

CHAPTER 5

How Christ Is to Be Made Use of as the Way for Sanctification in General

*H*aving shown how a poor soul, lying under the burden of sin and wrath, is to make use of Jesus Christ for righteousness and justification and so to make use of Him, go out to Him, and apply Him as He is made of God "unto us...righteousness" (1 Cor. 1:30), and that but briefly. This whole great business being more fully and satisfactorily handled in that forementioned great though small treatise—namely, "The Christian's Great Interest"—we will now come and show how a believer or a justified soul will further make use of Christ for sanctification, this being a particular about which they are oftentimes much exercised and perplexed.

That we may therefore in some weak measure through the help of this light and grace propose some things to clear up this great and necessary truth, we will first speak a little to it in the general and then come to clear up the matter more particularly.

Review and Summary
Before we speak of the matter in general, it would be remembered:

I. That the person who only is in case to make use of Christ for sanctification is one that has made use of Him already for righteousness and justification. For one who is a stranger to Christ and is living in nature has no access to Christ for sanctification. He must be a believer and within the covenant before he can make use of the grounds of sanctification laid down in the covenant. One must first be united to Christ and justified by faith in Him before he can draw any virtue from Him for perfecting holiness. He must first be in Him before he can grow up in Him or bring forth fruit in Him. And therefore the first thing that souls would go about should be to get a union made up with Christ and be clothed with His righteousness by faith, and then they have a right to all His benefits. First they should labor to get their state changed from enmity to peace and reconciliation with God through faith in Jesus.

II. Yet next it would be observed that, when it is said that one must be a believer before he can go to Christ and make use of Him for holiness and sanctification, it is not so understood and said that one must know that indeed he is justified by faith before he can make any use of Christ for sanctification. One may be justified and a believer, indeed, and growing in grace through Jesus Christ and so actually improving the grounds of sanctification and making use of Christ for this end and allowed to that and yet win to no certainty of his union with Christ, of his justification through faith in Him, nor of his faith.

III. But, thirdly, if it be said, "How can a soul with confidence approach to Christ for use-making of Him in reference to sanctification, that is, still doubting of his state and regeneration?" then I answer [that] it is true: a clear sight of our interest in Christ by faith would be a great encouragement to our confident approaching to and use-making of Him in all things. And this consideration should move all to a more earnest search and study of the marks and evidences of their interest. A good help to this they will find in the forementioned book. I will only say this here: that if the soul have an earnest desire to be sanctified wholly and to have on the image of God that he may glorify Him and pants after holiness as for life that he may look like Him that is holy and makes this his work and study, sorrowing at nothing more than at his shortcoming, crying out and longing for the day when he will be delivered from a body of death and have the old man wholly crucified—[then] he needs not question his interest in Christ and warrant to make use of Him for every part of sanctification. For this longing desire after conformity to God's law and panting after this spiritual life to the end [that] God may be exalted, Christ glorified, and others edified will not be readily found in one that is yet in nature. It is true, I grant, some who design to establish their own righteousness and to be justified by their own works and inherent holiness may wish that they may be more holy and less guilty. And for some other corrupt ends they may desire to be free of the power of some lust, which they find noxious and troublesome, and yet retain with love and desire some other beloved lusts and so have a heart still cleaving to the heart of some detestable thing or other. But gracious souls, as they have respect to all the commands of God, so they have not that design of being justified before God by their works, nor do they study mortification and sanctification for any such end. Indeed, they no sooner discover any bias of their false, deceitful hearts to any such end but as soon they disown it and abhor it. So that hence believers may get some discovery of the reality of their faith and interest in Christ and of their warrant, indeed, and duty to make use of Christ for sanctification.

Making Use of Christ for Sanctification
This premised, we come to speak something in the general of [a] believer use-making of Christ as made of God to us

sanctification. And for this end, we will only speak a little to two things. First, we will show on what account it is that Christ is called our sanctification, or, made of God to us sanctification, as the apostle's phrase is (1 Cor. 1:30); or, what Christ has done as mediator to begin and carry on to perfection the work of sanctification in the soul. And, secondly, how the soul is to demean itself in this matter, or how the soul is to make use of and improve what Christ has done for this end: that it may grow in grace and perfect holiness in the fear of God.

How Is Christ Made Our Sanctification?
As to the first, we would know that though the work of sanctification be formally ours, yet it is wrought by another hand as the principal efficient cause, even by the Father, Son, and Holy Ghost. The Father is said to purge the branches that they may bring forth more fruit (John 15:1). Hence we are said to be sanctified by God the Father (Jude 1). The Son is also called the sanctifier (Heb. 2:21). He sanctifies and cleanses the church with the washing of water by the word (Eph. 5:26). The Spirit is also said to sanctify (Rom. 15:16; 2 Thess. 2:13; 1 Peter 1:2). Hence we are said to be washed and sanctified by the Spirit of God (1 Cor. 6:11). But more particularly, we are said to be sanctified in Christ (1:2), and He is made of God to us sanctification (v. 30). Let us then see in what sense this may be true. And:

I. He has by His death and blood procured that this work of sanctification will be wrought and carried on. For He suffered without the gate "that he might sanctify the people with his own blood" (Heb. 13:12). We are saved by the washing of regeneration and renewing of the Holy Ghost, "which he shed on us abundantly through Jesus Christ our Saviour" (Titus 3:5–6). He "gave himself for us, that he might redeem us from all iniquity, and purify unto himself a peculiar people, zealous of good works" (2:14). Thus our sanctification is the fruit of His death and purchased by His blood. He gave Himself for His church that He might sanctify it (Eph. 5:25–26).

II. He dying as a cautioner and public person, believers are [therefore] accounted in law to be dead to sin in Him. Hence the apostle tells us (Rom. 6:3–6) that as many of us as are baptized into Jesus Christ were baptized into His death, and that therefore we are buried with Him by baptism into death and are planted together in the likeness of His death—indeed, and that our old man is crucified with Him that the body of sin might be destroyed that henceforth we should not serve sin. From this believers are warranted and commanded to reckon themselves "to be dead indeed unto sin" (v. 11), and therefore [that] sin should "not reign in your mortal body, that ye should obey it in the lusts thereof" (v. 12). This is a sure ground of hope and comfort for believers: that Christ died thus as a public person, and that by virtue of this, being now united to Christ by faith, they are dead to sin by law. And sin cannot challenge a dominion over them, as before their conversion it might have done and did—for the law has dominion over a man as long as he lives, but no longer. Wherefore, believing brethren, becoming "dead to the law by the body of Christ;… [should be] married to another, even to him who is raised from the dead, that we should bring forth fruit unto God" (7:1–4).

III. Hence it follows that our "old man is crucified with [Christ], that the body of sin might be destroyed" (6:6). So that this old tyrant that oppresses the people of God has got his death wounds in the crucifixion of Christ and will never recover his former vigor and activity to oppress and bear down the people of God as he did. He is now virtually through the death of Jesus killed and crucified, being in Christ nailed to the cross.

IV. His resurrection is a pawn and pledge of this sanctification. For as He died as a public person, so He rose again as a public person. "We are buried with him by baptism...that like as Christ was raised up from the dead by the glory of the Father, even so we also should walk in newness of life" (Rom. 6:4). And believers are said to be "planted together...in the likeness of his resurrection" (v. 5). And "they shall also live with him" (v. 8). And therefore they are to "reckon [themselves]... alive unto God through Jesus Christ our Lord" (v. 11). We are raised up together (Eph. 2:6).

V. This sanctification is an article of the covenant of redemption between the Father and the Son (Isa. 52:15). So will He sprinkle many nations. "He shall see his seed...and the pleasure of the LORD shall prosper in his hand" (53:10). Christ then, having this promised to Him, must see to the accomplishment of it and will have it granted to Him, seeing He has fulfilled all that was engaged to by Him—having made His soul an offering for sin.

VI. This sanctification is promised in the covenant of grace. "And I will cleanse them from all their iniquity" (Jer. 33:8). Compare Ezekiel 37:23, "And I will cleanse them." So Ezekiel 36:25: "Then will I sprinkle clean water upon you, and ye shall be clean: from all your filthiness, and from all your idols, will I cleanse you." Now all the promises of the covenant of grace are confirmed to us in the mediator, for in Him all the promises of the covenant "are yea...[and] Amen" (2 Cor. 1:20).

VII. He has purchased and made sure to His own the new nature and the heart of flesh, which is also promised (Jer.

32:39; Ezek. 11:19; 36:26). This is the new and lively principle of grace, the spring of sanctification, which cannot be idle in the soul but must be emitting vital acts natively. Indeed, through Him are believers made partakers of the divine nature, which is a growing thing—young glory in the soul: "According as his divine power hath given unto us all things that pertain unto life and godliness, through the knowledge of him that hath called us to glory and virtue: whereby are given unto us exceeding great and precious promises: that by these ye might be partakers of the divine nature" (2 Peter 1:3–4).

VIII. The Spirit is promised to cause us [to] walk in His statutes (Ezek. 46:27). Now all these promises are made good to us in Christ, who is the cautioner of the covenant. Indeed, He has gotten now the dispensing and giving out of the rich promises of the covenant committed to Him, so as He is the great and glorious custodier of all purchased blessings.

IX. There are new waterings, breathings, and gales of the Spirit given in Christ (Isa. 27:3). He must water His garden or vineyard every moment. This is the north wind and the south wind that blows on the garden (Cant. 4:16). He must be as the dew to Israel (Hos. 14:5).

X. Through Christ is the believer brought into such a covenant state as gives great ground of hope of certain victory. He is not now under the law but under grace. And hence infers the apostle that sin shall not have dominion over them (Rom. 6:14). Being now under that dispensation of grace by which all their stock is in the mediator's hand and at His disposal and not in their own hand and power as under the covenant of works, there is a sure ground laid down for constant supply and furniture in all necessities.

XI. Christ has prayed for this, "Sanctify them through thy truth" (John 17:17), where the Lord is praying that His disciples might be more and more sanctified and so fitted and qualified for the work of the ministry they were to be employed in. And what He prayed for them was not for them alone but also for the elect proportionably, who are opposed to the world, for which He did not pray (v. 9).

XII. He stands to believers in relation of a vine or a root, in which they grow as branches, so that by abiding in Him, living by faith in Him, and drawing sap from Him, they bring forth fruit in Him (15:1–2, 4–5). Their stock of grace is in Him, the root. And He communicates sap and life to His branches by which they grow, flourish, and bring forth fruit to the glory of God.

XIII. Christ has taken on Him[self] the office of a prophet and teacher to instruct us in the way in which we ought to go, for He is that great prophet whom the Lord promised to raise up and who was to be heard and obeyed in all things (Deut. 18:15; Acts 3:22; 7:37). He is given for a witness and a leader (Isa. 55:4). And we are commanded to hear Him (Matt. 17:5; Mark 10:7).

XIV. He has also taken on Him the office of a king (Ps. 2:6; Isa. 9:7; Matt. 28:5; Phil. 2:8–11) and thereby stands engaged to subdue all their spiritual enemies, Satan, and corruption (Psalm 110). He is given for a leader and commander (Isa. 55:5) and so can cause His people [to] walk in His ways.

XV. When we defile ourselves with new transgressions and failings, He has provided a fountain for us to wash in: "a fountain opened to the house of David and to the inhabitants of Jerusalem for sin and for uncleanness" (Zech. 13:1). And this fountain is His blood, which cleanses from all sin (Heb. 9:14; 1 John 1:7; Rev. 1:5).

XVI. He is set before us as a copy and pattern that we should walk even as He walked (1 John 2:6). He left us an example that we "should follow his steps" (1 Peter 2:21). But we should beware to separate this consideration from the preceding, as anti-Christian Socinians do, who will have Christ only to be a copy.

XVII. He has overcome Satan, our archenemy, and has destroyed his works (1 John 3:8). He came to destroy the works of the devil and in particular his works of wickedness in the soul. Thus He is a conqueror and the captain of our salvation.

XVIII. As He has purchased, so has He appointed ordinances for the laying of the foundation and carrying on this work of sanctification. Both word and sacraments are appointed for that. The word to convert and to confirm: "Sanctify them through thy truth: thy word is truth," said Christ (John 17:17). The Word is given as the rule and also through the means of it is life and strength conveyed to the soul to perfect holiness in the fear of God ([2 Cor. 7:1[1]]). And the sacraments are given to strengthen and confirm the soul in the ways of God.

XIX. As He has laid down strong encouragements to His followers to hold on in the way of holiness many great and precious promises by which they may be made partakers of the divine nature (2 Peter 1:4) and by which they are encouraged to cleanse themselves from all filthiness of the flesh and spirit (2 Cor. 7:1), and many motives to hold on and continue—so

---

1. Original, 1 Peter 2:2.

has He rolled difficulties out of the way, whether they be within us or without us. And by this [He has] made the way easy and pleasant to such as walk in it, so as they may now run the way of His commandments and walk and not weary and run and not be faint.

XX. Indeed, we would remember for our encouragement and confidence that in carrying on of this work lies the satisfaction of the soul and the pleasure of the Lord that must prosper in His hand, and thus He sees His seed and has of the travail of His soul and is satisfied.

These particulars rightly considered will discover to us what a noble ground for sanctification is in Christ laid down for believers, which they may and must by faith grip so that they may grow in grace and grow up in Christ and perfect holiness. And what a wonderful contrivance of grace this is in which all things are made so sure for believers, Christ becoming all things to them and paving a royal and sure way for them—sure for them, and glorious to Himself!

How Should Believers Make Use of Christ?
As to the second particular, that is, how believers are to carry in this matter, or how they are to make use of Christ, and of those grounds of sanctification in Christ, which we have mentioned:

First, there are some things which they should beware of and guard against, as:

I. They should beware of a heartless despondency and giving way to discouragement and hearkening to the language of unbelief or to the suggestion of Satan by which he will labor to persuade them of the impossibility of getting the work of sanctification throughed or any progress made in it to purpose. Satan and a deceitful heart can soon muster up many difficulties and allege that there are many lions, many insuperable difficulties in the way to discourage them from venturing forward. And if Satan prevail here, he has gained a great point. Therefore, the believer should keep up his head in hope and beware of multiplying discouragements to himself or of concluding the matter impossible, for then will he neither have heart nor hand for the work but sit down and wring his hands as overcome with discouragement and despondency of spirit.

II. They should beware of willfully rejecting their own mercies and forbearing to make use of the grounds of hope, of strength and progress in the matter of sanctification, which Christ has allowed them to make use of. There is such an evil among God's children that they scar at that which Christ out of great love has provided for them and dare not with confidence make use of nor apply to themselves the great and comfortable promises to the end they might be encouraged. They will not take their allowance, as thinking themselves unworthy and that it would be presumpt[uous] in them to challenge a right to such great things. And they think it commendable humility in them to stand back and so willfully refuse the advantages and helps that make so much for their growth in grace.

III. They should beware of a careless neglect of the means appointed for advancing in holiness; for, though the means do not work the effect, yet it is by the means that God has chosen to work the work of sanctification. Here that is to be seen that the hand of the diligent makes rich, and the field of the slothful is soon grown over with thorns and nettles, so that "poverty come as one that travelleth; and…want as an armed man" (Prov. 24:30[–34]). It is a sinful tempting of God to think to be sanctified another way than God has in His deep wisdom condescended on.

IV. Yet they should beware of laying too much weight on the means and ordinances, as if they could effectuate the business. Though the Lord has thought fit to work in and by the means, yet He Himself must do the work. Means are but means and not the principal cause. Nor can they work but as the principal agent is pleased to make use of them and to work by them. When we lean to the means and to instruments, we prejudge ourselves by disobliging of God and provoking Him to leave us that we may wrestle with the ordinances alone and find no advantage. Therefore, the soul should guard against this.

V. Even though the means can do nothing unless He breathe, yet we should beware not only of neglecting, as we said before, but also of a slighting way of performing them without that earnestness and diligence that is required—"Cursed be he that doeth the work of the LORD negligently"[2] (Jer. 48:10). Here then is the special art of Christianity apparent: to be as diligent, earnest, and serious in the use of the means as if they could effectuate the matter we were seeking, and yet to be as much abstracted from them in our hopes and expectation and to be as much leaning on the Lord alone and depending on Him for the blessing as if we were using no means at all.

VI. They should beware of slighting and neglecting the motions of the Spirit, for by this they may lose the best opportunity. They should be always on the wing, ready to embrace the least motion. And they should stand always ready, waiting

---

2. Note that the KJV has "deceitfully" instead of "negligently"— Brown is here quoting the Geneva Bible.

for the breathings of His Spirit and open at His call, lest afterward they be put to call and seek and not attain what they would be at, as we see in the spouse (Cant. 5:2–4, etc.).

VII. They should also guard against the quenching of the Spirit (1 Thess. 5:12) or grieving of the Spirit (Eph. 4:30) by their unchristian and unsuitable carriage, for this will much mar their sanctification. It is by the Spirit that the work of sanctification is carried on in the soul. And when this Spirit is disturbed and put from His work, how can the work go on? When the motions of this indwelling Spirit are extinguished, His work is marred and retarded. And when He is grieved, He is hindered in His work. Therefore, souls must guard against unbelief, despondency, [and] unsuitable and unchristian carriage.

VIII. Especially they should beware of wasting sins (Ps. 51:10)—sins against light and conscience, such as David called presumptuous sins (19:13). They should beware also of savoring any unknown corruption or anything of that kind that may hinder the work of sanctification.

Secondly, it were useful and of great advantage for such as would grow in grace and advance in the way of holiness to be living in the constant conviction:

I. Of the necessity of holiness, "without which no man shall see the Lord" (Heb. 12:14). Nothing enter[s] into the New Jerusalem that defiles (cf. Rev. 21:[2]7).

II. Of their own inability to do any one act right[ly], how they are not sufficient of themselves to think anything as of themselves (2 Cor. 3:5), and that without Christ they can do nothing (John 15:5).

III. Of the insufficiency of any human help or means or way which they might think good to choose, to mortify aright one corruption or to give strength for the discharge of any one duty—for our sufficiency is of God (ch. 3), and it is "through the Spirit" that we must "mortify the deeds of the body" (Rom. 8:13).

IV. And of the treachery and deceitfulness of the heart, which is bent to follow by-ways, being not only "deceitful above all things" but also "desperately wicked" (Jer. 17:9).

That by this means the soul may be jealous of itself and despair of doing anything in its own strength and so be fortified against that main evil which is an enemy to all true sanctification; namely, confidence in the flesh.

Thirdly, the soul will keep its eye fixed on these things:

I. On Christ's all-sufficiency to help—in all cases that He is able to save "to the uttermost" (Heb. 7:25).

II. On His compassionateness to such as are out of the way and readiness to help poor sinners with His grace and strength. And this will keep up the soul from fainting and despairing.

III. On the commands of holiness, such as these: "Cleanse your hands…and purify your hearts" (James 4:8); and, "Be ye holy; for I am holy" (1 Peter 1:15–16); and the like, that the authority of God and conscience to command may set the soul to work.

IV. On the great recompense of reward that is appointed for such as wrestle on and endure to the end and on the great promises of great things to such as are sanctified, of which the Scriptures are full—that the soul may be encouraged to run through difficulties, to ride out storms, to endure hardness as a good soldier, and to persevere in duty.

V. On the other hand, on the many sad threatenings and denunciations of wrath against such as transgress His laws, and on all the sad things that such as shake off the fear of God and the study of holiness have to look for, of which the Scripture is full—that by this means the soul may be kept in awe and spurred forward to duty and made the more willing to shake off laziness.

VI. On the rule, the Word of God, by which alone we must regulate all our actions. And this ought to be our meditation day and night and all our study, as we see it was David's and other holy men of God their daily work (see Psalms 1; 119).

Fourthly, in all this study of holiness and aiming at a higher measure of grace, the believer would level at a right end and so would not design holiness for this end that he might be justified by it or that he might by it procure and purchase to himself heaven and God's favor. For the weight of all that must lie on Jesus Christ, who is our righteousness. And our holiness must not dethrone Him nor rob Him of His glory, which He will not give to another. But [he] would study holiness to the end he might glorify God—Father, Son, and Holy Spirit—and please Him who calls to holiness and by this be "meet to be partakers of the inheritance of the saints in light" (Col. 1:10, 12) and be made a meet³ bride for such a holy bridegroom and a member to such a holy head—that by this others might be edified (Matt. 5:16; 1 Peter 2:12; 3:1–2); that the soul may look like a temple of the Holy Ghost and like a servant

3. *Meet*: fitting.

of Christ's bought with a price (1 Cor. 6:17–20) and have a clear evidence of His regeneration and justification; and also that he may express his thankfulness to God for all His favors and benefits.

Fifthly, the soul should by faith lay hold on and grip fast to the ground of sanctification—that is to say (1) to what Christ has purchased for His people [and] (2) to what as a public person He has done for them—and so by faith:

I. Challenge a right to and lay hold on the promises of grace, strength, victory, and thorough bearing in their combatting with corruption within and Satan and a wicked world without.

II. Reckon themselves "dead indeed unto sin" through the death of Christ and "alive unto God" through His resurrection (Rom. 6:4, 11). And that the old man is crucified with Him, "that the body of sin might be destroyed" (v. 6). And that they are now "not under the law, but under grace" (v. 14).

That by this means they may be encouraged to continue fighting against a vanquished enemy and not give over, despite disappointments, discouragements, prevailings of corruption, etc., and the believer may know on what ground[s] he stands and what is the ground[s] of his hope and expectation of victory in the end—and so he may run, "not as uncertainly," and so fight, "not as one that beateth the air" (1 Cor. 9:26).

Sixthly, in this work of sanctification, the believer should be much in the lively exercise of faith—fight by faith, advance by faith, grow up and bring forth fruit by faith. And so:

I. The believer would be often renewing his grips of Christ, holding Him fast by faith and so abiding in Him that he may bring forth fruit (John 15:4–5).

II. Not only would he be keeping his union fast with Christ, but he would also be eyeing Christ by faith as his storehouse and general Lord dispensator of all the purchased blessings of the covenant which he stands in need of and looking on Christ as standing engaged by office to complete His work of salvation and to present him with the rest to Himself holy, without blemish, indeed, and without spot and wrinkle or any such thing (Eph. 5:27).

III. He would by faith grip to the promises, both of the general stock of grace, the new heart and heart of flesh and the Spirit to cause us [to] walk in His statutes (Ezek. 36:26–27), and of the several particular acts of grace that he stands in need of, such as that "I will cleanse them from all their iniquities, etc." (Jer. 30:8). So Ezekiel 36:25 and Jeremiah 31:19. [This is] as the church does (Mic. 7:9), "He will subdue our iniquities, etc." And so having or gripping these promises, we are to cleanse ourselves from all filthiness of flesh and spirit and perfect holiness in the fear of God (2 Cor. 7:1).

IV. As the believer would by faith draw out of Christ, through the conduit of the promises which are all yea and amen in Him (2 Cor. 1:20), grace, strength, knowledge, courage, or whatever his fight in this warfare calls for, to the end he may be strong in "the Lord, and in the power of his might" (Eph. 6:10), so he would by faith roll the weight of the whole work on Christ and thus cast himself and his care and burden on Him who cares for him (Ps. 37:5; 55:22; 1 Peter 5:7), and so go on in duty without anxiety, knowing who bears the weight of all and who has undertaken to work both to will and to do according to His good pleasure. Thus should the work be easy and safe, when by faith we roll the burden on Him who is the chosen one fitted for that work and leave it on Him who is our strength, patiently waiting for the outgate in hope.

Thus the believer makes use of Christ, as made of God sanctification, when in the use of means appointed, eyeing the covenant of grace, and the promises of it, and what Christ has done to sanctify and cleanse His people. He rolls the matter on Him and expects help, salvation, and victory through Him.

Cautions
But lest some should be discouraged and think all this in vain because they perceive no progress nor growth in grace for all this but rather corruption as strong and troublesome as ever, I would say a few things to them.

I. Let them search and try whether their shortcoming and disappointment does not much proceed from this: that the matter is not so cleanly cast over on Christ as it should be. Is it not too often found that they go forth to the battle in their own strength, lippening[4] to their own stock of grace, to their own knowledge, or to their duties, or the like? How then can they prosper?

II. Let them mourn as they get any discovery of this and guard against that corrupt bias of the heart which is still inclining them to an engagement without the captain of their salvation and a fighting without the armor of God.

III. Let them try and see if in studying holiness they be not led by corrupt ends and do not more labor after sanctification that they may be more worthy and the better accepted of God and that they may have quietness and peace as to their

---

4. *Lippening:* entrusting.

acceptance with God, as if this were any cause, matter, or condition of their righteousness and justification before God than that they may show their obedience to the command of God (John 15:16; Eph. 2:10; 1 Thess. 4:3) and express their thankfulness to Him and glorify God (Mal. 1:6; Matt. 3:16; John 17:10; Eph. 4:30). And, if so, they ought to acknowledge God's goodness in that disappointment, seeing by this they see more and more a necessity of laying aside their own righteousness and of betaking themselves to the righteousness of Christ and of resting on that alone for peace and acceptance with God.

IV. They should try and see if their negligence and carelessness in watching and in the discharge of duties do not occasion their disappointments and shortcoming. God sometimes thinks fit to suffer a lion of corruption to set on them that they may look about them and stand more vigilantly on their watchtower, knowing that they have to do with a vigilant adversary, the devil, who, as a roaring lion, goes about seeking whom he may devour (1 Peter 5:8), and that they "wrestle not against flesh and blood, but against principalities, against powers, against the rulers of the darkness of this world, against spiritual wickedness in high places" (Eph. 6:12). It is not for naught that we are so often commanded to watch (Matt. 14:38; 24:42; 25:13; 26:41; Mark 13:33–37; Luke 21:36; 1 Cor. 16:13; Col. 4:2; 1 Thess. 5:6; 1 Peter 4:7). Through the want of this, we know what befell David and Peter.

V. They should try and see whether there be not too much self-confidence, which occasioned Peter's foul fall. God may in justice and mercy suffer corruption to break loose on such at a time and tread them under foot to learn them afterward to carry more soberly and to "work out their salvation with fear and trembling" (Phil. 2:12), remembering what a jealous, holy God He is with whom they have to do, what an adversary they have against them, and how weak their own strength is.

VI. This should be remembered that one may be growing in grace and advancing in holiness, when, to his apprehension, he is not going forward from strength to strength but rather going backward. It is one thing to have grace, and another thing to see that we have grace. So it is one thing to be growing in grace, and another thing to see that we are growing in grace. Many may question their growth in grace when their very questioning of it may evince the contrary. For they may conclude no growth but rather a back-going, because they perceive more and more violent and strong corruptions and hidden works of darkness and wickedness within their soul than ever they did before, while as that great discovery shows the increase of their spiritual knowledge, and an increase in this is an increase in grace. So they may question and doubt of their growth on mistakes, as thinking corruption always strongest when it makes the greatest stir and noise, or their complaints may flow from a vehement desire they have to have much more sanctification, which may cause them [to] over-look many degrees they have advanced. Or some such thing may occasion their darkness and complaints. Indeed, God may think it fittest for them, to the end they may be kept humble and diligent, to be in the dark as to their progress, whereas if they saw what advancement and progress they had made in Christianity, they might grow wanton, secure, and careless and so occasion some sad dispensation to humble them again.

VII. It should be remembered that perfect victory is not to be had here. It is true, in respect of justification through the impu-tation of the perfect righteousness of Christ and in respect of their sincerity and gospel simplicity and in respect also of the parts of the new man, believers are said to be perfect. Such a one was Noah (Gen. 6:9) and Job (1:1, 8). See also Psalm 37:37; 64:4; 1 Corinthians 2:6; Hebrews 5:14; and James 3:2. And it is true, we are to aim at perfection and to pray for it (as Matt. 5:48; 2 Cor. 13:11; Col. 4:12; Heb. 6:1; 13:21; James 1:4; 1 Peter 5:10). Yet as to the degrees of holiness and sanctification and in respect of the remnant of corruption within, there is no full perfection here (Jer. 9:20–21; Phil. 3:12). For even he who is washed and, as to justification, is clean every whit yet needs to wash his feet, because contracting filth in his conversation (Job 13:10). So that if the Lord should mark iniquity, no man should stand (Ps. 130:3; 143:2). There will still be in the best something, more or less, of that battle that Paul speaks of (Rom. 7:15–23). So that they will still have occasion to cry out with him, verse 24: "O wretched man that I am! who shall deliver me from the body of this death?" And the flesh will still lust against the Spirit, and the Spirit against the flesh, so that they will not be able to do what they would (Gal. 5:17). The place of perfection is above, where all tears are wiped away and the weary wrestler is at rest.

VIII. Let them not mistake and think that every stirring of corruption in the soul argues its dominion and prevailing power. Corruption may stir and make a great deal ado, where it cannot get leave to reign, and be as a violent and cruel invader, seeking the throne, putting the whole kingdom in a combustion, who is resisted with force of arms. Corruption may be more quiet and still, when indeed it has the throne of the soul—as a conqueror may be more quiet and still when he has overcome and is in peaceable possession of the kingdom than when he was but fighting for it. When the strong man keeps the house and is master, then all is quiet and at rest, till a stronger come and thrust him out and dispossess him.

IX. Sanctification does not always consist in a man's freedom from some corruptions. For there may be some corruptions that one has no natural inclination to, but, on the contrary, a great aversion for—as some world's wretches may have no inclination to prodigality and ranting or such like vices, which are contrary to their humor or to their constant education. And Satan may never tempt some man to such evils, knowing he will get more advantage by plying his temper and genius and so carrying him away to the other contrary evil. And so, though this man know not so much as what it is once to be tempted to those vices, yet that will not say that he is a sanctified man. Far less will it say that he has more grace than another man whose predominant that evil is and against which he is daily fighting and wrestling. From this it appears that wrestling and protesting against even an overcoming corruption may evidence more of grace than freedom from some evils, to which some are not so much tempted and to which they are naturally less inclined.

X. Nor should they think that corruption is always master of the soul and possessing the throne as a full conqueror when it prevails and carries the soul headlong at a time, for corruption may sometimes come in on the soul as an inundation with irresistible violence and, for a time, carry all before it, so that the soul cannot make any sensible resistance. As when a sudden, violent, and unexpected temptation sets on, so as the poor man is overwhelmed and scarce knows where he is or what he is doing, till he be laid on his back. At that time it will be a great matter if the soul dare quietly enter a protest against and dissent from what is done. And if there be an honest protestation against the violent and tyrannical invasion of corruption, we cannot say that corruption is in peaceable possession of the throne. If the spirit be lusting against the flesh, levying all the forces he can against the invader by prayer and supplication to God and calling in all the supply of divine help he can get and, when he can do no more, is fighting and groaning under that unjust invasion, resolving never to pay homage to the usurper nor to obey his laws nor so much as parley with him or make peace—we cannot say that the soul does consent fully to this usurpation. Indeed, if the soul will do this much at such a time when Satan sets on with all his force, it will be a greater evidence of the strength of grace in the soul than if the soul should do the same or a little more at a time when the temptation is not so strong.

XI. It is not good for them to say that grace is not growing in them because they advance not so far as some do and because they come not to the pitch of grace that they see some advanced to. That is not a sure rule to measure their growth in grace by. Some may have a better natural temper by which they are less inclined to several vices which these find a strong propension[5] to. They may have the advantage of a better education and the like, so that they should rather try themselves this year by what they were the last year, and that in reference to the lusts to which they have been most subject all their days.

XII. We must not think that every believer will attain to the same measure of grace. There is a measure appointed for every member or joint of this body. And every joint supplies according to the effectual working in the measure of every part (Eph. 4:16). God has more ado with some than with

---

5. *Propension*: propensity.

others. There is more strength required in an arm or leg than in a finger or toe. And everyone should be content with his measure, so far as not to fret or repine against God and His dispensations that makes them but a finger and not an arm of the body and do their duty in their station, fighting against sin, according to the measure or grace dispensed to them of the Lord, and that faithfully and constantly, and not quarrel with God that He makes us not as free of temptations and corruptions as some others. For the captain must not be blamed for commanding some of his soldiers to this post where they never once see the enemy and others to that post where they must continually fight. The soldier is here under command and therefore must be quiet and take his lot. So must the Christian reverence the Lord's dispensations in ordering matters so as they will never have one hour's quietness, while as others have more rest and peace and stand at their post fighting, resolving never to yield but rather to cover the ground with their dead bodies till the commander in chief think good to relieve them. Sure I am, as the only wise God has distributed to every member of the body as He has thought good, so it is the duty of every member to endeavor this holy submission to Him as to the measure of grace considered as His free gift bestowed on them, and to be humbled for the grudgings of his heart, because God has not given him more talents. And sure I am, though this submission make no great noise in the world, yet really this is one of the highest degrees of grace attainable here and such an ornament of a meek and quiet spirit as is in the sight of God of great price. So that whoever has attained to this has the very grace they seem to want and more. Yet, lest this should be abused, let me add a word or two of caution to qualify this submission:

1. There must be with it a high prizing even of that degree of grace which they want.

2. There must be a panting after grace, as it is God's image and a conformity to Him, and with so much singleness as they may be in case to say without the reproachings of their heart [that] they do not so much love holiness for heaven, as heaven for holiness.

3. There must be an unceasingness in using all means by which the growth of grace may be promoved to this end that they may be conformed to His image, rather than that they may be comforted.

4. There must be also a deep humiliation for the want of that degree of grace they would have, as it imports the want of so much conformity to Him to whose image they are predestinated to be conformed, which will very well consist with this submission we are speaking of.

XIII. It would be remembered that there may be a great progress even when it is not observed, when:

1. Hereby the man is made to lie in the dust, to loath himself, and cry, "Behold, I am vile!"

2. Hereby his indignation against the body of death is the more increased.

3. Hereby his esteem of a savior and of the blessed contrivance of salvation is the more heightened that he sees he is by this brought to make mention of His righteousness, even of His only.

4. Hereby his longing after immediate fruition is increased, where all these complaints will cease.

5. And hereby he is put to essay that much slighted duty of holding fast the rejoicing of his hope firm to the end, looking and longing for the grace that will be brought to him at the revelation of Jesus Christ, when he will be presented without spot and be made meet to be a partaker of the inheritance of the saints in light.

CHAPTER 6

How Christ Is to Be Made Use of in Reference to the Killing and Crucifying of the Old Man

*H*aving thus shortly pointed out some things in general serving to the clearing and opening up the way of our use-making of Christ for sanctification, we come now more particularly to the clearing up of this business. In sanctification we must consider, first, the renewing and changing of our nature and frame; and, next, the washing and purging away of our daily contracted spots. The first of these is commonly divided into two parts—namely, first, the mortification, killing, and crucifying of the old man of sin and corruption which is within; and, second, the vivification, renewing, quickening, and strengthening of the new man of grace. And this is a growth in grace and in fruitfulness and holiness.

As to the first of these—namely, the mortification or crucifying of the old man—we would know that there is such a principle of wickedness and enmity against God in man by nature now since the fall by which the man is inclined to evil and only to evil. This is called the old man, as being like the body made of so many parts, joints, and members, that is, so many lusts and corruptions and evil inclinations, which together make up a corpus. And they are fast joined and compacted together as the members of the body, each useful and serviceable to one another, and all of them concurring and contributing their utmost to the carrying on of the work of sin—and so it is the man of sin. And it is also called the old man, as having first possession of the soul before it is by grace renewed, and it is a dying more and more daily. Thus it is called the old man and the body of sin (Rom. 6:6). This old man has his members in our members and faculties so that none of them are free—understanding, will, affections, and the members of our body are all servants of unrighteousness to this body of sin and old man. So we read of the motions of sin (7:5), which work in our members to bring forth fruit to death, and of the lusts of the flesh (Rom. 13:14; Gal. 5:16, 24), and the lusts of sin (Rom. 6:12). So we hear of the desires of the flesh and of the mind (Eph. 2:3) and of affections and lusts (Gal. 5:24). And the old man is said to be corrupt according to the deceitful lusts (Eph. 4:22). All which lusts and affections are as so many members of this body of sin and of this old man. And, further, there is in this a considerable power, force, and efficacy which this old man has in us to carry us away and, as it were, command or constrain us as by a forcible law. Hence we read of the law of sin and death (Rom. 8:2), which only the law of the Spirit of life in Christ does make us free from. It is also called a law in our members warring against the law of our mind (7:23) and bringing us into captivity to the law of sin which is in our members. So it is said to lust against the Spirit and to war (Gal. 5:17). All which point out the strength, activity, and dominion of sin in the soul so that it is as the husband over the wife (Rom. 7:1). Indeed, it has a domineering and constraining power where its horns are not held in by grace. And as its power is great, so its nature is wicked and malicious—for it is pure "enmity against God" (8:7). So that it neither is nor can be reconciled and therefore must be put off and abolished (Eph. 2:15), killed and crucified (Rom. 6:6). Now in this lies the work of a believer to be killing, mortifying, and crucifying this enemy, or rather enmity, and delivering himself from under this bondage and slavery that he may be Christ's free man, and that through the Spirit (Rom. 8:13).

How to Use Christ to Crucify the Flesh
Now, if it be asked, "How will a believer make use of Christ to the end this old man may be gotten crucified?" or, "How should a believer mortify this old man and the lusts thereof through Christ, or by the Spirit of Jesus?" we will propose these things which may help to clear this:

I. The believer should have his eye on this old man as his archenemy, as a deadly cutthroat lying within his bosom. It is an enemy lodging within him in his soul, mind, heart, and affections, so that there is no part free, and therefore is acquaint[ed] with all the motions of the soul and is always opposing and hindering everything that is good. It is an enemy that will never be reconciled to God and therefore will not be reconciled with the believer as such. For it is called enmity itself, and so it is always actively seeking to promove the ruin of the soul, what by prompting, inclining, moving, and forcibly drawing or driving, sometimes with violence and rage, to evil; what by withstanding, resisting, opposing, counterworking, and contradicting what is good—so that the believer cannot get that done which he would do and is made to do that which he would not. Therefore, this being such an enemy and so dangerous an enemy, so constant and implacable an enemy, so active and close an enemy, so deadly and destructive, it is the believer's part to guard against this enemy, to have a vigilant eye on it, to carry as an irreconcilable enemy to it, and therefore never to come in terms of capitulation or agreement with it—never once to parley, let be make peace. And the believer would not have his vigilant eye on this or that member of this body of death so much as on the body itself or the principle of wickedness and rebellion against God—the head, life, spirit, or law of this body of death. For there lies its greatest wickedness and activity. And this is always opposing us, though not in every joint and member but sometimes in one, sometimes in another.

II. Though the believer should have a main eye on the body— this innate, strong, and forcible law of sin and death—yet should he have friendship and familiarity with no part, member, or lust of all this body. All the deeds of the body should be mortified (Rom. 8:13). The old man with his deeds should be mortified (Col. 3:6). And we should mortify our "members which are upon the earth" (v. 5), for all of them are against us, and the least of them countenanced, entertained, and embraced will work our ruin and cut our soul's throat. Therefore should the believer look on each of them and on all of them as his deadly enemies.

III. He should consider that, as it is a very unseemly thing for him to be a slave to that old tyrant and to yield his members as so many servants to iniquity, so it is dangerous and deadly. His life lies at the stake. Either he must get it mortified, killed, and subdued, or it will kill him. His life will go for its life. If this enemy escape, he is a gone man. The consideration of this should cause the believer to act here in earnestness and seriousness, with care and diligence, and set about this work of mortification with labor and pains.

IV. Much more must it be against all reason and Christianity for the believer to be making provision for the flesh, "to fulfil the lusts thereof" (Rom. 13:14). To be strengthening the hands of and laying provision to this enemy which is set and sworn against us can stand with no reason. And here is much of the Christian's prudence and spiritual wisdom required to discern what may make for fostering of this or that corruption or member of the body of sin and death, and to withdraw that, as we will labor to take away provision of any kind from an enemy that is coming against us. Paul acted in this as a wise gamester and combatant when he kept under his body and brought it into subjection (1 Cor. 9:27). It were but to mock God and to preach forth our own folly to be looking to Christ for help against such an enemy and, in the meantime, to be underhand strengthening the hands of the enemy. This would be double dealing and treachery against ourselves.

V. To the end their opposition to this enemy may be the stronger and more resolute, they should consider that this body of sin is wholly set against God and His interest in the soul, being very enmity itself against God (Rom. 8:7) and always lusting and fighting against the work of God in the soul (Gal. 5:17) and against everything that is good, so that it will not suffer, so far as it can hinder the soul, to do anything that is good, at least in a right manner and for a right end. Indeed, with its lustings, it drives constantly to that which is evil, raises evil motions and inclinations in the soul before the believer be aware, [and] sides with any temptation that is offered to the end that it may destroy the soul, like a traitor within—as we see it did in David, when he fell into adultery, and with Asaph (Ps. 73:2). Indeed, itself opposes and tempts (James 1:14) by setting mind, will, and affections on wrong courses. And thus it drives the soul to a course of rebellion against God or diverts it and draws it back that it cannot get God served aright. Indeed, sometimes it sets a fire in the soul, entangling all the faculties, filling the mind with darkness or prejudice, misleading or preventing the affections, and so miscarrying the will and leading it captive (Rom. 7:23)—so that the thing is done which the unregenerate soul would not do, and the duty is left undone which the soul would fain have done, indeed, and that sometimes despite the soul's watching and striving against this, so strong is its force.

VI. The believer should remember that this enemy is not for him to fight against alone and that his own strength and skill will make but a slender opposition to it. It will laugh at the shaking of his spear. It can easily insinuate itself on all occasions, because it lies so near and close to the soul, always residing there, and is at the believer's right hand, whatever he be doing, and is always openly or closely opposing, and that with great facility. For it easily besets (Heb. 12:1) because it lies within the soul and in all the faculties of it—in the heart, mind, will, conscience, and affections. So that on this account, the deceitfulness of the heart is great and passes the search of man (Jer. 17:9). Man cannot know all the windings and turnings, all the drifts and designs, all the lurking and retiring places, all the falsehoods and double dealings, all the dissimulations, lies, and subterfuges, all the plausible and deceitful pretexts and insinuations of his heart acted and spirited by this law of sin and death. And besides this slight and cunning, it has strength and power to draw by lusts into destruction and perdition (1 Tim. 4:9) and to carry the soul headlong, so that it makes the man's case miserable (Rom. 7:24). All which would say that the believer should call in other help than his own and remember that through the Spirit he must mortify the deeds of the body (8:13).

VII. And therefore the believer must lay aside all his carnal weapons in dealing with his adversary and look out for divine help and assistance, even for the promised Spirit, through which alone he can be instructed and enabled for this great work. For of himself he can do nothing, not so much as think a good thought as of himself (2 Cor. 3:5), far less will he be able to oppose such a mighty adversary that has so great and many advantages. And therefore all his carnal means, purposes, vows, and fightings in himself will but render himself weaker and a readier prey to this adversary, which gains ground while he is so opposed. It is Christ alone and His Spirit that can destroy the works of the devil and kill or crucify this enmity.

VIII. So that the believer must have his recourse for help and succor here to Jesus, the captain of salvation, and must follow Him and fight under His banners, make use of His weapons, which are spiritual, fight according to His counsel and conduct, taking Him as a leader and commander and lying open for His orders and instructions, waiting for the motions of His Spirit and following them, and thus oppose and fight against this deadly enemy with an eye always on Christ by faith, depending on Him for light to the mind, resolution to the will, and grace to the whole soul to stand in the battle and to withstand all assaults. And [he must] never engage in a dispute with this enemy or any lust or member of this body without Christ the principal—that is, the soul would despair in itself and be strong in Him and in the power of His might, by faith gripping to Him, as head, captain, and commander in chief, resolving to fight in His strength and to oppose through the help of His Spirit.

IX. And for this cause the believer would eye the covenant of redemption, the basis of all our hope and consolation, in which final and full victory is promised to Christ, as head of the elect; namely, that He will bruise the serpent's head. And so that in

Him, all His followers and members of His mystical body will lift up the head and get full victory at length over both sin and death. Now it is God that "giveth us the victory through our Lord Jesus Christ" (1 Cor. 15:57). The believer would also eye by faith the covenant of grace, in which particularly this same victory is promised to the believer, in and through Jesus. "And the God of peace shall bruise Satan under your feet shortly" (Rom. 16:20), and "sin shall not have dominion over you: for ye are not under the law, but under grace" (6:14). The believer, I say, would look out by faith to and lay hold on these and the like promises and by this get strength conveyed to himself, by which he may strive lawfully and fight valiantly and oppose with courage and resolution.

X. Further, the believer would eye Christ as a fountain of furniture, as a full and complete magazine, standing open and ready for every one of His honest soldiers to run to for new supplies of what they want. So that whatever they find wanting in their Christian armor, they must run away to the open magazine, Christ's fullness, that stands ready for them, and by faith take and put on what they want and stand in need of in their warfare. If their girdle of truth be slacked, loosed, or weakened, and they be meeting with temptations anent[1] their hypocrisy, and Satan objecting to them their double dealing, of purpose to discourage them and to make them faint and give over the fight—they must away to Him who is the truth, that He may bind on that girdle better and make their hearts more upright before God in all they do. And if their breastplate of righteousness be weakened and Satan there seem to get advantage by casting up to them their unrighteous dealings toward God or men, [then] they must flee to Him who

---

1. *Anent*: concerning.

only can help here and beg pardon through His blood for their failings and set to again afresh to the battle. If their resolution, which is understood by the preparation of the gospel of peace, grow weak, it must be renewed in Christ's armory, and the feet of new be shod with it. If their shield of faith begin to fail them, away must they get to Him who is the author and finisher of faith (Heb. 12:2). And if their helmet of hope begin to fail them, in this armory alone can that be supplied. And if their sword be blunted in their hand or they unable to wield it aright, the Spirit of Jesus can only teach their hands to fight and instruct them how to manage that useful weapon with advantage. Thus must the believer be strong in Him and "in the power of his might" (Eph. 6:10). He is their God that girds them with strength and makes their way perfect. He makes their feet like hinds' feet and sets them on their high places. He teaches their hands to war, so that a bow of steel is broken by their arms. He gives them the shield of salvation. His right hand upholds them. He girds with strength to the battle (Ps. 18:3[1], etc.).

XI. For the further strengthening of their hope, faith, and confidence, believers would eye Christ as hanging on the cross and overcoming by death [both] death and him that has the power of death, the devil, and so as meritoriously purchasing this redemption from the slavery of sin and Satan and particularly from the slavery of that body of death and of the law of sin and death—for the apostle tells us that the law of the Spirit of life in Christ Jesus does make us "free from the law of sin and death" (Rom. 8:2), and that because, as he says further, "What the law could not do, in that it was weak through the flesh, God sending his own Son in the likeness of sinful flesh, and for sin, condemned sin in the flesh: that the righteousness of the law might be fulfilled in us" (vv. 3–4). So that the believer may now look on that enemy, however fearful it may appear, as condemned and killed in the death of Christ. He, having laid down the price of redemption, has bought this freedom from the chains and fetters with which He was held in captivity. Faith, then, on the death of Jesus satisfying justice for the poor captive, may and should support and strengthen the hope and confidence of the believer that he will obtain the victory at length.

XII. And it will further confirm the hope and faith of the believer to look to Christ hanging on the cross and there vanquishing and overcoming this archenemy—as a public person, representing the elect who died in Him and virtually and legally did in Him overcome that jailor and break his fetter. And the soul now believing may, indeed, should reckon itself in Christ dying, as it were, on the cross and there overcoming all those spiritual enemies. "Likewise," the apostle says, "reckon ye also yourselves to be dead indeed unto sin" (Rom. 6:11). From hence, even while fighting, the believer may account himself a conqueror, indeed, more than a conqueror, through Him that loved him (8:37). Now faith acting thus on Christ as a public person, dying and overcoming death and sin, the believer may not only infer the certainty of victory, knowing that our old man is crucified with Christ (6:6), but also from the cross of Christ draw strength to stand and fight against the strugglings of this vanquished and killed enemy. "They that are Christ's have crucified the flesh with the affections and lusts" (Gal. 5:24). But how? Even by the cross of Christ. For by this is the world "crucified unto me," the apostle says, "and I unto the world" (6:14). Your old man "is crucified with him, that the body of sin might be destroyed" (Rom. 6:6).

XIII. The believer, being dead indeed to sin through the cross of Christ, is to look on himself as legally freed from that yoke of bondage under sin and death. "The law hath dominion over a man as long as he liveth" (Rom. 7:1). But by the body of Christ believers are "become dead to the law" (v. 4). That law of sin and death which has dominion over a man that lives still in nature and is not yet by faith planted in the likeness of Christ's death nor buried with Him by baptism into death (6:4–5) has not that dominion over believers it had once. "For the law of the Spirit of life in Christ Jesus hath made me free from the law of sin and death" (8:2). So that now the believer is free from that tyranny. And that tyrant can exercise no lawful jurisdiction or authority over him. And therefore he may with the greater courage repel the insolencies of that tyrant that contrary to all right and equity seeks to lord it over him still. They are no lawful subjects to that cruel and raging prince or to that spiritual wickedness.

XIV. So that the believer, renouncing that jurisdiction under which he was formerly and being under a new husband and under a new law, even the law of the Spirit of life in Christ Jesus, is to look on all the motions of sin as illegal and as treasonable acts of a tyrant. The old man being crucified with Christ that the body of sin might be destroyed, the believer is not any more to serve sin (Rom. 6:6). And being now dead, they are freed from sin (v. 7) and are "married to another, even to him who is raised from the dead," that they should not serve sin but "bring forth fruit unto God" (7:4). And therefore, [they should] look on all motions of the flesh and all the inclinations and stirrings of the old law of sin as acts of treachery and rebellion against the right and jurisdiction of the believer's new Lord and husband and are therefore obliged to lay hold on this old man, this body of death, and all the members

of it as traitors to the rightful king and husband and to take
them prisoners to the king that He may give out sentence and
execute the same against them as enemies to His kingdom
and interest in the soul—they being now no more servants
of sin but of righteousness, they ought no more to yield their
members servants to uncleanness, and iniquity unto iniquity
(6:18–19), and being debtors no more to the flesh, "to live after
the flesh" ([8]:12). They are to mortify the deeds of the body
"through the Spirit" (v. 13) and [are] to crucify "the flesh with
the affections and lusts" (Gal. 5:24)—that is, by bringing them
to the cross of Christ where first they were condemned and
crucified in their full body and power that a new sentence, as
it were, may go out against them, as parts of that condemned
tyrant and as belonging to that crucified body.

XV. So that the believer that would carry faithfully in this
matter and fight lawfully in this warfare and hope to obtain
the victory through Jesus Christ must bring these traitors that
appear in their sinful motions and lusts in the soul, working
rebellion against the just authority and equitable laws of the
lawful prince Jesus, before the tribunal of Him who has now
got all power and authority in heaven and in earth (Matt.
28:18) and "hath committed all judgment to him" (John 5:22).
And to this end [He] "both died, and rose, and revived, that he
might be Lord both of the dead and living" (Rom. 14:9), that
He may execute justice on the traitor, head, and members;
that He may trample these devils under and bruise the head of
these serpents within us. The believer then is by faith in prayer
to carry these open enemies to Christ and declare and witness
against them as traitors by what mischief they have done in the
soul, by their hindering the righteous laws of the king to be
obeyed, and constraining and forcing what by arguments and
allurements and what by forcible inclinations and pousings to

a disobedience and a counteracting of Christ. And he should urge and plead on the fundamental laws of the land—namely, the articles of agreement between the Father and the Son and the faithful promises of the covenant of grace and on Christ's office as king and governor and His undertaking as mediator; on the merits of His death and sufferings; on Him dying as a common person; on the constitution of the gospel by which they are in law repute[d] as dying in Him and so free from the law of sin and death; and on their relation to Him as their new Lord, head, husband, king, commander, etc. On these arguments, I say, to plead for justice against the rebel that is now brought to the bar, and so by faith leave the prisoner in His hand that He may in His own time and way give a second blow to the neck of this implacable and raging enemy that he may not rise up to disturb the peace of the soul as before or to trouble, impede, and molest the soul in paying the homage and obedience due to his lawful master and sovereign king Jesus.

Cautions and Directions
For further clearing of the premises, I would propose a few particulars for caution and direction, as:

I. This work of laying the burden of this business on Christ by faith would be gone about with much singleness of heart, aiming at the glory of God and the carrying on of His work in the soul, and not for self-ends and carnal by-respects, lest by this we mar all.

II. It would be carried on without partiality against all and every one of the lusts and motions of the old man. For if there be a compliance with and a sparing of any one known lust, the whole work may be marred. They may meet with a disappointment as to the particular lust they are desiring victory over. And the lust they are harboring, though it may seem little, may open a door to many stronger and so occasion sad days to the man, before he be aware.

III. As they would bring the particular lust or lusts to Christ as chief Lord justice, so they would always lay the ax to the root of the tree and crave justice against the main body that yet lies within the soul. And these particular corruptions and affections that are as members of that body of sin should put them in mind of the old man, for they should "[crucify] the flesh with the affections and lusts" (Gal. 5:24), the body and the members. These lusts are the lusts of sin or of that head sin, which has a law or the force and impulse of a law in the soul. And therefore their main design would be against this root where lies the strength and body of the enemy and which acts in those members. This is the capital enmity and should be mainly opposed. And the following of this course would prove more successful than that which many time[s] we take. Our nibbling at or wrestling against this or that member of the body of death is but of little advantage, so long as the main body of sin, the bitter root of wickedness, the carnal mind, this innate enmity is miskent[2] and not opposed. But, on the contrary, strike at this, [and] we strike at all.

IV. This would be the believer's constant work to be crucifying the flesh with the lusts thereof, to be mortifying their members in which the members of the old man quarter and lodge (Col. 3:5)—to be spiritually minded and to mind the things of the Spirit (Rom. 8:5–6). For "the carnal mind is enmity against God" (v. 7), and so is not subject to the law of God, neither

2. *Miskent*: misknown.

indeed can be. It is not only an enemy which may be reconciled but enmity in the abstract which never can be reconciled. And this enmity will never be idle, for it cannot till it be fully and finally destroyed. The flesh is always "lust[ing] against the Spirit" (Gal. 5:17), for they "are contrary the one to the other." So that though to our sense it may sometimes appear as sleeping, in regard that it does not by some particular lust so molest and perplex the soul as formerly it did, yet it is restless and may be more active in another lust and so by changing weapons on us deceive us. Here then is much spiritual wisdom and vigilancy required. When they think they have gotten one lust subdued, they must not think the war is at an end—but after all their particular victories, watch and pray, that they enter not into temptation.

V. This way of laying the weight of the matter on Christ should and will keep them humble and teach them not to ascribe the glory of any good that is done to themselves but to give Him all the glory who is jealous of His glory and will not give it to another, that the crown may alone flourish on His head who is the captain of their salvation and who by His Spirit works all their works in them.

VI. Nor would this way of carrying the matter to Christ and putting it over on Him cause the believer [to] become negligent in commanded duties, reading, hearing prayer, etc. For it is there He must expect to meet with Christ. There must he seek Him, and there must he wait for Him and His Spirit to do the work desired. For though He has not limited Himself to these means so as He cannot or will not any other way help, yet He has bound us to them. And it is our duty to wait there where He has commanded us to wait, though He should sometime[s] think good to come another way for the manifestation of the sovereignty of His grace.

VII. Yet while we are about the means, we would guard against a leaning to them, lest instead of getting victory over corruption we be brought more in bondage to them another way. We must not think that our prayers or our hearing or reading, etc., will bring down the body of death or subdue any one corruption. For that were but a yielding to corruption and opening a back door to the carnal mind and to another deadly lust and a beating corruption with a sword of straw. This is not to mortify the deeds of the body through the Spirit but through the flesh. And a fleshly weapon will never draw blood of this spiritual wickedness or old man or of any corrupt lust or affection thereof. And yet how many times does our deceitful heart bias us this way? Our work would be, as is said, to use the ordinances as means by which we may get the business laid on Christ and help from Christ to do the business. We must go to the means with our prisoner to find Christ there at His court and assizes that He may take course with the traitor.

VIII. In all this there would be a looking to and dependence on Christ for help and grace, because of ourselves, as of ourselves, we cannot do this much. We cannot complain aright of corruptions nor take them away to Christ nor ask for justice against them. As constables and other officers must carry malefactors to the courts of justice on public charges, so Christ will not have us doing or attempting this much on our own charges, for He gives noble allowance.

IX. In following of this course, we would not think always to come speed[3] at the first. Sometimes the Lord for the encouragement of His children may give them a speedy hearing and deliver them from the tyranny of some particular lust or other that has troubled them—so that for some time at least it will not so trouble them as it did. Yet He will not do so always but may think it good to keep them waiting on Him and hanging on His courts for some considerable time that He may by this exercise their faith, patience, desire, zeal, and diligence. So that it should not seem strange to us if we be not admitted at the first and get not our answer at the first cry.

X. When the Lord thinks good to delay the answer to our desires and the execution of justice on the malefactor and traitor or to deliver us from his tyranny and trouble, we would beware of thinking to capitulate with the enemy for our peace and quiet or to enter into a cessation of arms with him—that is, our enmity against him should never abate. Nor should our desire after the mortification and crucifixion of this lust grow less. Nor should we be at quiet and at peace, though it should seem to grow a little more calm and still or not to rage as formerly—for this looks but like a covenant or confederacy with lust, which will not stand.

XI. We would also know that what Christ said of devils holds good of these lusts; namely, that some of them do not go out but by fasting and prayer—that is, by Christ sought to and found in these means. There are some lusts that will not be so easily killed and mortified as others but will cost us more pains and labor, as being corruptions which possibly have some greater advantage of our natural temper and constitution of

---

3. *Come speed*: to make haste.

body or of long continuance and a cursed habit or the like. We must not then think it strange if some such lust be not subdued so easily as some others to which we have fewer and weaker and not so frequent temptations.

XII. As we cannot expect a full conquest of the body of death so long as we are here, as was shown above, neither can we expect a full and final victory over any one lust which ever we have been troubled with. It is true, believers may be kept from some gross outbreaking of a corruption which sometime prevailed, as Peter was from relapsing into an open and downright denying his master. Yet that same corruption did afterward stir, though not so violently as to carry him to such a height of sin, yet so far as to cause him do that which was a partial denying of his master when Paul withstood him to the face because he was to be blamed for withdrawing from the Gentiles for fear of them of the circumcision, etc. (Gal. 2:11–12). So, though a particular lust may be so far subdued through grace as that for some considerable time a man may not find it so violent as it was, yet he cannot say that it is totally killed, because it may stir thereafter in some weaker measure. Indeed, he cannot tell but before he come to die that same corruption may rise to be as violent as ever and that Satan may again think to enter the soul at that same breach which once he entered at. Indeed, and who can tell whether God may not suffer that corruption which lay long as dead to revive again for a time and for a time drive the soul as violently as ever and prevail for a time? And this should teach all to walk soberly, watchfully, and in fear and to have a vigilant eye, even on such lusts and carnal affections as they may suppose they have gotten the victory of.

XIII. We would not think that we gain no ground on corruption because we still perceive it stirring, less or more. For as corruption is not always strongest, as was said above, nor has the deepest footing in the soul when its motions and stirrings are most felt, so neither must we think that there is no ground gained on a lust because we are still troubled and molested with its stirrings. For it is a great advantage to be more sensible of the motions of this enemy, and our more faithful and active wrestling against it may make its least stirrings more sensible to us—as the motions and trouble which a malefactor, while in grips and in prison, makes may be thought more of than his greater ragings before he was apprehended, yet he may be sure in fetters for all that. A beast that has gotten death's blow may get out of grips and run more mad than ever and yet will die at length of the same blow.

XIV. Though we should find present ease and quiet by our following this way, yet we should think it much if the Lord help us to stand when we have done all we can, though we meet not with the hoped-for success presently. If He give us grace to continue without wearying or fainting and [we] be resolved never to give over, we have reason to bless Him. If we be kept still in the conflict with pursuit of the enemy, it is our great advantage. The victory will come in God's own time. If our opposition so continue that we are resolved never to take nor give quarter, though our trouble and exercise should be the greater and our ease and quiet the less, we ought to bless Him, indeed, and rejoice in hope of what He will yet do for us—for He that will come will come and will not tarry. Let us wait for Him in doing our duty and faithfully keeping our post.

XV. Indeed, if we get quietness or ease from the violence of raging lusts for any little time and be not continually driven and carried headlong with them, we ought to be thankful for this and to walk humbly before Him, lest He be provoked by our unthankfulness and pride and let these furious dogs loose on us again.

XVI. When we are bending our strength and all our forces against some one corruption or other which possibly has been most troublesome to us, we would not be secure as to all others or think that we are in hazard only on this side, for Satan may make a feint here and really intend an assault at another place by some other corrupt affection. Oh, what need have we of spiritual wisdom that we may be better acquainted with his stratagems and wiles. Let us so then fight against one member of this body of death as to have our eye on others, lest when we think to keep out Satan at the foredoor[4] he enter in at the backdoor. He can make use of extremities and play his game with both, indeed, and gain his point, if we be not aware.

Objections Answered

It will not be amiss for further explaining of the matter to remove a scruple or two.

Indwelling Corruption?

Some may say that they cannot perceive that all their pains in this matter come to any good issue, for they never found corruption stir more and act more lively and incessantly than since they began to fight against it in good earnest—so that this would seem not to be the right way. I answer: Though from what is said before, particularly cautions 9 and 13, a resolution of this doubt may be had, yet I will propose these things for further clearing of the matter:

---

4. *Foredoor*: front door.

I. May not much of this flow from you not laying the whole work so wholly off yourself and on Christ, as you ought to do? Try and see.

II. May not the devil rage most when he thinks before long to be ejected? May he not labor to create most trouble to the soul when he sees that he is like[ly] to be put from some of his strengths?

III. May not the devil be doing this of purpose to drive you to despair of ever getting corruption subdued and mortified or to a fainting and sitting up in the pursuit and to a despondency of spirit, that so instead of fighting or standing, you may cede and turn you back? And should we comply with him in his designs?

IV. May not the Lord give way to this for a time to try your seriousness, patience, submission, and faith and to sharpen your diligence and kindle up your zeal? And should we not submit to His wise dispensations?

V. How can you say that you gain no advantage as long as you are not made to lay aside the matter wholly as hopeless of any good issue but on the contrary are helped to stand and to resist sin, to cry out against it, to fight as you can, and at least not to yield?

VI. What if God see it for your advantage that you be kept so in exercise for a time, to the end you may be kept humble, watchful, and diligent? He may see more of you than you can see of yourself and so may know what is best for you. And should you not condescend to be disposed of by Him as He will and to let Him make of you and do with you what He will?

VII. What if God be about to chasten you thus for your former negligence, security, and unwatchfulness, and giving too much advantage to those lusts, which now, after His awakening of you, you would be delivered from? Should you not bear the indignation of the Lord because you have sinned against Him, as the church resolved to do (Mic. 7:9)?

VIII. Is it not your duty the more that corruption stirs to run with it the oftener to Christ, that He may subdue it and put it to silence? May not you improve this to your advantage by making many errands to Him?

IX. May it not come in a day that has not come in a year? Are you sure that all your pains will be in vain? Or think you that all His children have got[ten] victory alike soon over their lusts? What cause is there then to complain thus?

X. May not all this convince you that it is your duty to wait on Him in the use of His appointed means and to be patient, standing fast to your post, resolving, when you have done all, yet to stand?

XI. May not this satisfy you that God through grace accepts your labor and wrestling as your duty and accounts it service to Him and obedience?

Sinful Condition?
But again, it may possibly be objected thus: So long as I am in this condition, kept under with my lusts, I cannot get God glorified and served as He ought to be. I answer: Though so long as it is so with you, you cannot glorify and serve Him in such a particular manner as others who have got more victory over those evils under which you are groaning, yet God can get glory and service of you another way, as:

I. By your submission with calmness of spirit to His wise dispensations when you dare not speak against Him and say with Rebecca in another case, "If it be so, why am I thus?" But sweetly and willingly cast yourself down at His feet, saying, "Good is the will of the Lord. Let Him do what seems Him good, etc."

II. By your patient on-waiting when you are not wearying nor fainting but saying, "Why should I not wait on the great King's leisure? Is He not free to come when He will? Dare I set limits to the Holy One of Israel?"

III. By your humility when you bless Him for keeping you so long out of hell and think much of Him giving you grace to see and observe the stirrings of corruption, which carnal wretches never perceive, and helping you to withstand and complain of corruption, which they sweetly comply with.

IV. By your hatred of sin when all that Satan can do cannot make you comply with those lusts or sweetly embrace those vipers or lie down in peace with those rotten members of the old man, as others do.

V. By your watchfulness when all your disappointments cause you the more earnestly [to] watch against that enemy.

VI. By you acting faith when still you are carrying sin in its lusts to Christ to kill and subdue, as believing the tenor of the gospel and new covenant.

VII. By your hope, which appears by you not despairing and giving over the matter as a hopeless business and turning aside to wicked courses.

VIII. By you praying when you cry to Him continually for help who only can help.

IX. By you wrestling and standing against all opposition, for by this is His strength made perfect in your weakness (2 Cor. 12:9).

X. By your obedience, for it is His command that you stand and fight this good fight of faith.

So that if you have a desire to glorify Him, you want not occasion to do it, even in this condition in which you complain that you cannot get Him glorified. And if those grounds do not satisfy you, it is to be feared that it is not so much a desire to glorify Him that moves you to cry so earnestly for actual delivery from the trouble of the flesh and the lusts thereof, as something else which you may search after and find out— such as love to ease, quietness, applause and commendation of others, or the like.

Reigning Sin?
But, in the third place, it may be objected: Is it not promised that sin will not have dominion over us, as not being under the law but under grace (Rom. 6:14)? How can we then but be troubled when we find not this promise made good? I answer:

I. Sin is not always victorious and domineering when it seems to rage and stir most. Your opposition to it, fighting and wrestling against it, shows that it has not full dominion. So long as an invading usurper is opposed, he has not full dominion, not having peaceable possession of what he is seeking. And thus the promise is in part accomplished.

II. Victory and a full conquest over the flesh and lusts thereof is not promised to any believer at his first appearing in the fields to fight nor granted to all in any measure at their first putting on their armor.

III. Therefore, it is your part to fight on and wait for that full victory—namely, that sin will not have dominion over you, for it will come in due time.

IV. God has His own time and seasons in which He accomplishes His promises. And we must leave Him a latitude both as to the time when and as to the manner how and as to the degree in which He will make good His promises. And He is wise in His dispensations.

Therefore, though the promise as yet appears not to be accomplished, there is no true cause of trouble of mind, because it will be afterward fully accomplished. And the wrestling against sin says that it is in great measure accomplished already—because where it has a full dominion, it suppresses all opposition or contradiction, except some faint resistance which a natural conscience for carnal ends on carnal principles and grounds may, now or then, make against this or that particular corruption, which occasions shame, disgrace, loss, challenges of a carnal conscience, and disquietness that way, when yet it is not hated nor wrestled against as sin or as a member of the old man and the body of death. The objector would consider that having subjected his consent to Christ, he is delivered really from that natural state of bondage under sin as a lawful lord, even though the old tyrant, now wanting a title, is making new invasions to trouble the peace and quiet of the soul.

Sinking Soul?

Fourthly, it may be said: But what can then in the meantime keep up the heart of a poor soul from sinking? Answer: Several things, if rightly considered, might help to support the soul in this case, as:

I. That they are helped to wrestle against this body of death in all the members of it so soon as they discover themselves, were it their right eye and right hand.

II. That these lusts gain not ground on them; or, if they do seem to gain ground, yet they attain not to a full dominion, not gaining their consent.

III. That God is faithful, and therefore the promised victory will be had in due time, and Satan's head will certainly be bruised.

IV. That the wrestling soul is about his duty, carrying as a good soldier of Jesus Christ, fighting the battles of the Lord, and waiting on Him in faith and hope.

Rising Corruptions?
But further, fifthly, some may say: If I were kept from yielding, my wrestling and standing would yield me some comfort. But when lust so stirs as that it conceives and brings forth sin (James 1:15), what can support or comfort me then? Answer:

I. Corruption cannot stir in us, but in that we sin for the very first rise. The *motus primo-primi*,[5] as they are called, are sinful, being contrary to the holy law of God. And the very in-being of that old man is our sin. For it is sinful and rebellious against God; indeed, it is very enmity and rebellion itself. When Satan comes with a temptation from without, he finds always much in us to entertain the temptation. So that the very stirring

_____

5. *Motus primo-primi*: the very first motions.

of corruption, which is occasioned by the temptation from without, is our guilt.

II. It is true it is our duty to set against the first risings and motions of corruption when it first entices, before it has conceived or brought forth sin. And it will argue grace in life and in action to be able to hinder the motions of lust so far that it will not conceive and bring forth sin. Yet we may not say that there is no grace in the soul or no measure of mortification attained where lust sometimes not only entices but conceives and brings forth sin. The sad experience of many of God's worthies, registrated in the Word, clears this abundantly. We must not say, "Such a one is fallen; therefore, he is dead." Paul reasons otherw[ise] (Romans 7).

III. Yet even then, when lust conceives and brings forth sin, this may comfort and bear up the heart of a poor believer:

1. That though corruption prevail so far as to bear down all opposition and run down all that stands in its way, yet it gives not the full consent of the soul. There is still a party for God in the soul that opposes so far as to protest against it or at least to dissent from it and not to will that which yet is done and positively to will that which cannot be gotten effectuated.

2. And further, this may bear up the poor soul that there is a party within which, though for a time during the violent overrunning of corruption can do little more than sigh and groan in a corner, yet is waiting and longing for an opportunity when it may appear more for God and against that wicked usurper.

3. So also this may comfort the poor soul that as it perceives corruption stirring and the old man moving

one member or other, it runs away to the king. And when it is not able to apprehend the traitor and take him captive to the court of justice does there discover the traitor and tell the king that there is such or such a traitor acting such and such rebellion against Him and His laws and complain and seek help to take the rebel prisoner and bring him bound hand and foot to the king that He may give out sentence against him—that is, when he can do no more against that raging enemy, [he] makes his complaint to the Lord and lays before Him, sighing and groaning for help and strength to withstand and oppose more this enemy.

Prevailing Corruption?
Lastly, some may yet object and say: If it were not worse with me than it is with others, I could then be satisfied. But I see some mightily prevailing over corruption, and I am still at under and can get no victory. And can I choose but [to] be sad at this? I answer:

I. Do you know for a certainty that those persons whose condition you judge happy are altogether free of the inward stirrings of those lusts that you are brought under by? Or do you know for a certainty that they are not under the power of some other corruption, as you think yourself under the power of that corruption of which you complain? What know you, then, but they may be as much complaining on other accounts as you do on that?

II. But be it so as you suppose that there is a difference between your condition and the condition of others, know you not that all the members of the body are not alike great and strong, as not being equally to be employed in work requiring strength.

Are there not some young strong men in Christ's family, and some that are but babes? May not a captain send some of his soldiers to one post where they will possibly not see the enemy all the day long and some others to another post where they will have no rest all the day? And why, I pray, may not God dispose of His soldiers as He will? He knows what He is doing. It is not safe that every one of the soldiers know what are the designs of the commander or general, nor is it always fit for us to know or to inquire what may be the designs of God with us and what He may be about to do. He may intend to employ one in greater works than another and so exercise them other ways for that warfare and work. It may suffice that the prevailing of others may encourage you to hope that at last your strong corruptions will also fall by the hand of the grace of God.

III. If your sadness savor not of envy and fretting, you should bless Him that by this you are put to the exercise of spiritual sorrow.

IV. It is well if this bring you to bless God for the success of others, because by this His grace is glorified (1 Cor. 12:26).

V. Therefore, let this satisfy us: that He is the Lord who does what He will in heaven and in earth and may dispose of us as He will and make of us what He will for His own glory. And that we are to mind our duty and be faithful at our post, standing and fighting in the strength of the Lord, resolving never to comply with the enemy, and to rejoice in this: that the enemy is already conquered by the captain, and that we share in His victory, and that the very God of peace will quickly bruise Satan under our feet (Rom. 16:20).

CHAPTER 7

How Christ Is to Be Made Use of in Reference to Growing in Grace

I come now to speak a little to the other part of sanctification which concerns the change of our nature and frame and is called vivification, or quickening of the new man of grace, which is called the new man, as having all its several members and parts as well as the old man, and called "new," because posterior to the other and after regeneration is on the growing hand. This duty of growing in grace, as it is called (2 Peter 3, etc.), is variously expressed and held forth to us in Scripture; for it is called an abiding and bringing forth fruit in Christ (John 15:5); adding to "faith virtue: and to virtue knowledge" (2 Peter 1:5–7); a going on to perfection (Heb. 7:1); a growing up in Christ in all things (Eph. 4:15); a working out our salvation (Phil. 2:12); a perfecting of holiness (2 Cor. 7:1); a walking in newness of life (Rom. 6:4); a yielding of ourselves to God, as alive from the dead, and our members as instruments of righteousness to God (6:13, 18); a bringing forth fruit to God (7:4); a serving in newness of spirit (7:6); a being renewed in the spirit of our minds, and a putting on the new man, which after God is created in righteousness and true holiness (Eph. 4:23–24; Col. 3:10); and the like. Some of which do more immediately express the nature of this change as to the root, and some as to the fruit and effects of it, and some the progress and advancement that is made or to be made in it. And all of them point out a special piece of work which lies on all that would see the face of God—namely, to be holy, gracious, and growing in grace.

This, then, being a special piece of the exercise and daily work of a Christian, and it being certain, as some of the places now cited do also affirm, that without Christ they cannot get this work either begun or carried on—[then] the main difficulty and question is how they are to make use of Christ for this end.

How to Make Use of Christ for Growth in Grace
For answer to this, though by what we have said in our former discourse it may be easy to gather what is to be said here, yet I will briefly put the reader in mind of these things as useful here:

I. The believer would consider what an ornament this is to the soul to have on this new man which is created after the image of God (Eph. 4:23). What an excellency lies here, to recover that lost glory, holiness, and the image of God? And what advantage the soul reaps by this when it is made meet to be a partaker of the inheritance of the saints in light (Col. 1:12); and walking "worthy of the Lord unto all pleasing, being fruitful in every good work, and increasing in the knowledge of God" (1:10); and "strengthened with all might, according to his glorious power, unto all patience and longsuffering with joyfulness" (v. 11). And when the abounding of the graces of the Spirit makes them that they will "neither be barren nor unfruitful in the knowledge of our Lord Jesus Christ" (2 Peter 1:8) and to be a vessel "unto honour, sanctified, and meet for the master's use, and prepared unto every good work" (2 Tim. 2:21). What glory and peace is here, to be found obedient to the many commands given to be holy. What hazard is in the want of holiness, when without it we cannot see God (Heb. 12:14). How unanswerable it is to our profession, who are members to such a holy head, to be unholy. What profit, joy, and satisfaction there is in being temples of the Holy Ghost, in walking after the Spirit, in bringing forth fruit to the glory of the Father, etc. The consideration of these and other motives to this study of sanctification would arm the soul with resolution and harden it against opposition.

II. It would be remembered that this work, though it be laid on us as our duty and we be called to it of God, yet it is beyond our hand and power. It is true, at conversion, the seed of grace is cast into the soul, new habits are infused, a new principle of life is given, the stony heart is changed into a heart of flesh. Yet these principles and habits cannot act in themselves or be brought into act by anything that a believer considered in himself and without divine help can do. But this work of sanctification and growth in grace must be carried on by divine help by the Spirit of Jesus dwelling and working within. And therefore it is called the sanctification of the Spirit (2 Thess. 2:13; 1 Peter 1:2). The God of peace must sanctify us (1 Thess. 5:23). We are said to be sanctified by God the Father (Jude 1) and by the Holy Ghost (Rom. 15:16; see also 1 Cor. 6:11). We would remember that of ourselves we can do nothing (2 Cor. 3:5) and that He must work in us both to will and to do of His good pleasure (Phil. 2:13). Even though no believer will question the truth of this, yet it may be it will be found after trial that one main cause of their not growing in grace and making progress in this work is their not acting as believing this but setting about the work as if it were a work which they themselves could master and do without special divine help.

Therefore, the believer would abide, live, and act in the faith of this truth.

III. Therefore, believers would not in going about this work either trust to their own strength, to the habits of grace, to their former experiences, to their knowledge and parts, or the like. Nor yet would they trust to any external mean which they are to go about, because the wisdom, strength, and help which their case calls for is not to be found in them. Yet they should not think of laying these means and duties aside, for then should they sin against God. They should prejudge themselves of the help, strength, and supply which God uses to convey to the soul in and by the use of the means. And in addition, they should tempt the Lord by prescribing another way to Him than He has thought good to take. The believer, then, would use the means and duties prescribed and that diligently, seriously, and constantly, and yet would lean as little to them and expect help and relief as little from them as if he were not using them at all, as we said above. And indeed this would be a right way, indeed, the most advantageous and profitable way of going about duties: to be diligent in the use of them because of God's command and yet to place our hope and expectation in God alone and to look above the ordinances for our help.

IV. Even though it be true that the power and grace of God alone does begin and carry on this work of sanctification in the soul, yet, though He might, did He but see it for His glory, carry on and finish this work in the soul without the intervention of second causes or means, He has despite this thought it fit for the glory of His name to work this work by means and particularly by believers setting about the work. He works not in man as if he were a block or a stone but uses him as a rational creature, endued with a rational soul, having useful and necessary faculties and a body fired by organs to be subservient to the soul in its actions. Therefore, the believer must not think to lie by and do nothing, for he is commanded to work out his own salvation, and that because it is God that works in him both to will and to do. Because God works all, therefore he should work—so reasons the apostle. So that God's working is an argument and motive to the man to work and not an argument to him to lie by idle and do nothing. And here is the holy art and divine skill requisite in this business—namely, for the believer to be as diligent and active as if he could bring forth fruit in his own strength and by his own working, and yet to be as abstracted from himself, his own grace, ability, knowledge, [and] experience in his working as if he were lying by like a mere block and only moving as moved by external force.

V. The soul that would make progress in Christianity and grow in grace would remember that Christ is proposed to us as a copy which we are to imitate, and that therefore we should set Christ continually before us as our pattern that we may follow His steps (1 Peter 1:15; 2:21). But in addition it would be remembered that He is not like other samples or copies that can help the man that imitates them in no other way than by their objective prospect, for looking by faith on this copy will bring virtue to the man that studies to imitate, by which he will be enabled to follow his copy better. Oh! If we knew in experience what this were to take a look of Christ's love, patience, longsuffering, meekness, hatred of sin, zeal, etc., and by faith to pore in till, by virtue proceeding from that copy, we found our hearts in some measure framed into the same disposition or at least more inclined to be cast into the same mold!

VI. The believer would act faith on Christ as the head of the body and as the stock in which the branches are ingrafted and by this suck sap and life and strength from Him that he may work, walk, and grow as becomes a Christian. The believer must grow up in Him, being a branch in Him, and must bring forth fruit in Him, as the forementioned places clear. Now, Christ Himself tells us that the branches cannot bring forth fruit except they abide in the vine, and that no more can His disciples bring forth except they abide in Him (John 15). Therefore, as it is by faith that the soul as a branch is united to Christ as the vine, and as it is by faith that they abide in Him, so it is by faith that they must bring forth fruit. And this faith must grip Christ as the vine and the stock or root from which comes sap, life, and strength. Faith, then, must look to Christ as the fountain of furniture—as the head from where comes all the influences of strength and motion. Christ has strength and life enough to give out, for the fullness of the Godhead dwells in Him bodily. And He is also willing enough to communicate of His fullness, as the relations He has taken on do witness. The head will not grudge to give to the members of the body spirits for action and motion. Nor will a vine grudge to give sap into the branches. Indeed, life, strength, and furniture will, as it were, natively flow out of Christ to believers, except they through unbelief and other distempers cause obstructions— as life and sap do natively and kindly flow from the root to the branches or from the head to the members unless obstructions stop the passage. It is necessary, therefore, that believers eye Christ under these and the like relations and look on Him as standing, so to speak, obliged by His place and relation to grant strength and influences of life by which they may become fruitful in every good work and so with holy, humble, and allowed boldness press in faith for new communications of grace, virtue, strength, courage, activity, and what else they need—for from the head all the body, by joints and bands, having nourishment ministered, increase with the increase of God (Eph. 4:16; Col. 2:19).

VII. For this cause believers would lie open to the influences of Christ and guard against the putting of obstructions in the way through grieving of the Spirit, by which He conveys and communicates those influences to the soul, and through questioning and misbelieving Christ's faithfulness and unchangeable willingness, which as a violent humor stops the passage. So then believers would lie open by looking and waiting, drawing, seeking from Him what they need, and by guarding against everything that may provoke the Lord to anger, whether in omission or commission. Here is requisite a holy, humble, sober, and watchful walk, an earnest, serious, and hungry looking out to Him, and a patient waiting for supply and furniture from Him. This is to open the mouth wide that He may fill it, to lie before the Sun of Righteousness that the beams of it may beat on them and warm and revive them, and to wait as a beggar at this king's gate till He give the alms.

VIII. For the strengthening their hope and faith in this, they would lay hold on Christ dying and by His death purchasing all those influences of life and strength which are requisite for carrying on the work of grace and sanctification in the soul. For we must be blessed in Christ with all spiritual blessings (Eph. 1:3). The believer, then, would look on these influences as purchased at a dear rate by the blood of Jesus Christ, so that the divine power gives to us all things that pertain to life and godliness through the knowledge of Him that has called us to glory and virtue (2 Peter 1:3). And this will encourage the soul to wait on and expect the flowing down of influences and spiritual blessings and showers of grace to cause the soul to flourish and become fruitful and to urge and press more earnestly by faith the bestowing of the purchased benefits.

IX. Moreover, the believer would look on Jesus as standing engaged and obliged to carry on this work, both receiving them as for this end from the Father. Hence we are said to be chosen "in him before the foundation of the world, that we should be holy, etc." (Eph. 1:4), and as dying for them. For He gave Himself for the church that He might sanctify and cleanse it, that He might present it to Himself a glorious church, that it should be holy (Eph. 5:25–27). He has reconciled them in the body of His flesh through death to present them holy (Col. 1:2, 22). So that the noble covenant of redemption may found the certain hope and expectation of the believer on a double account: (1) on the account of the Father's faithfulness, who promised a seed to Jesus—namely, such as should be His children and so be sanctified through Him, and that the pleasure of the Lord, which in part is the work of sanctification, should prosper in His hand; (2) and on the account of Christ's undertaking and engaging, as is said, to bring His sons and daughters to glory, which must be through sanctification—for without holiness no man will see God. And they must look like Himself, who is a holy head, a holy husband, a holy captain. And therefore they must be holy members, a holy spouse, and holy soldiers. So that He stands engaged to sanctify them by His Spirit and word and therefore is called the sanctifier, "for both he that sanctifieth and they who are sanctified are all of one" (Heb. 2:11). Indeed, their union with Christ lays the foundation of this, for, being joined to the Lord, they become "one spirit" (1 Cor. 6:17) and are animated and quickened by one and the same Spirit of life and grace and therefore must be sanctified by that Spirit.

X. The believer likewise would act faith on the promises of the new covenant—[promises] of grace, strength, life, etc., by which they will walk in His ways, have God's laws put into their minds and wrote in their hearts (Jer. 31:33; Heb. 8:10), and of the new heart and new spirit and the heart of flesh and the Spirit within them to cause them [to] walk in His ways or statutes and keep His judgments and do them (Ezek. 36:26–27), and the like, of which the Scripture abounds—because these are all given over to the believer by way of testament and legacy, Christ becoming the mediator of the New Testament that by means of death for the redemption of the transgressions that were under the first testament they which are called might receive the promise of eternal inheritance (Heb. 9:15). Now, Christ by His death has confirmed this testament, "for where a testament is, there must also of necessity be the death of the testator. For a testament is of force after men are dead" (vv. 16–17). Christ, then, dying to make the testament of force, has made the legacy of the promises sure to the believer, so that now all the promises are yea and amen in Christ (2 Cor. 1:20). He was made a minister of "circumcision...to confirm the promises made unto the fathers" (Rom. 15:8). That the eyeing of these promises by faith is a noble mean[s] to sanctification is clear by what the apostle says, "Having therefore these promises...let us cleanse ourselves...perfecting holiness in the fear of God" (2 Cor. 7:1). And it is by faith that those promises must be received (Heb. 9:33). So that the believer that would grow in grace would eye Christ, the fundamental promise, the testator establishing the testament and the executor or dispensator of the covenant, and expect the good things through Him and from Him, through the conduit and channel of the promises.

XI. Yet further, believers would eye Christ in His resurrection as a public person and so look on themselves and reckon themselves as rising virtually in and with Him and take the resurrection of Christ as a certain pawn and pledge of their sanctification—for so reasons the apostle. We are buried, says he, with Him by baptism unto death, that like as Christ was raised up from the dead by the glory of the Father, even so we also should walk in newness of life—for we will be also planted in the likeness of His resurrection. And if we be dead with Christ, we believe that we will also live with Him. Therefore reckon you also yourselves to be alive to God, through Jesus Christ our Lord, and yield yourselves to God, as those that are alive from the dead, and your members as instruments of righteousness to God (Rom. 6:4–5, 11, 13). The right improving of this ground would be of noble advantage to the student of holiness, for then he might with strong confidence conclude that the work of sanctification should prosper in his hand— for he may now look on himself as quickened together with Christ (Eph. 2:5)—Christ dying and rising as a public person, and he by faith being now joined with Him and united to Him.

XII. Moreover, this resurrection of Christ may yield us another ground of hope and confidence in this work, for there is mention made of the power of His resurrection (Phil. 3:10). So that by faith we may draw strength and virtue from Christ as a risen and quickened head by which we also may live to God and bring forth fruit to Him and serve no more in the oldness of the letter but in the newness of the Spirit (Rom. 7:4, 6). He was quickened as a head; and when the head is quickened, the members cannot but look for some communication of life from it and to live in the strength of the life of the head (see Col. 3:1–2).

XIII. Faith may and should also look to Christ as an intercessor with the Father. For this particular: "Sanctify them through thy truth: thy word is truth" (John 17:17). And this will add to their confidence that the work will go on, for Christ was always heard of the Father (John 11:4–42) and so will be in His prayer, which was not put up for the few disciples alone.

The believer then would eye Christ as engaging to the Father to begin and perfect this work, as dying to purchase the good things promised and to confirm the same, as quickened and rising as head and public person to ensure this work and to bestow and actually confer the graces requisite, and as praying also for the Father's concurrence. And [he should] cast the burden of the work on Him by faith, knowing that He stands obliged by His place and relation to His people to bear all their burdens, to work all their works in them, to perfect His own work that He has begun in them, to present them to Himself at last a holy bride, to give them the Spirit to dwell in them (Rom. 8:9, 11) and to quicken their mortal bodies (v. 11) and to lead them (v. 14) till at length they be crowned, and brought forward to glory. This is to live by faith when Christ lives, acts, and works in us by His Spirit (Gal. 2:20). Thus Christ dwells in the heart by faith, and by this His people become rooted and grounded in love, which is a cardinal grace. And knowing the love of Christ which passes knowledge, they become filled with all the fullness of God (Eph. 3:17, 19). So that the believer is to commit by faith the work to Christ and leave the stress of all the business on Him who is their life. Yet the believer must not think he is to do nothing or to lay aside the means of ordinances but, using these diligently, would in them commit the matter to Christ and by faith roll the whole work on Him, expecting on the ground of His relations, engagements, promises, beginnings, etc., that He will certainly perfect the work (Phil. 1:6) and take it well off their hands and be well pleased with them for putting the work in His hands and leaving it on Him who is made of God to us sanctification.

Cautions

As in the former part, so here it will not be amiss to give a few words of caution for preventing of mistakes:

I. We would beware of thinking that perfection can be attained here. The perfect man and measure of the stature of the fullness of Christ is but coming, and till then the body will be a perfecting and edifying through the work of the ministry (Eph. 4:12–13). Believers must not think of sitting down on any measure of grace which they attain to here, but they must be growing in grace, going from strength to strength till they appear in the upper Zion with the apostle. Forgetting those things that are behind and reaching forth to those things which are before, they must press toward the mark for the prize of the high calling of God in Christ Jesus (Phil. 3:13). It must then be a dreadful delusion for any to think that they can reach to such a degree of perfection here as not to stand in need of the ordinance any more. Let all believers live in the constant conviction of their shortcoming and be humbled and so work out their salvation with fear and trembling.

II. Nor should every believer expect one and the same measure of holiness, nor can it be expected with reason that all will advance here to the same height of sanctity. For every part of the body has its own measure and an effectual working in that measure. And so every joint of the body supplies less or more according to its proportion and contributes to the increase of the body and to the edifying of itself in love, as the apostle clearly shows (Eph. 4:16). As in the natural body the diversity of functions and uses of the members requires diversity of furniture and strength, so in the mystical body of Christ the members have not all alike measure, but each has his proper distinct measure according to his place and usefulness in the body. Believers then would learn much sobriety here and submission, knowing that God may dispense His graces as He will and give them to each member in what measure He thinks good. Only they would take heed that their poverty and lean-ness be not occasioned through their own carelessness and negligence in not plying the means of grace with that faithful-ness and single dependence on Christ that they ought.

III. It would be remembered that there may be some progress made in the way of holiness when yet the believer may appre-hend no such thing—not only because the measure of the growth may be so small and indiscernible, but also because, even where the growth in itself is discernible, the Lord may think it good for wise ends to hide it from their eyes that they may be kept humble and diligent. Whereas, if they saw how matters stood indeed with them, they might (without a new degree of grace) swell and be puffed up, indeed, even forget God and misken themselves and others too. Likewise this may proceed from such an earnest desire after more that they forget any measure they have gotten and so despise the day of small things.

IV. There may be a great progress in holiness, though not in that particular which the believer is most eyeing to his sense and apprehension. For when he thinks he is not growing in love to and zeal for God, etc., he may be growing in humility, which is also a member of the new man of grace. And when he can perceive no growth in knowledge, there may be a growth in affection and tenderness. And if the work be carried on in any joint or member, it decays in none, though it may be better apprehended in one than another.

V. There may be much holiness, where the believer is complaining of the want of fruits, when under that dispensation of the Lord toward him he is made to stoop before the Most High, to put his mouth in the dust, if so be there may be hope, and pleasantly to submit to God's wise ordering without grudging or quarrelling with God for what He does and to accept sweetly the punishment of his iniquity, if he see guilt lying at the root of this dispensation. Where there is a silent submission to the sovereign and only wise disposing hand of God, and the man is saying, "If He will not have me to be a fruitful tree in His garden nor to grow and flourish as the palm tree, let me be a shrub. Only let me be kept within the precincts of His garden that His eye may be on me for good. Let me abide within His courts that I may behold His countenance"—[then] there is grace, and no small measure of grace. To be a hired servant is much (Luke 15:19).

VI. But in addition, it would be observed that this gracious frame of soul that is silent before God under several disappointments is accompanied with much singleness of heart in panting after more holiness and with seriousness and diligence in all commanded duties, waiting on the Lord who is their hope and their salvation in each of them, and with mourning for their own sinful accession to that shortcoming in their expectations.

VII. We would not think that there is no progress in Christianity or growth in grace because it comes not our way or by the instruments and means that we must expect it by. Possibly we are too fond on some instruments and means that we prefer to others. And we think [that] if ever we get good, it must be that way and by that means, be it private or public. And God may give a proof of His sovereignty and check us for our folly by taking another way. He would not be found of the bride, neither by her seeking of Him secretly on her bed by night, nor more publicly by going about the city in the streets and broad ways, nor by the means of the watchmen (Cant. 3:1–3).

VIII. Nor would we think that there is no growth in the work of grace because it comes not at such or such prelimited or foreset time. Nor would we think the matter desperate because of our looking long and waiting and asking and laboring and yet seeing no sensible advantage. "Such and such a believer," says the soul, "made great progress in a short time, but I come no speed, for as long as I have been at this school." Oh! We should beware of limiting the Holy One of Israel. Let us be at duty and commit the event to Him.

IX. It is not a fit time to take the measure of our graces as to their sensible growth and fruitfulness when devils are broken loose on us, temptations are multiplied, corruptions make a great noise, and we are meeting with a horrible tempest shaking us on all hands. For it will be strong grace that will much appear then. It will be strong faith that will say, "Though He kill me, yet will I trust in Him." At such a time it will be much if the man keep the ground he has gained, though he make no progress. It will be much for a tree to stand and not to be blown out of the ground in the time of a strong and vehement storm of wind, though it keep not its flourishes and yield not fruit. The trees which in a cold winter day bear neither leaves nor fruit must not be said to go back nor not to grow, because when the spring comes again they may revive and be as fruitful as ever.

X. We would not always measure our graces by what appears outwardly, for there may be some accidental occurrence that may hinder that, and yet grace be at work within doors, which few or none can observe. The believer may be in a sweet and gracious frame, blushing before the Lord, indeed, melting in love or taken up with spiritual meditations and wondering, when as to some external duties it can find no present disposition through some accidental impediment or other—so that to some who judge most by outward appearance, no such things as the active working of grace in life can appear.

XI. We would think it no small measure or degree of holiness to be with singleness of heart pursuing it, even though it should seem to flee from us to be earnestly panting after it and hungering and thirsting for it. Nehemiah thought this no small thing when he said, "O LORD, I beseech thee, let now thine ear be attentive to the prayer…of thy servants, who desire to fear thy name" (Neh. 1:11).

XII. Whatever measure of holiness the believer win to, he would take special heed that he place no part of his confidence of him being accepted and justified before God in it, as if that could come in any part of the price to satisfy justice. But when he has done all, let him call and account himself an unprofitable servant. Though believers will not be so gross as to speak thus, yet sure their justifying of them holding back from God because they find not such a measure of grace and holiness as they would have looks too much this way and says that they lean too much hereto in the matter of the acceptance of their persons before God. Now this should be specially guarded against, lest their labor be in vain.

Objections Answered

An objection or two must here also be removed.

No Advance?

Some may say that though they have been laboring and striving and working now for some long time, yet they can perceive no advancement. They are as far short as ever.

I. [I] answer [that] has it not been found that some have complained without cause? Have not some complained of their unfruitfulness and want of growth that other good Christians would have thought themselves very happy if they had but advanced half so far as they saw them to have done?

II. But be it so, as it is alleged—what if the fault be their own? What if the cause of this be that they attempt things in their own strength, leaning to their own understanding or habits of grace or means, etc., and that they do not go about duties with that single dependence on Christ that is requisite, nor do they suck life, strength, and sap from Him by faith through the promises nor give themselves up to Him by faith that He may work in them both to will and to do. Should not this be seen, mourned for, and helped?

III. If all this shortcoming and disappointment cause them [to] lie in the dust and humble themselves more and more before the Lord, the grace of humiliation is growing, and that is no small advantage to be growing downward.

IV. In addition, they would do well to hold on in duty, looking to Christ for help and rolling all difficulties on Him, give themselves away to Him as their head and Lord and so continue their life of faith or their consenting to let Christ live in them by faith or work in them by His Spirit what is well pleasing in His sight and wait for the blessing and fruit in God's own time.

Unedifying?

Next, it will be objected: Though we might wait thus, yet how unedifying are we to others when there appears no fruit of the spirit of grace in us. [I] answer: Christian behavior and deportment under the sense of fruitlessness, expressing a holy submission of soul to God as sovereign, much humility of mind before Him, justifying of God, and taking guilt to themselves with a firm resolution to wait on patiently in the use of means appointed—[this] cannot but be edifying to Christian souls, such exercises being really the works and fruit of the Spirit of grace working within.

Covenant Promises?

But, thirdly, some may say, "How then are the promises of the covenant made good?" Answer:

I. The same measure of sanctification and holiness is not promised to all.

II. No great measure is promised to any absolutely. So much indeed is secured to all believers as will carry them to heaven, as without which they cannot see God. But much as to the degree depends on our performing through faith the conditions requisite—namely, on condition of us abiding in the vine, of us acting faith on Him, etc. And when these and the like conditions are not faithfully performed by us, what can we expect? So the Lord has appointed a way in which He will be found and will have us to wait for strength and influence from Him. And if we neglect these means which He has appointed, how can we expect the good which He has promised in the use of these means?

III. The Lord has His own time of making good all His promises, and we must not limit Him to a day.

IV. Hereby the Lord may be trying and exercising your faith, patience, hope, dependence, submission, diligence, etc. And "if these things be in you, and abound, they make you that ye shalt neither be barren nor unfruitful in the knowledge of our Lord Jesus Christ" (2 Peter 1:[8]).

What Support?

But lastly, it will be inquired, What can support the believing soul in this case? Answer:

I. The consideration and faith of the covenant of redemption in which both the Father's engagement of the Son and the Son's engagement to the Father secures grace and holiness and salvation to the believer. And whatever we be, They will be true to each other. Our unbelief will not make the faith of God of none effect.

II. The consideration of the noble and faithful promises contained in the covenant of grace which will all be made good in due time.

III. If we be humbled under the sense of our failings and shortcomings and made to mourn before the Lord, stirred up to more diligence and seriousness—that may yield comfort to our soul. If we be growing in humility, godly sorrow, repentance, diligence, and be gripping faster by faith to the root, [then] we want not ground of joy and support. For if that be, we cannot want fruit.

IV. It should be matter of joy and thanksgiving that the believer is kept from turning his back on the way of God and kept with his face still Zionward. Though he make but little progress, yet he is still looking forward and creeping as he may, waiting at God's door, begging and asking, studying, laboring, and endeavoring for strength to go faster.

V. It is no small matter of peace and comfort if we be kept from fretting, grudging, and repining at the Lord's dispensations with us and be taught to sit silent in the dust, adoring His sovereignty and ascribing no iniquity to our maker.

CHAPTER 8

How to Make Use of Christ for Taking the Guilt of Our Daily Out-Breakings Away

*T*he next part of our sanctification is in reference to our daily failings and transgressions, committed partly through the violence of temptations, as we see in David and Peter and other eminent men of God, partly through daily infirmities because of our weakness and imperfections—for in many things we offend all (James 3:2). And "if we say we have no sin, we deceive ourselves, and the truth is not in us" (1 John 1:8). A righteous man falls seven times (Prov. 24:16). "There is not a just man upon earth, that doeth good, and sinneth not" (Eccl. 7:20). And Solomon further says that "there is no man that sinneth not" (1 Kings 8:46). This being so, the question is how Christ is to be made use of for taking these away.

For satisfaction to this, it would be considered that in those daily out-breakings there are two things to be noticed. First, there is the guilt which is commonly called *reatus paenae*,[1] by which the transgressor is liable to the sentence of the law or to the penalty annexed to the breach of it, which is no less than God's curse—for "cursed is every one that continueth not in all things which are…in the book of the law to do them" (Gal. 3:10). Next, there is the stain or blot, which is called *reatus*

---

1. *Reatus paenae*: state of punishment.

culpae,[2] by which the soul is defiled and made insofar incapable of glory (for nothing enters in there which defiles) and of communion and fellowship with God who is of purer eyes than He can behold iniquity. So that it is manifest how necessary it is that both these be taken away that they may not stand in our way to the Father. And as to both, we must make use of Christ, who is the only way to the Father.

Christ and His Use to Take Away Guilt
And this we will now clear and, first, speak of the taking away of the guilt that is contracted by every sin. And for this cause we will speak briefly to two things: (1) show what Christ has done as mediator for this end that the guilt contracted by our daily failings and outbreakings might be taken away; [and] (2) show what the believer should do for the guilt taken away in Christ, or how he should make use of Christ for reconciliation with God after transgressions, or, for the taking away of the guilt that he lies under because of his violation of the law.

What Christ Has Done
As to the first, we say Christ for taking away of guilt contracted daily has done these things:

I. Christ laid down His life a ransom for all the sins of the elect, both such as were past before they believed and such as were to be committed after. His blood was shed for the remission of sins indefinitely and without distinction (Matt. 26:28).

II. And this was done according to the tenor of the covenant of redemption in which the Father caused all our sins to meet together on Him (Isa. 53:6) and made Him sin or a sacrifice

---

2. *Reatus culpae*: state of guilt.

for sin indefinitely (2 Cor. 5:21) and so did not except the sins committed after conversion.

III. Having satisfied justice and being risen from the dead as a conqueror, He is now exalted to be a prince to give repentance and remission of sins (Acts 5:31). Now repentance and remission of sins His people have need of, after conversion as well as before conversion.

IV. There are promises of pardon and remission of sins in the new covenant of grace, all which are sealed and confirmed in the blood of Jesus, "For I will forgive their iniquity, and I will remember their sin no more" (Jer. 31:34). And 33:8: "And I will cleanse them from all their iniquity, whereby they have sinned against me; and I will pardon all their iniquities, whereby they have sinned, and whereby they have transgressed against me." Isaiah 43:25: "I, even I, am he that blotteth out thy transgressions for mine own sake, and will not remember thy sins."

V. Though there be no actual pardon of sins till they be committed and repented of according to the tenor of the gospel (Matt. 3:2; Luke 13:3; Acts 2:38; 8:22), yet while Christ bare all the sins of His people on the cross, they were all then virtually and meritoriously taken away, of which Christ's resurrection was a certain pledge and evidence. For then got He His acquittance from all that either law or justice could charge Him with in behalf of them for whom He laid down His life a ransom. Romans 8:33–34: "Who shall lay any thing to the charge of God's elect? It is God that justifieth. Who is he that condemneth? It is Christ that died, yea rather, that is risen again."

VI. So that by virtue of Christ's death there is a way laid down in the covenant of grace how the sins of the elect will be actually pardoned—namely, that at their conversion and first laying hold on Christ by faith, all the sins of which they then stand guilty will be actually pardoned and forgiven in their justification. And all their after-sins will also be actually pardoned on their gripping to Christ of new by faith and turning to God by repentance. And this way is agreed to by Father and Son and revealed in the gospel for the instruction and encouragement of believers—and all to the glory of His free grace: "In whom we have redemption," the apostle says (Eph. 1:7–9), "through his blood, the forgiveness of sins, according to the riches of his grace; wherein he hath abounded toward us in all wisdom and prudence; having made known unto us the mystery of his will, according to his good pleasure which he hath purposed in himself."

VII. Beside[s] Christ's death and resurrection, which give ground of hope, of pardon, of daily out-breakings, there is likewise His intercession useful for this end. For, so says the apostle, "If any man sin, we have an advocate with the Father, Jesus Christ the righteous; and he is the propitiation for our sins" (1 John 2:1–2). This intercession is a special part of His priesthood, who was the Great High Priest (Heb. 4:14, 1) and a completing part (8:4; 9:8). And on this account it is that "he is able also to save them to the uttermost that come unto God by him, seeing he ever liveth to make intercession for them" (7:25). For by His intercession is the work of redemption carried on, the purchased benefits applied, and particularly, new grants of remission are through His intercession issued forth—He pleading and interceding in a way suitable to His glorified condition on His death and propitiation made while He was on the cross, accepted of the Father, and declared to be accepted by His resurrection, ascension, and sitting at His Father's right hand. And thus, as believers are reconciled to

God by Christ's death, they are saved by His life (Rom. 5:10). So that Christ's living to be an intercessor makes the salvation sure, and so laying down a ground for taking away of daily out-breakings, which, if not taken away, would hinder and obstruct the believer's salvation.

VIII. And as for the condition requisite to renewed pardon—namely, faith and repentance—Christ is the worker of both. For He is a prince exalted to give repentance, first and last (Acts 4:30). And as He is the author of faith, so He is the finisher of it (Heb. 12:2).

What Believers Must Do
As to the second particular—namely, what believers should do for getting the guilt of their daily failings and out-breakings taken away by Christ, or how they should make use of Christ for this end—I will for clearing of it propose these things to consideration:

I. We would beware to think that all our after actual transgressions are actually pardoned either when Christ died or when we first believed in Christ, as some suppose. For sin cannot properly be said to be pardoned before it be committed. David was put to sue out for pardon after his actual transgression was committed, and not for the mere sense and feeling of the pardon or the intimation of it to his spirit, when he cried out, "Blot out my transgressions, wash me, etc." (Ps. 51:2). And verse 9: "Hide thy face from my sins, and blot out all my iniquities." And verse 14: "Deliver me from bloodguiltiness." Sure[ly] when he spoke thus he sought some other thing than intimation of pardon to his sense and conscience, for that he desired also but in far more clear expressions, verse 8, "Make me to hear joy and gladness, etc.," and verse 12, "Restore unto me the joy of thy salvation, etc." Scripture phrases to express remission import this—namely, covering of sin, pardoning of debts, blotting out of sins, hiding of God's face from sin, not remembering of them, casting of them behind His back, casting of them into the sea, removing of sin (Ps. 33:1–2). These and the like phrases, though many of them be metaphorical, yet do all of them clearly evince that sin must first have a being before it can be pardoned. The same is clearly imported by the gospel conditions requisite before pardon, such as acknowledgment of sin (1 John 1:9), which we see was practiced by the worthies of old: David (Ps. 32:51); Nehemiah (ch. 10); Ezra (ch. 10); and Daniel (ch. 9). Confessing and forsaking of it (Prov. 28:13). Sorrowing for it and repenting of it and laying hold on Christ by faith, etc.

The reason why I propose this is not only to guard against this antinomian error but also to guard the soul from security, to which this doctrine has a natural tendency. For if a person once think that all his sins were pardoned on his first believing so that many of them were pardoned before they were committed, he will never be affected for his after transgressions nor complain of a body of death nor account himself miserable on that account, as Paul did (Rom. 7:24). Nor will he ever pray for remission, though Christ has taught all to do so in that pattern of prayer. Nor will he act faith on the promise of pardon made in the covenant of grace for after transgressions or for transgressions actually committed (Jer. 31:34; 33:8; Heb. 8:12). And so there will be no use made of Christ for new pardons or remissions of new sins.

II. The believer would remember that among other things antecedently requisite to remission of posterior actual transgressions, gospel repentance is especially required (Ezek. 14:6; 18:28, 30; Hos. 2:6–7; 14:6; Matt. 3:2; Luke 13:3; 15:17–18), by which a sinner through the help of the Spirit, being convinced not only of his hazard by reason of sin but also of the hatefulness and filthiness of sin and having a sight of the mercy of God in Christ Jesus to sinners turning from their sin, does turn from those sins to God with a full purpose of heart in his strength to follow Him and obey His laws. And by this the soul is brought to loathe itself and sin and is made willing to desire, seek for, accept of, and prize remissions of sins. This makes them more wary and careful in time coming. "For behold," says the apostle (2 Cor. 7:11), "this selfsame thing, that ye sorrowed after a godly sort, what carefulness it wrought in you, yea, what clearing of yourselves, yea, what indignation, yea, what fear, yea, what vehement desire, yea, what zeal, yea, what revenge, etc." Thus is God glorified in His justice (Ps. 51:4), and His mercy is acknowledged in not entering with us into judgment nor casting us into hell, as He might have done in justice.

III. Yet it would be remembered that though it has seemed good in the Lord's eyes to choose this method and appoint this way of obtaining pardon of sins daily committed for the glory of His grace and mercy and likewise for our good, we must not ascribe too much to repentance in the matter of pardon. We must not make it a cause of our remission, either efficient or meritorious. We must not think that it has any hand in appeasing the wrath of God or in satisfying justice. Pardon must always be an act of God's free grace, unmerited at our hands and procured alone through the merits of Christ. We must not put repentance in Christ's room and place nor ascribe any imperfection to His merits, as if they needed any supply from any act of ours. We must beware of leaning to our repentance and godly sorrow, even so far as to think to commend ourselves to God by which we may obtain pardon.

IV. The believer would consider seriously the dreadfulness of their condition who are lying under the lash of the law for sin. The law says, "Cursed is every one that continues not in all things written in the law." And every sin is a transgression of the law. So that, according to law and justice, they are in hazard. For every sin in itself exposes the sinner to eternal wrath, sin being an offense against God, who is a righteous judge, and a breach of His law. A right sight and apprehension of this would serve to humble the sinner before God and make him more earnest in seeking out for pardon that this obligation to punishment might be removed.

V. The believer would not only consider the sin itself but also take notice of all its aggravations. There are peculiar aggravations of some sins taken from the time, manner, and other circumstances which, rightly considered, will help forward the work of humiliation. And the sins of believers have this aggravation above the sins of others: that they are committed against more love, and special love, and against more opposition and contradiction of the grace of God within the soul, against more light and conviction, etc. And therefore their humiliation on this account ought to be singular and serious. So was it with David when he took notice of the special aggravation of his sin (Ps. 51:4, 6, 14) and Ezra (ch. 9) and Nehemiah (ch. 9) and Daniel (ch. 9). This considering of sin with its due aggravations would help to prize mercies at a high rate and cause the soul more willingly [to] wait for and more seriously seek after remission, knowing that God is more angry for great sins than for sins of infirmity and may therefore pursue the same with sorer judgments, as He broke David's bones [and] withdrew His comforts, etc.

VI. The believer would be convinced of an impossibility of doing anything in himself which can procure pardon at the hands of God. Should he weep, cry, afflict himself, and pray never so—all will do nothing by way of merit for taking away of the least sin that ever he committed. And the conviction of this would drive him to despair in himself and be a mean[s] to bring him cleanly off himself and to look out for mere mercy in Christ Jesus. So long as through the deceitfulness of Satan the false heart inclines to the old bias and has its eye on anything in itself from which it draws its hopes and expectation of pardon and acceptance, it will not purely act faith on Christ for this end. And so he will lose all his labor and in the end be disappointed. Therefore, the believer would guard against this, and that so much the more, that the false deceitful heart is so much inclined to this, and that this deceit can sometime[s] work so cunningly that it can hardly be discerned, being covered over with many false glosses and pretexts, and that it is so dishonorable to Jesus and hurtful and prejudicial to the soul.

VII. The believer would act faith on the promises of pardon in the new covenant, as having a right to them through Jesus Christ, and challenge with humble boldness the fulfilling of the same, according to that 1 John 1:9: "If we confess our sins, he is faithful and just to forgive us our sins." So that the believer may not only take hold of mercy and grace in God as an encouragement and invitation to go to God for pardon but even of the justice and righteousness of God because of His faithful promises. And the believer would have here a special eye to Christ, in whom all the promises are yea and amen, and look for the accomplishment of them through Him and for His sake alone.

VIII. Faith would eye Christ as hanging on the cross and offering up Himself through the eternal Spirit a sacrifice to satisfy divine justice for all the sins of His own chosen ones. We cannot think that Christ bare but some of their sins or only their sins committed before conversion. And if He bare all as the Father laid all on Him, the believer is to lay hold on Him by faith as hanging on the cross as well for taking away of the guilt of sins committed after conversion as before. His sacrifice was a sacrifice for all, and He "bare our sins [without distinction or exception] in his own body on the tree" (1 Peter 2:24). David had his eye on this when he cried out (Ps. 51:7), "Purge me with hyssop"—hyssop being sometimes used in the legal purifications, which typified that purification which Christ really wrought when He gave Himself a sacrifice for sin (Lev. 14:6; Num. 19:18).

IX. The believer looking on Christ dying as a mediator to pacify the wrath of God and to make satisfaction to the justice of God for the sins of His people would renew his consent to that gracious and wise contrivance of heaven of pardoning sins through a crucified mediator that mercy and justice might kiss each other and be glorified together. And [he should] declare again his full satisfaction with Christ's satisfying of justice for him and taking away the guilt of his sins by that blood that was shed on the cross by taking those sins of which now he stands guilty and for which he is desirous of pardon and by faith nailing them to the cross of Christ and rolling them on His shoulders that the guilt of them as well as of the rest might be taken away through the merits of His death and satisfaction. Thus the believer consents to the noble act of free grace by which the Lord made all our sins to meet together on Christ when he takes those particular sins with which now he is troubled and casts them in into the heap [so] that Christ, as the true scapegoat, may carry all away. This is to lay our hands on the head of our sacrifice.

X. The believer has another ground of comfort to grip to in this case, and that is Christ's eternal priesthood by which He makes intercession for the transgressions of His people and as their advocate and attorney with the Father pleads their cause, by which He is able to save them to the last and uttermost step of their journey, and so to save them from the guilt of all casual and emergent sins that might hinder their salvation. So that the believer is to put those sins that now he would have pardoned into the hands of Christ, the everlasting intercessor and all-sufficient advocate, [so] that He by virtue of His death would obtain a new pardon of these their failings and transgressions and deliverance from the guilt thereof and their acceptance with the Father, despite these transgressions.

XI. Thus believers, eyeing Christ as dying, rising again, ascending, and as sitting at the Father's right hand, there to be a priest forever after the order of Melchizedek and to intercede for His own and to see to the application of what benefits, pardons, favors, and other things they need, from all which they have strong ground of comfort and of hope, indeed, and assurance of pardon—[that they] would acquiesce in this way and, having laid those particular sins under the burden of which they now groan on Christ the mediator, dying on the cross to make satisfaction and arising to make application of what was purchased, and, having put them in His hand who is a faithful high priest and a noble intercessor, [they] would remember that Christ is a prince exalted to give repentance and remission of sins. And so [they would] expect the sentence even from Him as a prince now exalted and as having obtained that of the Father, even a power to forgive sins, justice being now sufficiently satisfied through His death, indeed, and as having all power in heaven and in earth as being Lord both of the dead and of the living. Sure[ly] a right thought of this would much quiet the soul in hope of obtaining pardon through Him, seeing now the pardon is in His own hand to give out who loved them so dearly that He gave Himself to the death for them and shed His heart blood to satisfy justice for their transgressions. Since He who has procured their pardon at so dear a rate and is their attorney to agent their business at the throne of grace has now obtained the prayed-for and looked-for pardon and has it in his own hand, they will not question but He will give it and so absolve them from their guilt.

XII. The believer, having taken this course with his daily provocations and laid them all on Him, would acquiesce in this way and not seek after another that he may obtain pardon. Here he would rest, committing the matter by faith in prayer to Christ. And, leaving his guilt and sins on Him, [he would] expect the pardon, indeed, conclude that they are already pardoned and that for these sins he will never be brought to condemnation, whatever Satan and a misbelieving heart may say or suggest afterward.

Thus should a believer make use of Christ for the taking away of the guilt of his daily transgressions. And for further clearing of it, I will add a few cautions.

Cautions

I. However, the believer is to be much moved at and affected with his sins and provocations which he commits after God has visited his soul with salvation and brought him into a covenant with Himself, yet he must not suppose that his sins after justification do mar his state—as if by this he were brought into a nonjustified state or to a nonreconciled state. It is true: such sins, especially if gross, whether in themselves or by reason of circumstances, will darken a man's state and put him to search and try his condition over again. But yet we dare not say that they make any alteration in the state of a believer, for once in a justified state, always in a justified state. It is true likewise that as to those sins which now he has committed he cannot be said to be acquitted or justified till this pardon be got out by faith and repentance, as is said. Yet his state remains fixed and unchanged, so that though God should seem to deal with such in His dispensations as with enemies, yet really His affections change not. He never accounts them real enemies. Indeed, love lies at the bottom of all His sharpest dispensations. If they forsake His law and walk not in His judgments, if they break His statutes and keep not His commandments, He will visit their transgression with the rod and their iniquity with stripes. Nevertheless, His lovingkindness will He not utterly take from them nor suffer His faithfulness to fail. His covenant will He not break nor alter the thing that has gone out of His lips (Ps. 89:30–34). And again, though after transgressions may waken challenges for former sins which have been pardoned and blotted out and give occasions to Satan to raise a storm in the soul and put all in confusion, yet really sins once pardoned cannot become again unpardoned sins. The Lord does not revoke His sentence nor alter the thing that is gone out of His mouth. It is true, likewise, that a believer, by committing of gross sins, may come to miss the effects of God's favor and goodwill and the intimations of His love and kindness. And so [he may] be made to cry with David, "Make me to hear joy and gladness" (Ps. 51:8), and verse 12, "Restore unto me the joy of thy salvation, etc." Yet that really holds true that whom He loves He loves to the end. And He is a God that changes not. And His gifts are without repentance. Indeed, though grieving of the Spirit may bring souls under sharp throes and pangs of the spirit of bondage and the terrors of God and His sharp arrows, the poison of which may drink up their spirits and so be far from the actual witnessings of the Spirit of adoption— yet the Spirit will never be again really a spirit of bondage to fear nor deny His own work in the soul or the soul's real right to or possession of that fundamental privilege of adoption—I say, that the soul is no more a son nor within the covenant.

II. The course before mentioned is to be taken with all sins, though (1) they be never so heinous and gross; (2) though they be accompanied with never such aggravating and crying aggravations; (3) though they be sins frequently fallen into; and (4) though they be sins many and heaped together. David's transgression was a heinous sin and had heinous aggravations. Indeed, there was a heap and a complication of sins together in that one. Yet he followed this course. We find none of these kind of sins excepted in the new covenant. And where the law does not distinguish, we ought not to distinguish. Where God's law does not expressly exclude us, we should not exclude ourselves. Christ's death is able enough to take away all sin. If through it a believer be justified from all his transgressions committed before conversion, why may not also a believer be through virtue of it justified from his gross and multiplied sins committed after conversion? The blood of Christ cleanses from all sin. Christ has taught His followers to pray, "Forgive us our sins, as we forgive them that sin against us." And He has told us also that we must forgive our brother "seventy times seven" (Matt. 18:22). We would not be discouraged then from taking this course because our sins are such and such. Indeed, rather, we would look on this as an argument to press us more to this way, because the greater our sins be, the greater need have we of pardon and to say with David, "Pardon mine iniquity; for it is great" (Ps. 25:11).

III. We would not think that on our taking of this course we will be instantly freed from challenges because of those sins for pardoning of which we take this course. Nor should we think that because challenges remain that therefore there is no pardon had or that this is not the way to pardon. For, as we will show afterward, pardon is one thing, and intimation of pardon is another thing. We may be pardoned and yet suppose that we are not pardoned. Challenges will abide till the conscience be sprinkled and till the Prince of Peace command peace to the conscience and put the accuser to silence—who, when he can do no more, will mar the peace of a believer as long as he can and stop the current of his comforts, which made David pray that God would restore to him the joy of his salvation (Psalm 51).

IV. Nor would we think that on us taking of this course for the pardon of our sins we will never thereafter meet with a challenge on the account of these sins. It is true, when sins are pardoned, they are fully pardoned in God's court, and that obligation to condemnation is taken away, and the pardoned person is looked on as no sinner—that is, as no person liable to condemnation because of these sins. For being pardoned, he becomes just before God. Yet we dare not say, but conscience afterward, being alarmed with new transgressions, may mistake, as people suddenly put into a fight are ready to do. Nor dare we say that God will not permit Satan to upbraid us with those sins which have been blotted out long ago, as He suffered Shimei, who was but an instrument of Satan, to cast up to David his bloodguiltiness, which had been pardoned long before. The Lord may think good to suffer this that His people may be kept humble and made more tender and watchful in all their ways.

V. Believers would not misimprove or abuse this great condescendency of free grace and take the great liberty to sin because there is such a sure, safe, and pleasant way of getting those sins blotted out and forgiven. "Shall we sin, because we are not under the law, but under grace? God forbid," says the apostle (Rom. 6:15). This were indeed to turn the grace of God into lasciviousness. And it may be a question, if such as have really repented and gotten their sins pardoned will be so ready to make this use of it. Sure[ly] sense of pardon will work some other effect, as we see (Ezek. 16:62–63).

VI. The believer, in going about this work of nailing his sins to the cross of Christ and of improving Christ's death, resurrection, and constant intercession for the obtaining of pardon, would not think of going alone or of doing this in his own strength; for of himself he can do nothing. He must look to Christ for grace to help in this time of need and must go about this duty with dependence on Him, waiting for the influence of light, counsel, strength, and grace from Him to repent and believe—for He is a prince exalted to give repentance, first and last. And He is the author and finisher of faith, so that without Him we can do nothing.

VII. Let the believer beware of concluding that he has got[ten] no pardon because he has met with no sensible intimation of it by the flowing in of peace and joy in his soul. Pardon is one mercy, and intimation of it to the soul is another distinct mercy and separable from it. Will we therefore say we have not gotten the first because we have not gotten both? The Lord, for wise reasons, can pardon poor sinners and not give any intimation of it—namely, that they may watch more against sin afterward and not be so bold as they have been, and that they may find more in experience what a bitter thing it is to sin against God and learn in addition to depend on Him for less and more and to carry more humbly. For it may be, God sees, that if they saw their sins pardoned [that] they would forget themselves and rush into new sins again.

VIII. The believer must not think it strange if he find more trouble after greater sins and a greater difficulty to lay hold on Christ for pardon of those than for pardon of others. For as God has been more dishonored by these, so is His anger more kindled on that account. And it is suitable for the glory of God's justice that our sorrow for such sins be proportionally greater. And this will likewise increase the difficulty. And ordinarily the effects of God's fatherly displeasure make deeper wounds in the soul after such sins, and these are not so easily healed— all which will call for suitable and proportionally greater godly sorrow and repentance and acts of faith, because faith will meet with more opposition and discouragement there and therefore must be the more strong to go through these impediments and to lay hold on His cross. Yet though this should make all watchful and to guard against gross and crying sins, it should not drive any to despair nor to say with that despairing wretch [that] their sin is greater than it can be forgiven. The ocean of mercy can drown and swallow up greater as well as lesser sins. Christ is an all-sufficient mediator for the greatest sins as well as the least. "Oh, for Thy name's sake, pardon mine iniquity, for it is great!" will come in season to a soul ready to sink with the weight of this millstone tied about its neck.

IX. As the greater sins should not make us despair of taking this course for remission, so nor should the smallness of sin make us to neglect this way. For the least sin cannot be pardoned but through Jesus Christ, for the law of God is violated by this, justice provoked, God's authority vilified, etc., and therefore cannot be now pardoned by reason of the threatenings annexed to the law without a ransom. Death is the wages of sin, lesser and greater, and the curse is due to all sin, greater and smaller. There, the believer would not suffer one sin seen and discovered to lie unpardoned, but on the first discovery of it take it away to Christ and nail it to the cross.

X. The believer would not conclude that his sins are not pardoned because possibly temporal strokes, inflicted because of them, are not removed. For though David's sin was pardoned, yet because of that sin of his a temporal stroke attended him and his family to his dying day. For not only did God cut off the child (2 Sam. 15:14) but told him that the sword should never depart from his house and that He would raise up evil against him out of his own house and give his wives to one that should lie with them in the sight of the sun (vv. 10–11). So we read that the Lord took vengeance on their inventions whose sins He had pardoned (Ps. 99:8). God may see this fit and expedient for His own glory and for humbling of them and causing them to fear the more to sin against Him. Indeed, not only may temporal calamities be inflicted because of sin pardoned or continued after sin is pardoned, but even sense of God's displeasure may continue after pardon, as appears by that penitential Psalm 51 penned by David after Nathan had spoken to him concerning his sin.

Questions or Objections Answered
I. What course will we take with secret sins? I answer: This same course must be followed with them. There is an implicit repentance of sins that have not been distinctly seen and

observed—as who can see and observe all their failings? And
so there may be an implicit faith acting—that is, the believer,
being persuaded that he is guilty of more sins than he has got
a clear sight of, as he would bewail his condition before God
because of these and sorrow for them after a godly manner, so
he would take them together in a heap or as a closed bagful
and by faith nail them to the cross of Christ, as if they were all
distinctly seen and known. "Who can understand his errors,"
said David (Ps. 19:12). Yet says he moreover, "Cleanse thou me
from secret faults."

II. But what if after all this I find no intimation of pardon to
my soul? Answer: As this should serve to keep you humble, so
it should excite to more diligence in this duty of going with
your sins to Christ and to ply Him and His cross more in and
through the promises and keep your soul constant in this duty
of the running to Christ as an all-sufficient mediator and as an
intercessor with the Father—and thus wait on Him [who] waits
to be gracious, even in this particular of intimating pardon to
your soul. He knows when it is most fit for you to know that
your sins are forgiven.

III. But what can yield me any ground of peace while it is so,
that I see no pardon or remission granted to me? Answer: This
may yield you peace: that, following this course which has been
explained, you are about your duty. You are not at peace with
sin nor harboring that viper in your soul. You are mourning and
sorrowing over it and running to Christ, the prince of pardons,
through His blood and intercession, conform[ing] to the
covenant of redemption, and after the encouragement given
in the many and precious promises of the covenant of grace,
and having these promises and rolling your guilt on Christ as
your cautioner, conform[ing] to the manner expressed in the

gospel, you are allowed to believe that your sins are pardoned and that you are accepted in the beloved and so quiet your soul through faith—God abiding faithful and true, and His promises being all yea and amen in Christ.

IV. But so long as I find no intimation of pardon, I cannot think that I have taken the right gospel way of bringing my sins to Christ. Answer: Though that will not follow, as we cleared above—for a soul may take the right gospel way of getting the guilt of their sins taken away in Christ, and God may pardon on this and for all that not think it fit to give intimation of that pardon as yet for wise and holy ends. Yet the soul may humble itself for its shortcoming and still go about the duty, amending in Christ what it supposes to be amiss and renewing its act of repentance and faith, and beg of Christ understanding in the matter, and so continue carrying sin always to Christ's cross and eyeing His intercession, and wait for a full clearing of the matter in His good time.

V. But what will I do with the guilt of my weak repentance and weak faith? Answer: When with a weak and defective repentance and faith you are carrying away your sins to Christ and nailing them to His cross, let the imperfection of your faith and repentance go with the rest and leave all there.

VI. What will I do with my conscience that still accuses me of guilt, despite my taking and following this course? Answer: Despise not the accusation of conscience, but let these humble you the more and keep you closer at this duty. Yet know that conscience is but an underservant and God's deputy and must accuse according to law. (I speak not here of the irregular, furious, and turbulent motions of Satan, casting in grenades in the soul and conscience to raise a combustion and put all

in a fire.) Its mouth must be stopped by law, and so the soul
would stay and answer the accusations of conscience with this:
that he has fled to Christ, the only mediator and cautioner,
and cast his burden on Him and leans to His merits alone and
has put those sins in His hand as his advocate and intercessor
with the Father—and that the gospel requires no more of him.
And if conscience should say that both faith and repentance
are imperfect and defective and that guilt is by these rather
increased than taken away, [then] he must answer again:
"True; but I have done with the guilt of my faith and repentance as with the rest, taken all to Christ and left all on Him.
And in this only do I acquiesce—I look not for pardon for
my imperfect faith and repentance, indeed, nor would I look
for pardon of my sins, for my faith and repentance, were they
never so perfect, but only in and through Jesus Christ, the only
cautioner, redeemer, and advocate." But further, this deputy
would be brought to his master who can only command him to
silence—that is to say, the believer would go to Christ with the
accusing conscience and desire Him to command its silence
that he may have peace of conscience and freedom from
those accusations that are bitter and troublesome. Remember,
in addition, that if these accusations drive you to Christ and
endear Him more to your soul, they will do no harm, because
they drive you to your only resting place and to the grand
peacemaker. But if otherwise they discourage or forslow[3] you
in your motion Christward, then be sure conscience speaks
without warrant, and its accusations ought not, insofar and as
to that end, to be regarded.

---

3. *Forslow*: to slow down.

CHAPTER 9

How to Make Use of Christ for Cleansing of Us from Our Daily Spots

*H*aving spoken of the way of making use of Christ for removing the guilt of our daily transgressions, we come to speak of the way of making use of Christ for taking away the guilt that cleaves to the soul through daily transgressions. For every sin "defileth the man" (Matt. 15:20). And the best are said to have their spots and to need washing, which presupposes filthiness and defilement (John 13:8–10; Eph. 5:27). Hence we are so often called to this duty of washing and making us clean (Isa. 1:16; Jer. 4:14; Acts 22:16). David prays for this washing (Ps. 51:2–7). And it is Christ's work to wash (1 Cor. 6:11; Eph. 5:26; Rev. 1:5; see Titus 3:5).

Christ and His Use in Taking Away Our Daily Sin

Now, in speaking to this, we will observe the same method and first show what Christ has done to take away this filth, and next what way we are to make use of Him for this end: to get our spots and filthiness taken away that we may be holy.

What Christ Has Done

As to the first, for the purging away of the filth of our daily failings and transgressions, Christ has done these things:

I. He has died that He may procure this benefit and advantage to us. And thus He has washed us meritoriously in His own blood which He shed on the cross. Thus He loved us and washed us from our sins in His own blood (Rev. 1:5). And this is from all sins as well such as are committed after as such as are committed before conversion. Thus, "he had by himself purged our sins" (Heb. 1:3)—namely, by offering up of Himself as an expiatory sacrifice to make an atonement and so procure this liberty. So also it is said (Eph. 5:25–27) that Christ gave Himself for His church that He might sanctify and cleanse it—that He might present it to Himself a glorious church, not having spot or wrinkle or any such thing, but that it should be holy and without blemish. So Titus 2:14: "[He] gave himself for us, that he might…purify unto himself a peculiar people, zealous of good works." Here then is the foundation and ground of all cleansing and purification: Christ's death procuring it.

II. As He has procured, so He sends the Spirit to effectuate this and to work this washing and sanctification in us. Hence it is said that we are sanctified and washed in the name of the Lord Jesus and by the Spirit of our God (1 Cor. 6:11). We are said to be saved "by the washing of regeneration, and renewing of the Holy Ghost; which he hath shed on us abundantly through Jesus Christ our Saviour" (Titus 3:5–6). The sending then or shedding of the holy and sanctifying Spirit on us by which we are sanctified and consequently purified and purged from our filth is a fruit of Christ's death and mediation, being purchased by it, and is an effect of His resurrection and glorification and intercession in glory.

III. He has made a fountain of His blood for this end: that we may go to it daily and wash and be clean. Thus His blood cleanses from all sin (1 John 1:7–9). This is the "fountain opened to the house of David and to the inhabitants of Jerusalem for sin and for uncleanness" (Zech. 13:1).

IV. He has purchased and provided the external means by which this cleansing and sanctification is brought about—namely, the preaching of the gospel, which He Himself preached and by this sanctified. "Now ye are clean through the word which I have spoken unto you" (John 15:3). The church is sanctified and cleansed "with the washing of water by the word" (Eph. 5:26).

V. So has He procured and works in the soul those graces that promove and carry on this work of sanctification and purifying—such as faith, which purifies the heart (Acts 15:9), of which He is the author and finisher (Hebrews 12); and hope, which whoever has "purifieth himself, even as he is pure" (1 John 3:3).

VI. He has confirmed and ratified all the promises of the covenant which are ample and large touching this cleansing and washing: "And I will cleanse them from all their iniquity, whereby they have sinned against me" (Jer. 33:8). "Then will I sprinkle clean water upon you, and ye shall be clean: from all your filthiness" (Ezek. 36:25). So Ezekiel 37:23: "And [I] will cleanse them." And all the other promises of the covenant apprehended by faith have no small influence on our cleansing (2 Cor. 7:1): "Having therefore these promises, ...let us cleanse ourselves, etc."—all which promises are yea and amen in Christ (1:20).

Thus Christ made all sure for the cleansing and washing of His people, conform[ing] to that article of the covenant of redemption. So will He sprinkle many nations (Isa. 52:15).

What Believers Must Do

Secondly, as to the way of our use-making of Christ for the purging away of our filth and daily pollutions, believers would take this course:

I. They would remember and live in the conviction of the exceeding abominableness and filthiness of sin, which is compared to the vomit of a dog and to the mire in which the sow wallows (2 Peter 2:22), filthy rags (Isa. 64:6), to a menstruous cloth (30:22), and the like, that this may move them to seek with greater care and diligence to have that filth taken away.

II. They would remember also how abominable sin makes them in the eyes of a holy God, who cannot behold iniquity, being a God of purer eyes than to behold it (Hab. 1:13). Nor can He look on it. And how therefore nothing can enter into the New Jerusalem nor anything that defiles. And this will make them so much the more to abhor it and to seek to be washed from it.

III. They would look by faith on the blood of Christ that is shed for this end: to wash filthy souls into. And [they would] run to it as a fountain opened for this end: that they might come to it and wash and be clean.

IV. For their encouragement, they would grip by faith to the promises of the new covenant, which are large and full.

V. And remember the end of Christ's death—namely, to purchase to Himself a holy people, zealous of good works, to present them to Himself holy and without spot or wrinkle or any such thing. And this will be further ground of encouragement.

VI. They would put the work by faith in His hand, who has best skill to wash a foul soul and to purge away all their spots, and by faith pray for and expect the Spirit to sanctify and cleanse them from all their filthiness. That is, they would make known and spread forth their abominations before the Lord and, eyeing Christ as the only Great High Priest whose blood is a fountain to wash in, would lay the work on Him and by faith put Him to wash away that filth and to purify their souls by His Spirit, pardoning their bygone iniquities and renewing them in the Spirit of their minds by grace, that they may walk before Him in fear. Thus they would roll the work on Him and leave it there.

Cautions and Directions

I. First, the believer would in all this work be kept in the exercise of these graces following:

1. Of humility, seeing what a vile, filthy wretch he is that stands in need of washing and purging daily, because of his daily pollutions and transgressions.

2. Of love, considering with what a loving God he has to do that has provided so liberally all things for him and particularly has provided a fountain, and such a fountain to which he not only may but is commanded to resort daily.

3. Of thankfulness, remembering how great this mercy is, how unworthy he is on whom it is bestowed, and who He is that does grant it.

4. Of fear, lest God's goodness be abused and He provoked who is so gracious to us.

5. Of sincerity and godly ingenuity, avoiding all hypocrisy and formality, knowing that we have to do with Him who will not be mocked.

6. Of holy hatred, loathing, and abhorrence of sin, which makes us so filthy and odious in the eyes of the Lord.

II. Secondly, this course would be followed for the purging away of the least sins. For till they be purged away, we remain in our filth and cannot expect God's favorable countenance nor His warm embracements nor the hearty intimations of His love and kindness. And a small inconsiderable like spot may grow greater and provoke God to let the accuser of the brethren, Satan, who always waits for his opportunity, loose on us. And a conscience wakened may make much of a little defilement to keep the soul from approaching to God.

III. This course would be followed with every sin quickly without delay. For the longer those spots continue, it will be the more difficult to get them taken away. The soul will after some time become the less troubled about them and possibly forget them, and so they will remain. And this may occasion at last a sad distance and provoke God to hide His face, which will cause more bitterness and sorrow. It were good, then, to keep up a spirit of tenderness and fear.

IV. Let this be our daily work and exercise, for we are daily contracting new filth. Yesterday's cleansing will not save us from new filth today. Nor will our running to the fountain today serve to take away new spots tomorrow—new spots call for new washing. So that this must be our very life and exercise to be daily and continually running to the fountain with our souls and giving Christ, the great purger, much to do.

V. We must not think to be perfectly washed so long as we are here. For we will be contracting new filth daily. Our feet will still be to wash (John 13:10). We will not be without spot or wrinkle till we come home to that place in which enters nothing that defiles.

VI. Let the believer's recourse in this matter be wholly to Jesus Christ and His blood and lay no weight on their sorrow, repentance, or tears, or on any outward means which they are commanded to use. Yet would they not lay aside these means but go through them to the fountain to Jesus there, and there only to be cleansed.

VII. They should not be discouraged or despair when their spots appear great and not like the spots of His children. For Christ's blood can purge from all sin and wash away all their filth, of however deep a dye it be. Christ's blood is so deep an ocean that a mountain will be sunk out of sight in it as well as a small pebble stone.

VIII. Though Christ's blood be strong enough to purge from all sin, even the greatest, yet they should know that scandalous spots or a deep stain may cost them more frequent running to the fountain through humiliation, godly sorrow, prayer, and supplication. David's scandalous blot cost him more trouble and pains before he got it purged away than many others, as we see (Psalm 51).

IX. When all this is done, we must think of having on another righteousness as our clothing and covering in the day of our appearance before our judge—even the righteousness of Jesus Christ, which only is perfect and able to save us from the wrath of God. Let us be never so washed in the matter of sanctification and cleansed from our spots—we cannot for all that be accounted righteous before God. Nor will that satisfy justice or take away the guilt so much as of one transgression before God. Christ's righteousness will be our upper garment for all eternity. This is the fine linen of which His bride is busked[1] in heaven.

X. At every time we run to the fountain with our daily contracted filth, we would not forget to carry along with us the mother corruption, which is the sink and puddle of all filthiness. I mean our natural corrupted rottenness and pollution from which flow all our other actual pollutions. We would do well to carry mother and daughter both together to the fountain. David prayed to be washed and purged as well from his original filthiness in which he was conceived and born as from his bloodguiltiness (Ps. 51:5, 7).

XI. Let not this occasion our carelessness in watching against sin. For that would be to turn His grace into wantonness. But rather let it sharpen our diligence in watching against all occasions of sin, lest we again defile our soul.

XII. Not only must we have our bodies or our outward conversation washed but our soul within—the frame of our heart, our understanding, will, affections, and conscience—sprinkled with that blood. The blood of Christ, who through the eternal Spirit "offered himself without spot to God," must purge our consciences from dead works to serve the living God (Heb. 9:14), and we must "have our hearts sprinkled from an evil conscience" (10:22).

XIII. Finally, if the believer fear that he will not be able to remember all these particular duties, let him remember this— namely, to put a foul soul, defiled with original and actual pollutions, in Christ's hand daily and leave it to Him to wash by His blood and Spirit, and yet remember to lay the weight of

---

1. *Busked*: dressed.

his acceptance before God on the imputed righteousness of Jesus Christ and not on his own cleanness when thus sanctified and washed, which is but imperfect.

Questions or Objections Answered

I. But, alas, some may object and say that their very faith which must carry the rest of their filth to the fountain of Christ's blood is defiled. How, then, can they expect to be made clean? Answer: The blood of Jesus Christ is sufficiently able to wash all our filth away—and the filth of faith, as well as of other actions. Therefore, when faith, as a hand, is carrying the filth of the soul away to Christ to be washed in His blood, let the foul hand go with the foul handful. Give Christ faith and all to wash.

II. But what will I do, when, despite all this, my conscience will still accuse me of uncleanness and cry out against me as filthy and abominable? Answer: Take it away also to the blood of Jesus that there it may be purged (Heb. 9:14). And here alone will we get "our hearts sprinkled from an evil conscience" (10:22). The conscience must be steeped, so to speak, in the blood of Jesus, and so it will be clean. And taking our filthy hearts to this cleansing fountain to be washed, we will get them delivered and sprinkled from an evil conscience, that it will no more have ground of accusation against us. When we have it to say that we have put our filthy souls in the hand of the great cleanser Jesus Christ and brought all our pollutions to His blood, what can conscience say to us? The Lord, it is true, may suffer our conscience still to bark on us and cast up our filthiness to us that we may be the more humbled and be put to lie more constantly at the fountain. Yet when we have fled to Christ and taken our filthiness to the open and appointed fountain, we can answer the accusations of conscience in law and have peace.

III. But I am apt to think, some will say, that if I had once taken the right way to get my sins and filthiness purged away, my conscience would trouble me no more. But now, so long as it dogs[2] me thus, I cannot think that the way which I have taken is the right way. Answer: Though the Lord may think good to suffer conscience to trouble a man for a time, though he has taken the right way, as is said, for a further exercise and trial to Him; yet the believer will have no less disadvantage by examining his way and trying whether he has laid the matter cleanly over on Christ or whether he has laid too much weight on his own humiliation, sorrow, and pains and whether he be leaving the matter on Jesus and expecting to be washed alone in His blood or looking into himself and expecting some help in the matter from self, and after trial would mourn for any failing he gets discovered and still be about that work of running with filth to the fountain. But in addition, they would go to Christ for help, because without Him they cannot come to Him. They cannot come or carry their soul to the fountain opened for sin and for uncleanness. So that in all this work there would be a single dependence on Christ for understanding and strength to go about this work aright.

Conclusions

Thus have we endeavored to clear up Christ being the way to the Father, first and last, and how all believers or unbelievers are to make use of Him as the way to the Father, whatever their condition be—from all which we may see:

_____

2. *Dogs*: original, "doggeth."

I. That such are in a wretched and forlorn condition who are still strangers to Christ and will not lay hold on Him nor come to Him and walk in Him and make use of Him. They are unrighteous and unholy and daily contracting more guilt and more filth. And they know no way either for justification or sanctification but a way of self, which will prove like the brooks which run dry in summer and disappoint the weary traveler when he has most need. They are without Christ, and so without the way, the only way, the safe and sure way to the Father. And, oh! If all that is here spoken could induce them to think once of the misery of their condition and to seek out for relief that they might not only be saved from their state of sin and misery but brought into a state of salvation through Jesus Christ so that they might be justified before God from all that justice, the devil, the law, or conscience could lay against them and thoroughly sanctified and so at length brought home to the Father, fair and spotless.

II. On the other hand, we see the noble advantage of believers, who, through grace, are entered in this way; for it is a full and complete way that will carry them safe home. They will find that He is able to save to the uttermost all that come to God through Him. And, oh! If they were sensible of this, how would it excite them to thankfulness! How would it encourage them to run through difficulties great and many!

III. We see what a special duty lies on believers to make special use of Christ in all things as the way to the Father and so march to heaven in Him as the only way—march in His hands, or rather be carried in His arms and bosom. This were to go from strength to strength till at length they appeared in Zion and landed in that pleasant place of rest, where the weary are at rest and yet rest not day nor night but sing praises to Him that has redeemed them by His blood, "out of every kindred, and tongue, and people, and nation...saying, Blessing, and honour, and glory, and power, be unto him that sitteth upon the throne, and unto the Lamb for ever and ever" (Rev. 5:9, 13).

IV. Hence we may see the cause of the leanness of believers of their wanderings, of their shortcomings, of their many defilements, etc.—namely, their not constant making use of Christ as the way in all things, according to the tenor of the gospel. Oh, if this were laid to heart and mourned for and if grace were sought to help it!

This one point of truth that Christ is the way, well understood and rightly put into practice, would do all our business both as to justification and sanctification. And were poor sinners once entered into this way and had they grace from this way to walk in it, it would prove their life and salvation— for it is the marrow and substance of the whole gospel. So that there needs little more to be said. Yet we will speak a little to the other particulars in the text.

CHAPTER 10

"The Truth": Some Particulars Proposed

That what we are to speak to for the clearing and improving this noble piece of truth that Christ is the truth may be the more clearly understood and edifying, we will first take notice of some generals and then show particularly how or in what respects Christ is called the truth and finally speak to some cases in which we are to make use of Christ as the truth.

Some General Ways Christ Is the Truth

As to the first, there are four general things here to be noticed:

Our Case by Nature

This supposes what our case by nature is and what we are all without Christ, who is the truth, as:

I. It supposes that without Christ we are in darkness, mistakes, errors. Indeed, we are said to be darkness itself. "Ye were sometimes darkness, etc." (Eph. 5:8) and of darkness (John 1:5; 1 Thess. 5:5), indeed, under the power of darkness (John 12:35; Col. 1:13; 1 John 2:11), "walk[ing] in darkness" (1 John 1:6), and "abid[ing] in darkness (John 12:46; 1 Thess. 5:4; 1 Peter 2:9). We wander and go astray as soon as we are born, speaking lies (Ps. 58:3). Indeed, we go astray in the greatness of our folly (Prov. 5:23). We are all gone astray (Ps. 119:67–176; Isa. 53:6), so far are we from any knowledge of or acquaintance with truth or with the way of truth.

II. It supposes that we cannot turn into the right way. A spirit of error and untruth leads us continually wrong. Like the sheep, we wander still, and we weary ourselves in our wandering and so spend all our labor and pains in vain. Being under the power of untruth and error, we cannot walk one step right.

III. Though all other ways beside[s] Him who only is the way and the truth be false ways and byways, leading us away from the true resting place and from that way which is the truth, yet we are prone and ready to cleave to those false and erroneous ways and grip to shadows and to lean to them as if they were the ways of truth—such as:

1. A good heart, which many may imagine they have when they have nothing less.

2. Good intentions and purposes for time to come, which such as were not under the power of error and untruth would never deceive themselves with.

3. A harmless life without scandalous out-breakings to the reproach of Christianity, a foundation on which no wise man, led by truth, would build his salvation or hopes of eternal happiness.

4. An outward, moral, civil, and discreet carriage, which no man can blame and in which a heathen can outstrip many called Christians. So that it must be a poor ground to found our hopes on, and yet many are so blinded that they lean all their weight on such a rotten staff.

5. Outward exercise of religious duties in which a Pharisee may outstrip many—and yet, oh how many build all their hopes of heaven on this sandy foundation, which none but blinded persons would do!

6. The commendation and applause of ministers and Christians is that which many rest on, which is a sad proof of the blindness of their hearts.

7. The way of good works and alms-deeds blindfolds many and shows that they were never led by truth or taught of Christ, who is the truth.

8. Some pinching grief and sorrow for sin is another way which people, strangers to the truth, deceive themselves with.

9. A common sort of repentance backed with some kind of amendment and outward reformation is a way that many rest secure in, though it lead to destruction.

10. Freedom from challenges of conscience deceives many.

Though these and such like ways be dangerous, indeed, deadly, yet how many are there to be found among Christians that have no better ground of their hope of salvation and will cleave to them so fast as no preaching will make them so much as once question the matter or suspect that these ways will in the end deceive them, so strong is their inclination to the way of error, though not as the way of error.

IV. It presupposes also an inclinableness in us by nature to wander out of the way; for being nothing but a mass of error, made up of darkness, ignorance, and mistakes, we have a strong bias to error, which agrees best with our natural, corrupted temper. Hence it is that we have such a strong propension to errors and mistakes, whether concerning God and His way of dealing with His church or with ourselves. Oh, how ready are our hearts by nature to hatch and foment wrong, unseemly, untrue, indeed, unchristian if not blasphemous thoughts and conceptions of His nature, attributes, word, and works? And how ready and prone are we to receive and entertain wrong apprehensions of all His ways and dealings with His church and people? And as for His works in and about ourselves— oh, what unsuitable, erroneous, false, ungodly, absurd, and abominable opinions do we with greediness drink in and foster, indeed, feed on with delight? Who is able to recount all the errors and mistakes which our heart by nature is ready to admit and foster with complacency? Are we not by nature ready to say that there is not a God—as the fool (Ps. 14:1)— or that He is not such a God as His word and works declare Him to be—a holy, just, righteous, omnipotent, omnipresent, omniscient God, etc.? Or that He is a changeable God and actually changed, not being the same now which sometime[s] He was. That He has forgotten to be gracious and remembers not His people in adversity and so is not tender and merciful. That He has forgotten His promises and so is not faithful and true. That He approves of sin because He suffers the way of the wicked to prosper and so is not a holy God, etc. Indeed, do not oftentimes such thoughts as these lodge within the heart of the truly godly? All which shows how prone we are to receive and entertain erroneous and false thoughts of God.

Or concerning ourselves, supposing ourselves to be born again and reconciled to God when yet we are living in black nature. And who so bold and confident that they are right, as they that are furthest out of the way? Or, on the other hand, supposing ourselves to be in a bad state and in nature and darkness, when the daystar from on high has visited us and brought our souls from death to life. And who more ready to complain than such as have least cause? Or supposing ourselves in a good condition, lively, active, diligent, watchful, etc., when it is just otherwise with us. Or, on the contrary, complaining of deadness, formality, upsitting, fainting, heartlessness in the ways of God, when it is not so. Or, in questioned matters, taking truth to be error and error to be truth.

Or concerning others. How ready are we to run either to the one extremity or the other in judging their persons and actions?

Oh! Where is the faith of this natural condition? Where is the real conviction of it? Sure[ly] there is but little real believing of this when:

1. There are so many that never so much as suspect themselves or question either their state or condition at one time or other—never once imagine that their blinded hearts may deceive them, never once dream of a possibility of mistaking and of dying with a lie in their right hand.

2. And so many that are not lamenting and bewailing this their condition nor crying out and complaining of a false, deceitful, and desperately wicked heart.

3. And so few that are indeed humbled under the sense of this and made therefore to walk more watchfully and soberly with an eye always on their treacherous and deceiving hearts.

4. And so few, crying for help from God against this deceitful adversary, through daily experience of the atheism, hypocrisy, ignorance, misconceptions of God and of His ways and deceitfulness of our hearts, might sufficiently put it out of doubt with us.

Next, how miserable must their condition be who are yet strangers to Christ. For they are living in darkness, lying in darkness, walking in darkness, indeed, very darkness itself, a mass of error, mistakes, ignorance, and misconceptions of all things that are good, and still wandering out of the way.

V. Should not this preach out to and convince us all of a necessity of having more acquaintance with truth, with Jesus Christ, who is the truth, that we may be delivered from this woeful and wretched condition—for truth only can set us free from this.

All Other Ways Are False Ways

The second general thing to be noticed here is that all other ways and courses which we can take or follow that we may obtain life, beside[s] Christ, are but lies, false and deceitful ways—there is no truth in them. For He only is the truth. No other whatever can bear this epithet, for:

1. He only can satisfy the soul in all points otherways. Whatever we can imagine and dream can yield no true satisfaction in this matter.

2. He only can secure the soul from destructive ruinous courses which will undo the soul. All other ways will fail here. None of them can give the least security to the soul that they will not bring him, in end, to destruction and everlasting perdition.

3. He only can bring the soul safe through all opposition and difficulties in the way. No other way can do this but will leave us in the mire before ever we come to the end of our journey.

4. He will not deceive nor disappoint the soul. All other ways in end will prove treacherous and give the traveler a doleful and sad disappointment.

Oh, what a warning should this be to us all to take heed that we embrace not a lie instead of Him who is the truth and sit not down with a shadow instead of the substance. How ready are we to put other things in His place? But whatever it be that gets His room in the soul, though good and worthy in itself, will prove a lie—even (1) all our outward holiness and duties; indeed, (2) all our experiences and great attainments; indeed, (3) all our gifts and endowments; indeed, (4) our very graces. None of these are Christ's. And if we place that hope and confidence in them which we should place on Him, they will not prove the truth to us—He alone is the truth.

How sure then should we labor to be that we do not die with a lie in our right hand. And how carefully should we guard against the trusting in or leaning to anything that is not Christ, and whole Christ, and only Christ, and Christ as offered in the gospel—seeing this way is only the truth, and no other way will be found so in end, though at present we may find in it:

1. Some inward peace and quietness of heart, as if all were right.
2. Some satisfaction of mind, things being right as we apprehend, but falsely, through the deceitfulness of the heart.
3. Something like assurance and confidence that all will be right with us.
4. And hope founded on this, which may help to ride through some storms and yet fail us at length.

Christ Is the Truth for Us
The third general is this: Christ Jesus is not only the truth in Himself but also in reference to us. The scope of the place clears this. As He is the way and the life for our use, so He is

the truth, not only as God equal with the Father but also as mediator and our Immanuel.

As God, He is (1) essentially truth, being God equal with the Father in power and glory. (2) In respect of veracity, He is the God of truth (Deut. 32:4), faithful in all His sayings (Ps. 31:5), keeping truth forever (Ps. 146:6). (3) He is the fountain and springhead of all created truth, for He is the first truth.

As mediator and in reference to us, He is "full of grace and truth" (John 1:14). He received not the Spirit in measure (3:34). And this Spirit is a spirit of truth. But of this more when we come to show more particularly how and in what respects He is called the truth as mediator.

Christ Is the Truth

The fourth general which is here observable is that He is not only called "truth" but "the truth," as He is the way and the life—and not only true but truth in the abstract, which says:

1. That He is every way truth, however we consider Him, as God or as mediator.

2. That all truth is in Him. All truth of salvation for us is to be found in Him.

3. That all that is in Him is truth. His natures, offices, performances, words, works, etc.—all are true.

4. That He is pure and unmixed truth—no lie in Him, no error or mistake there.

5. That truth in Him is in its perfection and excellency. In the truest of men it is very imperfect.

Oh what an excellent one must He be! How completely fitted and furnished for us! Oh! If our souls could love Him and close with Him and rest on Him as all-sufficient!

CHAPTER 11

More Particularly in What Respect Christ Is Called the Truth

*B*ut for further explaining of this matter, we would see more particularly in what respects it is that He is called the truth. And this will make way to our use-making of Him. So:

I. He is the truth in opposition to the shadows and types of Him under the law. Hence, as "the law," the whole Levitical and typical dispensation, came "by Moses, but grace and truth came by Jesus Christ" (John 1:17). They were all shadows of Him, and He is the substance and body of them all (Col. 2:17). And this is true in these respects:

1. All these shadows and types pointed at Him and directed, as with a finger, the Israelites, who were under that dispensation, to look to Christ, the promised Messiah, and to rest and to lay all their weight on Him. So that the law was a shadow of good things to come (Col. 2:17; Heb. 10:1).

2. They all terminate in Him, He putting an end by His coming and performing His work to all those types which only related to Him and to what He was to do. The body being come, there is no more need of the

shadow and the thing typified existing. There is no more need or use of the type.

3. They are all fulfilled in Him. He answers them all fully so that whatever was shadowed forth by them is completely to be found in Him. This the apostle in his epistle to the Hebrews abundantly evinces. And Paul to the Colossians tells us [that] we are complete in Him and therefore need no more follow the shadows.

II. He is the truth in reference to the prophecies of old—all which did principally point at Him and His concernments, His person, nature, offices, work, kingdom, etc. And whatever was foretold in these prophecies is perfectly fulfilled in Him or done by Him or will in due time be effectuated by Him. He is that great prophet spoken of (Deut 18:15, 18–19). So said the Jews themselves (John 6:14). All the prophets from Samuel spoke of Him and of His days (Acts 3:22–24). "To him gave all the prophets witness" (10:43). And whatever they prophesied or witnessed of Him was or is in due time to be fulfilled in Him. Hence, we find the evangelists and apostles frequently applying the sayings and prophecies of the Old Testament to Him. And Luke (4:18) himself said the prophecy of Isaiah 61:1, etc., was fulfilled in Him (see 1 Peter 10:11–12). And Himself expounded to the two disciples going to Emmaus in all the Scriptures, beginning at Moses and all the prophets, all the things concerning Himself (Luke 24:27). And thus is He the truth of all the prophecies.

III. He is the truth in reference to His undertaking with the Father in that glorious covenant of redemption. For whatever the Father laid on Him to do, that He did fully and faithfully. He was to bear our griefs, to carry our sorrows—and that He did. He was to be wounded for our transgressions and bruised for our iniquities. The chastisement of our peace was on Him, and by His stripes we were to be healed (Isa. 53:5)—and so it was (Rom. 4:25; 1 Cor. 15:3; 1 Peter 2:23). His soul was to be made an offering for sin (Isa. 53:10)—and so it was; for He offered up Himself a sacrifice for sin. Indeed, all that He was to do by virtue of that covenant He did it perfectly, so as He cried out while hanging on the cross, "It is finished" (John 19:30). And in His prayer (John 17), He told His Father (v. 4) that He had glorified Him on earth and had finished the work which He gave Him to do, so that the Father was well pleased with Him (Matt. 3:17; 13:18; 17:5; Mark 1:11; Luke 3:22).

IV. He is the truth in respect of His offices which He took on Him for our good. For all the duties of these offices which He was to do and what remains to be done, He will perfect in due time. Did He take on Him the office of a prophet? He did fully execute the same in revealing mediately and immediately the whole counsel of God (John 1:18; 15:15; Acts 20:32; Eph. 4:11–13; Heb. 1:2; 1 Peter 1:10–12). Did He take on Him the office of a priest? So did He fulfill the same, offering up Himself an expiatory sacrifice to God (Heb. 2:17; 9:28) and becoming a priest and living forever to make intercession for us (7:25). And did He take on the office and function of a king? So does He execute the same, calling a people to Himself out of the world by His word and Spirit (Ps. 110:3; Isa. 55:4–5; Acts 15:14–16), erecting a visible church, a company of visible professors to profess and declare His name, which as His kingdom He rules with His own officers, laws and penalties, or censures—so that the government is on His shoulders (Isa. 9:6–7), who is the head of the body, the church (Eph. 1:22–23; Col. 1:18). And this His kingdom He rules in a visible manner by His own officers, etc. (Isa. 33:22; Matt. 18:17–18; 1 Cor. 5:4–5; 12:28; Eph. 4:11–12). And further, He executes this office by effectually calling the elect, giving them grace (Acts 5:3); rewarding the obedient (Rev. 2:10; 22:12); chastising the disobedient (3:19); bringing His own home at length through all their temptations [and] afflictions; and overcoming all their enemies (Psalm 110; 1 Cor. 15:25). And at length He will do the part of a king, when He will judge [the] quick and dead at the last day (Acts 17:31; 2 Thess. 1:8–9; 2 Tim. 4:1).

V. He is the truth in this regard: that He fully answers all the titles and names which He had got. As He was called Jesus, so did He save His people from their sins (Matt. 1:21). As He was called Christ, so was He anointed with the Spirit without measure (Ps. 45:7; John 3:34) and separated for His work and endued with all power for that effect (Job 6:27; Matt. 28:18–20) and established to be a prophet (Luke 4:18, 21; Acts 3:21–22), a priest (Heb. 4:14–15; 5:5–7), and a king (Ps. 2:6; Isa. 9:6–7; Matt. 21:5; Phil. 2:8–11). Was He called "Immanuel" (Isa. 7:14)? So was He indeed God with us, being God and man in one person forever. Was He called "Wonderful" (9:6)? So was He indeed in His two distinct natures in one person, at which the angels may wonder (Eph. 3:10–11; 1 Tim. 3:16; 1 Peter 1:12). Was He called "Counselor"? So was He indeed, coming out from the Father's bosom with the whole counsel of God concerning our salvation (John 1:14, 18; 3:13; 5:20; 15:15). Was He called "the mighty God"? So was He indeed (Ps. 45:6; 83:18; 110:1; Jer. 23:6; 33:16; Mal. 3:1; Matt. 11:10; 22:44; Luke 1:76; John 1:1; 5:20; 14:1; Rom. 9:5; Titus 2:13; Heb. 1:8, 13). Was He called the "everlasting Father"? So is He the Father of eternity, being (as some interpret the word) the author of eternal life, which He gives to all that believe in Him (John 6:39–40, 47, 51; 8:51; 10:28; 11:25–26; Heb. 5:9; 7:25). Was He called the "Prince of Peace"? So is He the Prince of Peace indeed, being our peace (Mic. 5:5; Eph. 2:14), making up peace between God and us (Isa. 53:5, 19; Eph. 2:17; Col. 1:20). Hence His gospel is the gospel of peace; and His ministers, ambassadors of peace (Isa. 52:7; Rom. 10:15; 2 Cor. 5:19–20; Eph. 6:15). And He gives peace to all His (Zech. 9:10; John 14:27; 17:33; Rom. 5:1; 8:16; 14:17; 2 Thess. 3:17). Was He called the "Lord our Righteousness" (Jer. 23:6)? So is He the same indeed, bringing in everlasting righteousness (Dan. 9:24) and being made of God to us righteousness (1 Cor. 1:30) and making us righteous (2 Cor. 5:21).

VI. He is the truth in reference to the promises, which:

1. Center all in Him and lead to Him as the great promise.

2. Are founded all on Him, who is the only mediator of the covenant of promises.

3. Are confirmed all by Him and made yea and amen in Him (1:20). He confirmed the promises made to the fathers (Rev. 15:8).

4. Are all dispensed and given out by Him, who is the executor of His own testament and the great dispensator of all that we need—so that what we ask of the Father, He gives it Himself (John 14:13–14).

VII. He is the truth in that He fully answers all the hopes and expectations of His people. He will not be found a liar to them, whatever Satan may suggest to them or a misbelieving heart may prompt them to conceive and their jealousy may make them apprehend and whatever His dispensations may now seem to say. In [the] end, they will all find that He is the truth, fully satisfying all their desires and granting all that ever they could hope for or expect from Him. They will at length be satisfied with His likeness (Ps. 17:15), indeed, abundantly satisfied with the fatness of His house (36:8) and with His goodness (65:4), and that as with marrow and fatness (63:5). One sight of His glory will fully satisfy and cause them to cry out, "Enough!" Jeremiah is now saying, as once he did in the bitterness of his soul through the power of corruption and temptation (15:18), "Wilt thou be altogether unto me as a liar, and as waters that fail?"—for:

VIII. He is the truth in opposition to all other ways of salvation:

1. There is no salvation now by the law of works, that covenant being once broken cannot anymore save. The law cannot now do it in that it is weak through the flesh (Rom. 8:3).

2. There is no salvation now by the law of Moses without Christ. Hence Israel, which followed after the law of righteousness, did not attain to the law of righteousness because they sought it not by faith but as it were by the works of the law (9:31–32). They went about to establish their own righteousness and did not submit themselves to the righteousness of God (10:3).

3. There is no salvation by anything mixed in with Christ, as the apostle fully clears in his epistle to the Galatians.

4. There is no salvation by any other way or medium which man can invent or fall on, of which there are not a few, as we showed above—for there is not another name given under heaven by which we can be saved but the name of Jesus (Acts 4:12). No religion will save but this. So that He is the true salvation, and He only is the true salvation. And He is the sure and safe salvation. Such as make use of Him will not be mistaken nor disappointed (Isa. 35:8).

IX. He is the truth in respect of His leading and guiding His people in the truth. Hence He is called a teacher from God (John 3:2) and one that teaches the way of God in truth (Matt. 22:16), [and] a prophet mighty in deed and word (Luke 24:19). And in this respect He is the truth on several accounts:

1. Of His personal teaching. God spoke by Him (Heb. 1:2). He revealed the Father's mind (Matt. 11:27; John 1:18).

2. Of His messengers sent by Him, as prophets of old [and] apostles and ministers of late, whom He sends forth to make disciples (Matt. 28:18) and to open the eyes of the blind (Acts 26:18).

3. Of His Word, which He has left as our rule and which is a sure word of prophecy, more sure than a voice from heaven (2 Peter 1:19).

4. Of His ordinances, which He has established as means to guide us in the way of truth.

5. Of His Spirit by which He makes the word clear (John 14:26). This Spirit is sent to teach all truth and to lead and guide us in all truth (17:13; 1 John 2:27) and sent by Him and by the Father in His name (John 14:26; 15:16; 16:14).

6. Of His dispensations of providence within us and without us, by which likewise He instructs in the way of truth.

X. He is the truth in respect of Him bearing witness to the truth. And this He does:

1. By Himself, who was given for a witness (Isa. 55:4) and came to bear witness to the truth (John 3:11; 18:37) and was a faithful witness (Rev. 1:5; 3:14).

2. By His ministers, who witness the truth of the gospel by publishing and proclaiming the same.

3. By His martyrs, who seal the truth with their blood and so bear witness to it (Acts 22:20; Rev. 2:13; 17:6).

4. By His Spirit, sealing the truth of grace in a believer and his interest in God through Christ and his right to all the benefits of the new covenant—"in whom also after that ye believed, ye were sealed with that holy Spirit of promise, which is the earnest of our inheritance" (Eph. 1:13–14).

XI. He is the truth in respect that He carries toward poor sinners in all things, according to the tenor of the gospel and the offers of it. He offers Himself to all freely and promises to put none away that come to Him. And this He does in truth, for no man can say that he had a sincere and true desire to come to Jesus and that He rejected him and would not look on him. He gives encouragement to all sinners to come that will be content to quit their sins and promises to upbraid none that come. And is there any that in their own experience can witness the contrary? He offers all freely, and did He ever reject any on the want of a price in their hand? Indeed, has not the cause of them getting no admittance been that they thought to commend themselves to Christ by their worth and would not take all freely for the glory of His grace? Let believers and others speak here out of their own experience in truth and in uprightness. And it will be found that He was and is the truth.

XII. He is the truth in that in all His dispensations in the gospel and in all His works and actions in and about His own people He is true and upright. All His offers, all His promises, all His dispensations are done in truth and uprightness. Indeed, all are done out of truth and uprightness of love, true tenderness and affection to them, whatever the corruption of jealousy and misbelief think and say to the contrary. He is the truth and so always the same—unchangeable in His love, whatever His dispensations seem to say. And the believer may rest assured of this: that His being the truth will be to him whatever His word holds him forth to be, and that constantly and unchangeably.

CHAPTER 12

Some General Uses from This Useful Truth That Christ Is the Truth

Having thus cleared up this truth, we should come to speak of the way of believers making use of Him as the truth in several cases in which they will stand in need of Him as the truth. But before we come to the particulars, we will first propose some general uses of this useful point:

The Woeful Condition of Unbelievers

First, this point of truth serves to discover to us the woeful condition of such as are strangers to Christ the truth. And oh, if it were believed! For:

I. They are not yet delivered from that dreadful plague of blindness, error, ignorance, mistakes under which all are by nature—a condition that if rightly seen would cause the soul [to] lie low in the dust.

II. Whatever course they take till they come to Christ, and while they remain in that condition, is a lie and a false, erroneous, and deceitful way. For still they are turning aside to lies (Ps. 40:4) and seeking after them (4:2).

III. Whatever hopes and confidence they may have that their way will carry them through, yet in [the] end they will be found to inherit lies (Jer. 16:19) and meet with the saddest disappointment that can be. For instead of the fellowship of God, Christ, angels, and glorified spirits, they will take up their lodging with devils and damned souls—and that because they have made no acquaintance with the way of truth. And the way in which they are is but a lie and a falsehood and so of necessity must deceive them.

IV. All their literal and speculative knowledge will not avail them so long as they are strangers to Him who is the truth. Their knowledge is but ignorance, because it is not a knowledge of Him who is the truth.

V. They have none to go to for help and light in the day of their darkness, confusion, and perplexity; for they are not reconciled to the truth, which alone can prove steadable[1] and comfortable in that day.

VI. They can do nothing to help themselves out of that state of darkness and ignorance. And whatever they do to help themselves will but increase their darkness and misery, because there is no truth there, and truth, even the truth alone, can dispel these clouds of error, mistakes, ignorance, etc.

The Blessed Condition of Believers
Secondly, hence we see the happy and blessed condition of believers who have embraced this truth and gotten their souls opened to Him who is the truth, for:

I. They are in part delivered from that mass of lies, mistakes, misapprehensions, errors, deceitfulness, and ignorance under which they lay formerly, and all the unregenerate do yet lie.

---

1 *Steadable*: serviceable.

And though they be not fully delivered from it, yet the day is coming when that will be. And the begun work of grace and truth in them is a pledge of this. And at present they have ground to believe that that evil will not again have dominion over them, they being now under grace and under the guidance of truth.

II. Even though they have many perplexing thoughts, doubts, and fears of their state and condition and think many a time that they will one day or other perish by the way, and all their hopes and confidence will vanish; yet having given up themselves to truth, and to the truth, they will not be disappointed in the end. The truth will land them safe on the other side. The truth will prove no lie.

III. They have a fast and steadable friend to go to in a day of darkness, clouds, doubts, when falsehood and lies are like[ly] to prevail, even the truth, who alone can help them in that day.

IV. Even though the knowledge they have of God and of the mysteries of the gospel be but small, yet that small measure being taught by Him who is the truth and flowing from truth will prove sanctifying and saving.

V. They have ground to hope for more freedom from errors and deceitful lies than others, for they have chosen the way of truth and given themselves up to the leading of truth.

Objection: But do not even such drink in and receive and plead for errors as well as others. And is it not sometime[s] found that they even live and die in some mistakes and errors?

Answer: I grant [1] the Lord may suffer even some of His own to fall into and to continue for some time in errors—indeed, and it may be all their days as to some errors—that by this all may learn to tremble and fear and to work out their salvation with fear and trembling. (2) Some may be tried by this (Dan. 11:35). (3) Others may break their neck of this. (4) To punish themselves for not making that use of truth and of the truth that they should have done. Yet we would consider these few things:

1. That there are many more unregenerate persons that fall into error.

2. If His people fall into error at any time, they do not always continue in that to the end. God for His own glory makes, sometime[s] or other, truth shine in on their soul, which discovers that mistake, and presently the grace of God in their soul makes them to abhor the same.

3. Or if some continue in it to their dying day, yet they repent of it by an implicit repentance, as they do of other unknown and unseen evils that lie in their soul—so that that error does not destroy their soul.

4. There are some gross errors which a regenerate soul cannot readily embrace; or, if through a mistake or the power of a temptation they do embrace them, yet they cannot heartily close with them, whatever for a time through corruption and pride they may seem outwardly to do. And that because the very daily exercise of grace will discover them, and so they will be found to be against their daily experience—as some opinions of the papists, Arminians, and Socinians, together with the abominable Quakers, which a gracious soul, when not carried away with the torrent of corruption and with the tempest of a temptation, cannot but observe to contradict the daily workings of grace in their soul and the motions of their sanctified soul in prayer and

other holy duties. And so such as they cannot but find to be false by their own experience.

The Reproof to the Wicked

Thirdly, here is ground of a sharp reproof of the wicked who continue in unbelief and:

I. Will not believe nor give any credit to His promises with which He seeks to allure poor souls to come to Him for life.

II. Nor will they believe His threatenings with which He uses to alarm souls and to urge them forward to their duty.

III. Nor will they believe and receive His offers as true.

IV. Nor will they believe that He is the true prophet, priest, and king that must save souls from hell and death. And therefore they will not give Him employment in His offices.

All which cannot but be a high provocation, for in effect it is to say that He is not the truth nor worthy to be believed. Let them consider this and see how they think He will take this off their hands. No man will take it well that another should either call or account him a liar. And can they think that Christ will take it well at their hands to be accounted by them a liar? What will they think to be challenged for this in the great day? Now, the truth is all unbelievers [are ones] as they make God a liar. (Oh horrid and abominable crime! Whose hair would not stand on end to hear this?) 1 John 5:10–11: "He that believeth not God hath made him a liar; because he believeth not the record that God gave of his Son. And this is the record, that God hath given to us eternal life, and this life is in his Son." So do they make the Son of God a liar in all His sayings, in all His offices, and in all His works. And they make the Holy Ghost a liar in not believing that truth that He has sealed as firm truth.

They make the covenant of suretyship between the Father and the Son a mere lie and a forgery. Oh dreadful! They make the word of truth a lie, and they make all the saints liars. And all the officers of Jesus Christ who declare this truth and the saints who believe it and rest on it—liars.

The Reproof to the Godly

Fourthly, hence is there ground of reproof to the godly in that:

I. They do not firmly enough believe His sayings neither His promises nor His threatenings, as appears too often on the one hand by their faintings and fears and, on the other hand, by their carelessness and loose walk.

II. They make not use of Him in all cases as they ought. His offices lie by and are not improved. Nor is He gone to as the truth in cases requiring His help as the truth—that is, in cases of darkness, doubtings, confusion, ignorance of their case and condition, and the like.

III. They do not approach to Him nor to God through Him heartily and cordially as the very truth and true way.

IV. Nor do they rest with confidence on Him in all difficulties as being the truth that will not fail them nor disappoint them.

V. Nor do they rejoice in Him as satisfied with Him who is the truth in the want of all other things.

The Duties in Response

Fifthly, the right consideration of this truth should keep us in mind of several great duties, such as these:

I. Of pitying those places where this truth is not heard of, as among Turks and heathens; or where it is darkened with superstition and men's inventions, as among papists; or where it has been clearly shining but now is darkened, as in some churches now under the prevailing power of corruption; or, lastly, where it is not received in its power and luster, as, alas, it is too little received in the best and purest churches.

II. Of being thankful to Him for making this truth known in the world and particularly in the place where we were born or had our abode—and yet more for that He has determined our hearts to a believing of this truth in some weak measure, to an embracing of it and to a giving of ourselves up to be led, ruled, and guided by this.

III. Of esteeming highly of every piece of truth for His sake who is the truth, studying it for His sake, loving it for His sake, holding it fast for His sake, witnessing to it, as we are called, for His sake. We should buy the truth and not sell it (Prov. 23:23). And we should plead for it and be valiant for it (Isa. 59:4, 14; Jer. 7:28; 9:3).

IV. Of taking part with Him and His cause in all hazards, for truth is always on His side. And truth will prevail at length.

V. Of giving Him employment in our doubts and difficulties, whether:

1. They be about some controverted points of truth which come to be debated or to trouble the church.

2. Or about our own estate and condition quarreled at by Satan or questioned by the false heart.

3. Or about our carriage in our daily walk.

In all these and the like, we should be employing truth that we may be led in truth and taught by truth to walk in sure paths.

VI. Of carrying in all things before Him as true, for He is truth, and the truth, and so cannot be deceived. And therefore we should walk before Him in sincerity and singleness of heart, without guile, hypocrisy, or falsehood, that we may look like children of the truth, and of the day, and of light, and children that will not lie or dissemble (Isa. 63:8)—not like these that lied to Him (Ps. 78:38; Isa. 59:13).

VII. Of taking Him only for our guide to heaven by denying our own wit, skill, and understanding and looking to and resting on Him who alone is the truth, and so acknowledging Him in all our ways, depending on Him for light and counsel, for singleness of heart, humility, diligence, and truth in the inward parts.

VIII. Of giving up ourselves daily to Him and His guidance and denying our own wills, humors, parties, or opinions; for He alone is truth and can only guide us aright. And for this cause, we would acquaint ourselves well with the Word, which is our rule, and seek after the Spirit, whom Christ has promised to lead us into all truth.

The Inducement to Lay Hold of Christ
Sixthly, should not this be a strong inducement to all of us to lay hold on and grip to Him who is the truth and only the truth?—seeing:

I. All other ways which we can take will prove a lie to us in the end.

II. He is substance and no shadow, and all that love Him will inherit substance—for He will fill all their treasures (Prov. 8:21).

III. Such as embrace Him will not wander nor be misled, for His "mouth shall speak truth; and wickedness is an abomination to [his] lips" (v. 7). "All the words of [his] mouth are in righteousness; there is nothing froward or perverse in them" (v. 8). He is wisdom and dwells with prudence and finds out "knowledge of witty inventions" (v. 12). Counsel is His and sound wisdom; He has understanding and strength (v. 14).

IV. He will make good all His promises in due time and give a subsistence and a being to them all—for He is the truth, and the truth must stand to His promises and fulfill them all.

V. He will never, nay, never leave His people, nor forsake them (Heb. 13:5). He is truth and cannot deceive. He cannot forsake nor disappoint. He is a spring of water, whose waters fail not (Isa. 58:11). Therefore, they cannot be disappointed in the end and perish who trust to Him.

VI. The truth will make them free (John 8:32, 36) and so deliver them from their state of sin and misery in which they lay as captives and from that spiritual bondage and slavery under which they were held.

The Consolation to Believers
Seventhly, this to believers may be a spring of consolation in many cases, as:

I. When error and wickedness seem to prosper and prevail. For though it prevail for a time, yet truth will be victorious at length, and the truth will overcome all. He is truth and will plead for truth.

II. When friends, acquaintances, relations fail them, and father and mother forsake them, truth will take them up. He who is the truth will answer His name and never deceive, never forsake.

III. When riches, honors, pleasures, or what else their heart has being going out after prove like summer brooks, for the truth will be the same to them in all generations. There is no shadow of turning with Him. The truth is always truth and true.

IV. When we fear that either ourselves or others will fall away in a day of trial and turn from the truth. Though all men prove liars and deceivers, truth will abide the same and stand out all the blasts of opposition.

V. When unbelief would make us question the truth of the promises, the faith of Him being truth itself and the truth, even truth in the abstract, would shame unbelief out of countenance. Will truth fail? Will not the truth be true? What a contradiction were that?

VI. When we know not how to answer the objections of Satan and of a false treacherous heart, for truth can easily answer all cavils. And He who is the truth can repel all objections against truth. Truth is impregnable and can stand against all.

VII. When we cannot know nor discover the wiles and subtlety of Satan. Truth can discover the depths of Satan and make the poor soul more acquaint[ed] with them. So that they will not anymore be ignorant of his devices who look to Him.

VIII. When the thoughts of the deceitfulness of our hearts trouble us, the depth of which we cannot search. This then may comfort us: that truth may search the heart and the reins (Jer. 17:9–10).

IX. When we cannot tell what our disease and distemper is and so cannot seek suitable remedies or help from God. Oh what a comfort is it to know and believe that He is the truth with whom we have to do, and so [He] knows our distemper perfectly and all its causes and symptoms. Truth cannot be at a stand in discerning our disease, so nor can He be ignorant of the fittest and only safest cures.

X. When we know not what to ask in prayer as not knowing what is best for us, it is a comfort to remember that we have to do with the truth, who is perfectly acquainted with all that and knows what is best.

XI. When we know not how to answer the calumnies of adversaries, it is comfortable to know that He is the truth that will hear truth when men will not and will own and stand for the truth when enemies do what they can to darken an honest man's good cause. It is comfortable to know we have the truth to appeal to, as David had (Ps. 7:17).

XII. When we think on our own covenant breaking and dealing deceitfully with God, it is comfortable to remember that, though we and all men be liars and deal deceitfully with Him, yet He is the truth and will keep covenant forever. He will not, He cannot deny Himself (2 Tim. 2:13).

The Prevailing of Christ's Cause

Eighthly, hence we may certainly conclude that truth, which is Christ's cause, will at length prevail. For He is truth, indeed, the truth, and so abides truth. Therefore must He prevail, and all the mouths of liars must be stopped. So then let us remain persuaded that truth at length will be victorious and that the cause of Christ will have the victory—[even] though:

I. The enemies of truth and the cause of Christ be multiplied, and many there be that rise up against it.

II. These enemies should prosper, and that for a long time, and carry on their course of error and wickedness with a high hand.

III. There should be few found to befriend truth and to own it in an evil day.

IV. Indeed, many of those that did sometime[s] own it and plead for it should at length turn their backs on it, as did Demas.

V. And such as continue constant and faithful be loaded with reproaches and pressed under with sore persecution for adhering to truth and owning constantly the good cause.

VI. Indeed, though all things in providence should seem to say that truth will not rise again, but seem, on the contrary, to conspire against the same.

The Need to Stay Close to the Truth
Ninthly, may we not hence read what should be our way and course in a time when a spirit of error is gone abroad and many are carried off their feet with it, or when we are doubtful what to do and what side of the dispute to take? Oh then is the fit time for us to employ truth, to live near to Him who is the truth, to wait on Him and hang on Him, with singleness of heart.

Objection: But many even of His own people do err and step aside.

Answer: That is true. But yet (1) that will be no excuse to you; indeed, (2) that should make you fear and tremble more; (3) and it should press you to lie near to Christ and to wrestle more earnestly with Him for the Spirit of light and of truth and to depend more constantly and faithfully on Him with single-ness of heart and to give up all your soul and way to Him as the God of truth and as the truth, that you may be led into all truth.

The Need to Make Use of Christ
Tenthly, this should stir us up to go to Him and make use of Him as the truth in all cases in which we may stand in need of truth's hand to help us. And for this cause we should mind these particulars:

I. We should live in the constant conviction of our ignorance, blindness, hypocrisy, readiness to mistake and err. This is clear and manifest and proved to be truth by daily experience. Yet how little is it believed that it is so with us? Do we see and believe the atheism of our hearts? Do we see and believe the hypocrisy of our hearts? Are we jealous of them as we ought to be? Oh that it were so! Let this then be more minded by us.

II. Let us live in the persuasion of this: that He only and nothing below Him will be able to clear our doubts, dispel our clouds, clear up our mistakes, send us light, and mani-fest truth to us—not our own study, pains, prayers, duties, learning, understanding, nor ministers, nor professors, and experienced Christians, and the like.

III. We should be daily giving up ourselves to Him as the truth in all the forementioned respects and receiving Him into our souls as such, that we may dwell and abide there. Then will the truth make us free. And if the Son make us free, we will be free indeed (John 8:36).

IV. There should be much single dependence on Him for light, instruction, direction, and guidance in all our exigencies.

V. In addition, there should be a waiting on Him with patience, giving Him liberty to take His own way and time, and a leaving of Him to it.

VI. We should by all means guard against such things as are hindrances and will prove obstacles to us in this matter, such as:

1. Prejudices against the truth. For then we will undervalue light and reject all the directions and instructions of the Spirit as not agreeing with our prejudicate opinion.

2. A willful turning away from truth, as these (2 Tim. 4:4; Titus 1:14).

3. Addictedness to our own judgments and opinions, which causes pertinaciousness, pride, and conceit, as thinking ourselves so wise as that we need no information. And this occasions a self-confidence.

4. Looking too much to and hanging too much on men, who are but instruments, crying them up as infallible and receiving without further examination all that they say—not like the Bereans (Acts 17). This is a great hindrance to the receiving of truth and very prejudicial.

5. A neglecting of the use of the means which God has appointed for this end.

6. Or a hanging too much on them and so misplacing them, giving them His room, etc.

7. Leaning too much to our own understanding, wit, and knowledge.

8. A resisting of the truth (2 Tim. 3:8).

These and the like hindrances should be guarded against, lest they mar our attaining to the knowledge of truth.

VII. There should be much of the exercise of prayer, for this is the main conduit and mean[s] through which light is conveyed into the soul. There should also be a serious and Christian reading and hearing of the Word, which is truth and the Word of truth and the Scripture of truth. And those duties should be gone about with (1) much self-denial; (2) with much singleness of heart; (3) with much humility; (4) with much willingness and readiness to be instructed; (5) with much seriousness and earnestness; and (6) with faith and dependence on God for His blessing and breathing.

VIII. We should beware of trusting to our own understandings or to the judgments of other men. Nor should we look to what suits most our own humors nor to what appears most specious and plausible, for that may deceive us.

IX. We should lie open to the influences and rays of light by exercising faith in earnest desires, as also patient waiting for and single looking to Him, minding His name and His relations, promises, and engagements, and the strengthening of our faith and confidence.

X. We should labor to keep fast whatever He teaches us by His word and Spirit and not prove leaking vessels. This the apostle exhorts to: "Therefore we ought to give the more earnest heed to the things which we have heard, lest at any time we should let them slip" (Heb. 2:1). Indeed, and we should be established in the truth (2 Peter 1:12).

XI. We should beware of resting on a form of the truth, as those did of whom we read (Rom. 2:20), and of holding the truth in unrighteousness, as those (1:18), and of disobeying it, as those mentioned in Romans 2:8 (see also Gal. 3:1; 5:7).

XII. But on the contrary, we should so receive truth as that it might rule and be master in us, captivate judgment, will, and affections, and break out into the practice. And this recommends several duties, such as:

1. To have the truth in us. While as, if we practice otherwise, "the truth is not in us" (1 John 1:8; 2:4).

2. To be of the truth, as belonging to its jurisdiction, power, and command (John 18:37; 1 John 3:19).

3. To do the truth by having true fellowship with Him (1 John 1:6) and "to walk in the truth" (Ps. 86:11; John 4; 2 John 4:3).

4. To have the loins girt with truth (Eph. 1:14).

5. To receive the love of the truth (2 Thess. 2:10).

6. To be instructed of Him, "as the truth is in Jesus" (Eph. 4:21).

7. To purify the soul in obeying the truth (1 Peter 2:22).

This will suffice for clearing up and applying in the general this excellent truth that Christ is the truth. We will now come and make some more particular use of this precious point by speaking to some particular cases (which we will instance in, by which the understanding Christian may be helped to understand how to carry and how to make use of Christ in other the like cases), in which Christ is to be made use of as the truth, and show how believers are to make use of Him in these cases as the truth.

CHAPTER 13

How to Make Use of Christ as the Truth for Growth in Knowledge

*I*t is a commanded duty that we grow in the knowledge of Jesus Christ (2 Peter 3:18) and the knowledge of Him being life eternal (John 17:3). And our measure of knowledge of Him here being but imperfect, for we know but in part, it cannot but be a useful duty and a desirable thing to be growing in this knowledge. This is to walk worthy of the Lord unto all pleasing, to be increasing in the knowledge of God (Col. 1:10). Knowledge must be added to virtue. And it lays a ground for other Christian virtues (2 Peter 1:5–6). In this knowledge we must not be barren (1:2). And this being so necessary, so desirable, so useful, and so advantageous a grace, the believer cannot but desire to have more and more of it, especially seeing it is a part of the image of God (Col. 3:10).

Now it is the truth that must teach them here, first and last. The light of the knowledge of the glory of God must be had in the face of Jesus Christ (2 Cor. 4:6). The question therefore is how we should make use of Jesus Christ for this end: that we may attain to more of this excellent knowledge.

Live in Constant Conviction

First, it is good to live in the constant conviction of a necessity of Him teaching us. And this takes in these particulars:

I. That we should be conscious of our ignorance, even when we know most or think we know most, remembering that the best knows but in part (1 Cor. 13:9). The more true knowledge we attain to, the more will we see and be convinced of our ignorance—because the more we know, the more will we discover of the vastness and incomprehensibility of that object which is proposed to our knowledge.

II. That we should remember how deceitful our hearts are and how ready they are to sit down on a shadow of knowledge, even where we know nothing as we ought to know (1 Cor. 8:2). And this will keep us jealous and watchful.

III. And to help forward our jealousy of our own hearts and watchfulness, we should remember that our hearts naturally are averse from any true and saving knowledge—whatever desire there be naturally after knowledge of hidden things out of curiosity and of things natural or of things spiritual, as natural, for the perfection of nature, as might be pretended, by which in effect those that increase knowledge, increase sorrow (Eccl. 1:18). Yet there is no inclination after spiritual and saving knowledge in us naturally, but an aversion of heart from it.

IV. That we should study and know the absolute necessity of this knowledge—how necessary it is for our Christian communion with God and Christian walk with others; how necessary for our right improving of dispensations, general and particular; what a noble ornament of a Christian it is and a necessary piece of the image of God which we have lost.

Be Convinced of Our Inadequacy

Secondly, on these grounds mentioned, we would also be convinced of this: that of ourselves and by all our natural parts, endowments, quickness, and sagacity, we cannot attain to this saving knowledge which is a special and saving grace and so must be wrought in the soul by a divine hand, even the mighty power of God. By our private study and reading, we may attain to a literal, heady, and speculative knowledge that will puff us up (1 Cor. 8:1). But by this will we never attain to this knowledge which is spiritual, hearty, and practical, and so saving. We must have the anointing here, which teaches us all things (1 John 2:27). And of this we should be persuaded, that we may look to a higher hand for light and instruction.

See Christ's Fitness
Thirdly, there should be an eyeing of Christ's furniture and fitness for this work of teaching of us, namely:

I. An eyeing of Him as the substantial wisdom of the Father (Proverbs 8).

II. An eyeing of Him as one come out of the bosom of the Father (John 1:18) and so sufficiently enabled to acquaint us with the mysteries of God for salvation.

III. An eyeing of Him as mediator, fully endued with all necessaries for this piece of His work, and so having received the Spirit without measure for this end (John 3:34), and as having hid in Him all the treasures of wisdom and knowledge (Col. 2:3), and as having all fullness dwelling in Him (1:19; and also Isa. 11:2; 61:1–2).

IV. An eyeing of Him as having power to send the Spirit, that anointing that teaches us all things and is truth and is no lie (1 John 2:20–27)—not only by way of intercession and entreaty, begging it of the Father (John 15:16–17), but also authoritatively, as conjunct with the Father. The Father sends Him in

Christ's name (14:26), and Christ sends Him from the Father (15:26). And this Spirit of truth which guides into all truth will receive of Christ's [truth] and show it to us (16:13–15).

See Christ's Readiness

Fourthly, there should be an eyeing of Christ's readiness, willingness, and engagement to help in this case. And this will encourage the soul to go forward. And for this cause we would remember these things:

I. That He stands obliged to help us with instruction by virtue of His office as a prophet, a witness, a leader, and a commander (Isa. 55:4).

II. That He is commissioned of the Father for this end and so is the Father's servant and is given for "a light to the Gentiles" (Isa. 42:6; 49:6). And the Father is said to speak by Him or in Him (Heb. 1:1).

III. That He received His gifts and qualifications for this end and purpose: that He might give out and dispense to His members according to their necessity, as is clear from Psalm 68:18, compared with Ephesians 4:8. What He is said to have received in the one place, He is said to have given in the other.

IV. That He has begun this work already by His Spirit in His followers and therefore stands engaged to see it perfected—for all His works are perfect works.

V. That He has a love to His scholars and a desire to have them all thriving and making progress in knowledge—this being His glory who is their master and teacher.

VI. That He laid down ways and means and a constant course for instructing of His people, for:

1. He has given His Word and settled and established ordinances for this end.

2. He has established a ministry for instructing His people (Eph. 4:8–13).

3. He has gifted persons for this work of the ministry (1 Cor. 12:4–11).

4. He makes these officers in the faithful administration of their function and through His blessing and Spirit makes their work prosperous and effectual in His own, as He sees fit.

See the Promise of the Covenant
Fifthly, there should be an eyeing of the promises of the covenant of grace made for this end, whether general or particular or both—such as those which we have (Isa. 2:9): "The earth shall be filled with the knowledge of the Lord," or of "the glory of the Lord, as the waters cover the sea" (Hab. 2:14); and that "the heart also of the rash shall understand knowledge, etc." (Isa. 32:4); and, "They shall all know me" (Jer. 31:34).

Use the Means of Knowledge
Sixthly, there should be a constant, diligent, serious, and single using of the means of knowledge with a faithful dependence on Christ by faith, gripping to Him in His relations, offices, engagements, and promises, and waiting on His breathing in hope and patience (Ps. 25:5).

Guard against All Obstructions
Seventhly, there should be a guarding against everything that may obstruct this work and grieve Him in it. And therefore we would beware:

1. To undervalue and have a little esteem of knowledge, for this will grieve Him and (to speak so) put Him from work.
2. To misimprove any measure of knowledge He gives.
3. To weary of the means and ordinances by which He uses to convey knowledge into the soul.
4. To limit the Holy One of Israel to this or that mean[s] to this or that time or to this or that measure, who should have a latitude as to all these.
5. To despise the day of small things because we get not more.
6. To be too curious in seeking after the knowledge of hidden mysteries, the knowledge of which is not so necessary.
7. To lean too much to and to depend too much on the ordinances or instruments, as if all or anything could come from them.

Improve Any Measure of Knowledge
Eighthly, there should be a right improving of any measure of knowledge we get to His glory and to the edification of others, with humility and thankfulness, and so a putting of that talent in use to gain more to His glory. Whatever measure of knowledge we get, we should in all haste put it into practice and set it to work. So will it increase and engage Him to give more.

Be Open to Christ's Instructions

Ninthly, there should be a lying open to Christ's instructions and to the shinings of the Spirit of light and of truth and a ready receiving of what measure He is pleased to grant or infuse—which includes those duties:

1. A serious and earnest hungering and thirsting after more spiritual knowledge.

2. A diligent use of every approve[d] mean[s] for this end.

3. A going about the means with much self-denial, spirituality, singleness of heart, and sincerity, looking to and depending on Him who must breathe on the means and make them useful.

4. A greedy receiving, drinking in, and treasuring up in the soul what is gotten.

5. A guarding against selfish and bye-ends, with a single eyeing of His glory.

6. A guarding against pride in the heart and a studying of humility and meekness, for the "meek will he guide in judgment: and the meek will he teach his way" (Ps. 25:9).

7. A putting of the heart or understanding in His hand, together with the truth that is heard and received, that He may write the truth and cause the heart [to] receive the impression of the truth.

Place Faith in Him

Tenthly, there should be a rolling of the whole matter by faith on Him as the only teacher, a putting of the ignorant, blockish, averse, and perverse heart into His hand, that He may frame it to His own mind, and a leaving of it there, till He by the Spirit write in it what He thinks meet, to His own glory and our good.

And sure[ly] were this way followed, growth in knowledge would not be so rare a thing as it is.

Cautions
For further direction and caution in this matter, the believer would take notice of these particulars:

I. That he should not sit down on any measure of knowledge he has attained to or can attain to here, as if he had enough and should labor for no more. But he should still be minding his duty of seeking and pressing for more.

II. Whenever he is about any mean[s] of knowledge such as preaching, reading, conference, etc., his heart should be only on Christ. He should be hanging on His lips for a word of instruction. And with greediness, looking for a word from His mouth, he should be sending many posts to heaven, many ejaculatory desires for light and understanding, and that with singleness and sincerity and not for base ends or out of hypocrisy.

III. Let him not think that there is no growth in knowledge, because possibly he perceives it not or is not satisfied as to the measure of it—indeed, though possibly he perceive more ignorance than ever he did before. If he grow in the knowledge of his own ignorance, it is a growth of knowledge not to be despised. And in a manner, what can we else know of God but that He far transcends all our knowledge and that He is an incomprehensible one in all His ways.

IV. Let him not think that there is no growth in knowledge because he perceives not a growth in the knowledge of such or such a particular which he desires most. For if there be a truth in the knowledge of other particulars necessary to be known, there is no reason to complain. If one grow not, as he supposes, in the knowledge of God and of the mysteries of the gospel, yet if he grow in the discovery of the treachery and wickedness of his own heart, he cannot say that he grows not in knowledge.

V. Let him not measure his growth in knowledge by his growth in the faculty of speaking and discoursing of such or such points of religion. Many measure their knowledge by their tongue and think they know little because they can express little. And so they think they attain to no increase or growth in knowledge because they perceive no increase or growth in this faculty of discoursing and talking of such or such points of truth. It is safer to measure their knowledge by the impression that the truth has on their spirits and the effects of it on all their carriage than by their ability and skill to talk and dispute of it.

VI. Let them beware to imagine that they will be able to search out the Almighty to perfection: "Canst thou" said Zophar (Job. 11:7–9), "by searching find out God? canst thou find out the Almighty unto perfection? It is as high as heaven; what canst thou do? deeper than hell; what canst thou know? The measure thereof is longer than the earth, and broader than the sea." Or that they will be able ever to win to the bottom of their own false, deceitful heart, which, as Jeremiah says, "is deceitful above all things, and desperately wicked: who can know it?" (17:9), and which it is God's prerogative alone to search and try (v. 10). Neither let them think, so long as they are here, to win to an exact and perfect knowledge of the mysteries of God in which is the manifold wisdom of God (Eph. 3:10), which very principalities and powers in heavenly places are learning, and which the angels are poring and looking into with desire (1 Peter 1:12). There is no perfection in knowledge to be had here, for here the best but knows in part and prophesies in part (1 Cor. 13:4).

VII. Let them not think that everyone will have the same measure of knowledge. Everyone has not the like use for it or the like capacity for it. There is a measure proportioned to everyone. They should not then complain because they have not such a measure of knowledge as they perceive in some others. It may be the Lord has some harder piece of service which calls for more knowledge to put others to. Let everyone then mind his duty faithfully and conscientiously, and let him not quarrel with God that he attains not to such a measure of knowledge as he sees others attain to.

VIII. Neither let them think that the same measure is required of all. For more is required of some by reason of their office and charge in the house of God, being called to teach and instruct others. And so more is required of such as have larger capacities and a better faculty of understanding than others, who naturally are but of a narrow reach and of a shallow capacity. More also is required of such as live under plain, powerful, and lively ordinances and under a more powerful and spiritual dispensation of the grace of God than of others that want such advantages. So likewise, more is required of old Christians than of new beginners. Old men, of much and long experience, should know more than such as are but babes in Christ and but of yesterday.

IX. Let their desires run out after that knowledge, not which puffs up—for there is a knowledge which puffs up (1 Cor.

8:1)—but which humbles and drives the soul farther from itself and nearer to Christ.

X. They should carefully distinguish between the gift of knowledge and the grace of knowledge. That ordinarily puffs up; this humbles. That brings not the soul to Jesus; this does. That is but a form (Rom. 2:20) and does not retain God (1:28); this is a real thing, laying hold on God and holding Him fast, having the fear of the Lord for its principle—for this fear of the Lord is the beginning of wisdom (Job. 28:28; Ps. 111:10; Prov. 1:7; 9:10). That lies most in the head and vents most in discourses, words, indeed, and sometimes vanishes into vain notions. But this goes down to the heart and lodges there and appears in the man's walk and conversation. As these two would be distinguished, so the one would not be measured by the other.

XI. When they do not profit, indeed, let them beware of quarrelling with Christ or of blaming Him in any manner of way. But let them lay the blame of their shortcoming on themselves for not making more use of Him by faith and single dependence on Him. It is true, none will be so bold as in words to quarrel with or blame Him. Yet the heart is deceitful and tacitly may raise and foment such thoughts of Him and His dispensations as can pass under no other notion than a quarrelling with Him. Now these would be guarded against.

XII. Beware of urging for or expecting immediate revelation or extraordinary manifestations. For we should not tempt the Lord nor set limits to Him. Neither should we prescribe means and ways to Him. We must be satisfied with the ordinary means which He has appointed and wait at wisdom's doors with our ears nailed to His posts.

XIII. Whatever point of truth they learn or whatever measure of knowledge they get, they would do well to give that back again to Christ to keep for them against a time of need and wait on Him for grace to improve it for His glory.

XIV. Let them beware of minding things too high (Ps. 131:1). It is better to fear and to stand in awe and to seek to lay the foundations well to get the saving knowledge of things necessary to salvation. This will yield most peace and satisfaction.

CHAPTER 14

_____

How to Make Use of Christ as Truth for Comfort When Truth Is Oppressed and Borne Down

There is another difficulty in which believing souls will stand in need of Christ as the truth to help them. And that is when His work is overturned, His cause borne down, truth condemned, and enemies in their opposition to His work prospering in all their wicked attempts. This is a very trying dispensation, as we see it was to the holy penman of Psalm 73, for it made him to stagger so that his feet were almost gone and his steps had well nigh slipped. Indeed, he was almost repenting of his being a godly person, saying, "Verily I have cleansed my heart in vain, and washed my hands in innocency" (v. 13). It was something like this which made Jeremiah say, "When I would comfort myself against sorrow, my heart is faint in me" (8:18). The harvest was past, and the summer was ended, and yet they were not saved (v. 20). And they looked for peace, but no good came; and for a time of health, but behold trouble (v. 15)—and this was fainting and vexatious. And what made Baruch, Jeremiah's faithful companion in tribulation, say, "Woe is me now! for the LORD hath added grief to my sorrow; I fainted in my sighing, and I find no rest" (45:3), but this: that all things were turning upside down. God was breaking down that which He had built and plucking up that which He had planted. Tribulation and suffering for a good cause is even fainting to some, as the apostle hints (Eph. 3:13) when he says, wherefore, "I desire that ye faint not at my tribulation for you." And that which evinces the danger of this dispensation is the fainting and backsliding of many in such a time of trial as sad experience too often clears.

Now the believer's stay in this case must be the Rock of Ages, Jesus the truth. It is He alone who can keep straight and honest in such a reeling time. So that a sight of Christ as the truth in reference to the carrying on of truth in the earth and advancing His cause and work will be the only support of a soul shaken by such a piece of trial.

How to Make Use of Christ in Difficult Times

But the question is, How should believers make use of Christ in such a time to the end they may be kept from fainting and succumbing in such a storm? To which I answer that the faith and consideration of these particulars would help to establishment:

I. That Christ in all this great work of redemption and in every piece of it is the Father's servant. So is He frequently called His "servant" (Isa. 42:1; 49:3, 5–6; 52:13; 53:11; Zech. 3:8). And therefore this work is a work [e]ntrusted to Him, and He stands engaged as a servant to be faithful to His trust. Moreover, add to this that He has a commission to perfect that work. And we need not doubt, but He who is the truth will be true to His trust. "Him hath God the Father sealed" (John 6:27). And He often tells us Himself that He is sent of the Father (4:34; 5:23–24, 30, 36–37; 6:38–40, 44, 57; 8:16, 18; 12:44–45, 49; 7:16; 9:4; 10:36; 11:42).

II. That while He was on the earth, He finished that work that was committed to Him to finish here, having purchased all that was to be bought by His blood, paying all the price that justice did ask (John 17:4; 19:30). By which price He has purchased a people to Himself (Luke 1:68; Rev. 5:9). So that His work, cause, and interest is a purchased work bought with His blood.

III. That His resurrection and glorification is an undoubted proof of this: that justice is satisfied, and that the price is fully paid. And also that His exaltation at the Father's right hand is a sure evidence and ground of hope that He will at last triumph over all His enemies and that His work of truth will prosper. The Father said to Him, "Sit thou at my right hand, until I make thine enemies thy footstool" (Ps. 110:1). Being highly exalted, He has got "a name which is above every name: that at the name of Jesus every knee should bow, of things in heaven, and things in earth, and things under the earth; and that every tongue should confess that Jesus Christ is Lord, to the glory of God the Father" (Phil. 2:9–11).

IV. That the Father stands engaged to make good to Him all that was promised and to give Him all that He purchased (Isa. 53:10–12). Christ, having now fulfilled His undertaking by making His soul an offering for sin and so satisfying justice, which is openly declared by His resurrection and admission to glory—as the head of His elect, [He] is to expect the accomplishment of what was conditioned to Him. His work, therefore, on the earth must prosper. And the Father has undertaken to see it prosper. Surely the faith of this would much support a poor soul, staggering at the thoughts of the prosperity of the wicked and of their evil cause.

V. That Christ Himself is now thoroughly furnished and enabled for the carrying on of His work over the belly of all adversaries, for all power in heaven and earth is given to Him

(Matt. 28:18) and every knee must bow to Him (Phil. 2:10). All judgment is committed unto Him (John 5:22, 27). Angels, powers, and authority are made subject unto Him (1 Peter 3:22). Yea, all things are under Him (Eph. 1:22). How then can His work miscarry? Or who can hinder that truth should flourish on the earth?

VI. That Christ is actually at work employing this power for the carrying forward of His design for the glory of the Father and for His own glory and for the good of His poor people. The Father worked by Him, and He by the Spirit, which is His great vicegerent, sent from the Father and from Him. And His work is to glorify the Son, and He will receive of His and show it to us (John 16:14).

VII. That Christ on many accounts stands engaged to perfect this work which He has begun and is about. His honor is engaged to go through, seeing now He is fully furnished for it and has all the creation at His command. He must then perfect His work as to the application, as well as He did perfect it as to the purchase. His love to His Father's and His own glory and to His own people's good and salvation may assure us that He will not leave the work unperfected. And His power and furniture may give us full security that no stop which His work meets with will be able to hinder it.

VIII. That hence it is clear and manifest that His wheel is in the midst of the wheels of men, and that therefore He is ordering all their motions and reelings to the best. His wheel keeps an even pace and moves equally and equitably in the midst of men's contrary motions.

IX. And that, therefore, all the eccentric and irregular motions of devils and wicked men being in His hand and ordered by Him cannot hinder but further His end—so that even enemies, while opposing and seeking to destroy the cause and interest of Christ, that His name and truth should no more be mentioned, are promoving His work. His wheel is the great wheel that orders all the lesser and subordinate wheels, whatever contrary motions they may have the one to the other, and all or many of them may seem to have to this great wheel. So that, do they what they will, the work of our Lord goes on. Their opposition is setting His work forward, though they intend the contrary. However their faces look, they row to the port He would be at. This is an undoubted truth and confirmed in all ages and yet is not firmly believed. And a truth it is, which, if believed, would do much to settle our staggering souls in a stormy day.

X. That at last He will come to be glorified in His saints (2 Thess. 1:10), "when the Lord Jesus shall be revealed from heaven with his mighty angels" (v. 7). Then will it be seen whose counsel will stand—His or men's—and whose work will prosper—His or Satan's.

Cautions

Yet, let me add a few words for caution and direction here:

I. The consideration of these things mentioned should not make us slacken our diligence in prayer and other duties. And when they are aright considered, they will rather prove a spur and a goad in our side to set us forward than a bridle to hold us back.

II. We would not think that Christ's work and interest is going backward always when it seems so to us. Even when He is casting down what He has built up and plucking up what He has planted, His work is prospering—for all that is in order to the laying of a better foundation and to the carrying on of a more glorious work, when He will lay all the stones with fair colors and the foundations with sapphires and make the windows of crystal, etc. (Isa. 54:11–12).

III. Though His work be always going on and His truth prospering, yet we would not think that it will always prosper alike in our apprehensions. Many times we judge by rules of our own making and not by the rule of truth. And hence it is that we mistake oftentimes. We walk little by faith and too much by sense. And hence we judge too much by sense and so pass a wrong judgment to His dishonor and the saddening of our own hearts.

IV. Nor would we think that His truth and interest is ruined and gone because it is sore oppressed in this or that particular place of the world—as if His work were not of a universal extent and in all the churches. If His truth thrive and prosper in some other place of the world, will we not say that His kingdom is coming? Or will we limit all His work and interest to one small part of the world?

V. We would not think the worse of His work because it is carried on with so many stops and does meet with so many impediments in its way. We are not acquainted with the depths of His infinite wisdom and counsel. And so we see not what noble ends He has before Him in suffering those impediments to lie in the way of His chariot. We think He should ride so triumphantly all along that none should once dare to cast the least block in His way. But we judge carnally, as unacquainted with the many noble and glorious designs which He has in ordering matters. As Himself was for a stone of stumbling and a rock of offense, so will He have the way of the carrying on of His work prove in His holy and spotless justice a stumbling stone to many that will stumble at it and fall and never rise anymore.

VI. We should beware to think that Christ has forgotten His work because He seems to take no notice of our prayers, which we are putting up now and then for His work. He may be doing that which we are desiring in the general and yet not let us know that He is answering our prayers—and that for wise and holy ends to keep us humble and diligent. He may seem to disregard our suits and yet be carrying on His work and granting us our desires on the matter.

VII. Hence we should beware of desponding and growing heartless and faint when we see few owning truth or standing on Christ's side, for He needs not man's help to carry on this work, though He sometimes thinks good to condescend so far as to honor some to be instrumental in setting of it forward, who yet have nothing but as He gives. Let us not then think that His work cannot prosper because great ones and mean ones oppose it, and such as should stand for it and own it are few and fainting, without strength, courage, or zeal.

CHAPTER 15

How to Make Use of Christ for Steadfastness in a Time When Truth Is Oppressed and Borne Down

When enemies are prevailing and the way of truth is evil spoken of, many faint, and many turn aside and do not plead for truth nor stand up for the interest of Christ in their hour and power of darkness. Many are overcome with base fear and either side with the workers of iniquity or are not valiant for the truth but, being fainthearted, turn back. Now the thoughts of this may put some who desire to stand fast and to own Him and His cause in a day of trial to inquire how they will make use of Christ who is the truth so as to be enabled to stand in the day of temptation and keep fast by truth when it is loaded with reproaches and buried under a heap of obloquy.

How to Continue Trusting Christ in Trouble
For satisfaction to this question, I will shortly point out those directions which, if followed, may prove helpful to keep the soul from fainting, misbelieving, doubting, quarrelling at the Lord's dispensations, and from yielding to the temptations in such a day.

I. The believer should live in the conviction of his hazard through the sleight of Satan, the strength of temptation, the wickedness and treachery of the heart, the evil example of others, and the want of sanctified courage, zeal, and resolution. And this will keep the soul humble and far from boasting of its own strength, which was Peter's fault.

II. They should live in the faith and persuasion of this: that it is Christ alone who is the truth, who can help them to stand for truth in a day of temptation, and that all their former purposes, vows, resolutions, solemn professions, and the like will prove but weak cables to hold them fast in a day of a storm, and that only the Rock of Ages must save them. And their being a leeward of Him and partaking of His warm and safe protection will do their business. That all their stock of grace and knowledge, and that confirmed with resolutions and sincere purposes, will help but little in that day. And that new influences of grace and truth from the fountain that is full of grace and truth will only prove establishing to the soul and confirm it in the truth in that day.

III. Therefore, they should eye Christ in His offices, particularly as the great prophet who can teach as never man taught, so teach as to make the soul receive the doctrine and to hold it fast—to receive it in love and lay it up in the heart as a rich and enriching treasure.

IV. They should eye Him in His relations to His people as their head, husband, brother, leader, commander, captain, etc. For those give ground of approaching to Him with confidence in the day of darkness and mists for light and direction and for strength and courage in the day of temptation and give ground of hope of help in that day of trial and difficulty.

V. They should eye and act faith on the promises of assistance and through-bearing in the day of calamity—such as those (Isa. 43:2), "When thou passest through the waters, I will be with thee; and through the rivers, they shall not overflow thee; when thou walkest through the fire, thou shalt not be burned; neither shall the flame kindle upon thee." And Isaiah 41:13: "For I the LORD thy God will hold thy right hand, saying unto thee, Fear not; I will help thee." And particularly they would eye the promises of light in the day of darkness (2 Sam. 22:29; Isa. 58:8, 10; 60:20).

VI. They should look on Christ as an exalted conqueror, now risen and glorified, as a victorious captain that has fought and overcome, that they as His followers may be made partakers of His victory and conquest and so reap the fruit of His resurrection and ascension in their establishment in the truth, when it is borne down and questioned, indeed, and condemned by men. He abode steadfast and immoveable in the midst of all the storms that blew in His face. And as He came to bear witness to the truth, so did He faithfully and zealously avow truth, even to the death, and in death got the victory of the arch liar and deceiver. Now the believer should eye this for the strengthening of his faith and hope of victory also, through Him. And therefore [he] would wait patiently for His help and not make haste, for they who believe make not haste (Isa. 28:16), knowing that He is true and faithful and will not disappoint His followers that trust in Him. And moreover it would be of advantage to them in this case to eye that gracious and comfortable word—John 14:19: "Because I live, ye shall live also"—and so by faith conclude that seeing Christ now lives as a conqueror over darkness, untruth, reproaches, calumnies, and opposition of liars, indeed, of the father of lies, they through Him will also live and ride out that storm. And this will give much courage to the soul to endure temptation and to wait in patience for an outgate.

VII. They should study much and suck at the grand promise of His coming again and of finally dispelling all clouds and of fully clearing up His glorious truths that are now covered over with obloquy and buried under reproaches. And this will encourage the soul to stand to truth in the midst of opposition, believing that at length truth, however much opposed now, will be victorious.

VIII. They should be single in their dependence on Him for strength and through-bearing in that day of trial—not leaning to their own understanding but acknowledging Him in all their ways (Prov. 3:8). And when they see no hope of outgate in the world nor appearance of the clearing up of the day, they would comfort themselves and encourage themselves in the Lord, as David did in a great strait (1 Sam. 20:6).

IX. On the forementioned grounds they would cast all the care of their through-bearing on Him who cares for them (1 Peter 5:7), rolling all their difficulties on Him, consulting only with Him and His Word and not with flesh and blood. And so they would commit their ways to Him who disposes of all things as He sees good, forbearing to limit the Holy One of Israel or to quarrel with Him for anything He does, and patiently wait for His outgate and delivery.

X. It were good in this time of trial to be remembering the worth of truth and entertaining high thoughts of the smallest piece of truth that is questioned for His sake who is the truth—that a sight of the glorious worth thereof may make them account the less of all they can lose in the defense and maintenance of it.

XI. So were it good at this time, when truths come to be questioned, to be lying near to the truth for light and to be keeping fast what He by His Spirit clears up to be truth, though the light should not be so full as to dispel all objections. This were to depend on Him for light with singleness of heart and in godly simplicity and sincerity to follow His direction and torch, though it should not shine so bright as they could wish.

Cautions

A few words of caution will be useful here also, as:

I. The believer, though taking this course, would not think to be altogether free of fear of stepping aside, in less or in more. God may think good to let much of this abide, to the end He may be kept watchful, tender, and diligent. For fear makes the soul circumspect and watchful. And this is a good preservative from defection.

II. Nor would the believer think that by this he will be kept altogether free of fainting. The heart now and then through fear and misbelief may fall into a fit of fainting and think all is gone. And yet He may carry poor souls through and make His strength perfect in their wickedness (2 Cor. 12:9), that when they are supported and carried through the temptation, they may sing praise to Him and not ascribe anything to themselves, remembering how often they were fainting and almost giving over the cause as desperate and hopeless.

III. They would not think it strange if, in the time of their wrestling with difficulties, the Lord hide His face from them and give not them that joyful access to Him in prayer that sometimes they have met with. For the Lord may see it fit to put them to this point of trial among the rest to see if the love of His glory and truth will keep them standing when they want the encouragement that might be expected in that way, and if pure conscience to the command and authority of God will keep from siding with an evil way when the soul is destitute of all sensible encouragement, both from within and from without.

IV. In all this business, believers should carry singly with an eye to God's glory and should not be acted with self-ends or drawn by carnal and selfish motives. They should not desire stability and through-bearing to be seen of men or to gain applause and praise of men, lest God be provoked to leave them to themselves, and they at length come off with discredit, as did Peter. Therefore, they should strive against these carnal motions of the heart and labor for spirituality, singleness of heart, and truth in the inward parts, which the Lord desires (Ps. 51:6).

CHAPTER 16

How to Make Use of Christ as the Truth When Error Prevails and the Spirit of Error Carries Many Away

There is a time when the spirit of error is going abroad, and truth is questioned, and many are led away with delusions. For Satan can change himself into an angel of light and make many great and fairlike pretensions to holiness and under that pretext usher in untruths and gain the consent of many to them. So that in such a time of temptation many are stolen off their feet and made to depart from the right ways of God and to embrace error and delusions instead of truth. Now the question is how a poor believer will make use of Christ, who is the truth, for keeping him steadfast in the truth in such a day of trial and from embracing of error, however plausible it may appear.

How to Continue in the Way of Truth
For satisfaction to this we will propose these few things:

I. In such a time when a spirit of error is let loose and rages and carries several away, it were good for all who would be kept straight and honest to be walking in fear. It is not good to despise such a sly and subtle enemy, especially in the hour and power of darkness. Then all are called to be on their guard and to stand on their watchtower and to be jealous of their corrupt hearts that are ready enough of their own accord to drink in error and to receive the temptation at any time, and much more then.

II. They should not think that their knowledge and ability to dispute for truth will keep them steadfast, if there be not more. For if the temptation grow, they may come to reason and dispute themselves out of all their former knowledge and skill. The father of lies is a cunning sophister and knows how to shake their grounds and cast all loose.

III. They should renew their covenant grips of Christ and make sure that main business—namely, their peace and union with God in Christ and their accepting of Christ for their head and husband. They would labor to have the foundation sure and to be united to the chief cornerstone [so] that, blow the storm as it will, they may ride safely, and that by this they may have access to Christ with boldness in their difficulty and may with confidence seek light from Him in the hour of darkness.

IV. To the end they may be kept more watchful and circumspect, they should remember that it is a dishonorable thing to Christ for them to step aside in the least matter of truth. The denying of the least point of truth is a consequential denying of Him who is the truth. And to lose a foot in the matters of truth is very dangerous, for who can tell when they who once slip a foot will recover it again? And who can tell how many and how dreadful errors they may drink in who have once opened the door to a small error? Therefore, they should beware of tampering in this matter and to admit any error on the account that it is a small and inconsiderable one. There may be an unseen concatenation between one error and another and between a small one and a greater one, so as if the little one be admitted and received, the greater will follow. And it may be feared that, if they once dally with error and make a gap in their consciences, that God will give them up to judicial blindness, that, before all be done, they will embrace that opinion which sometime[s] they seemed to hate as death.

V. They should eye the promises suiting that cause—namely, the promises of God's guiding "the blind by a way that they knew not"; of making darkness light before them, and crooked things straight (Isa. 42:16) and of guiding continually (58:11; see also 49:10; 57:18). And they would act faith on these and the like promises, as now made sure by Jesus.

VI. Particularly, they should fix their eye on that principal promise of the Spirit of truth to guide into all truth (John 16:13).

VII. With singleness of heart, they should depend on Christ and wait for light from Him and beware of prejudice at the truth. With singleness of heart, they should lie open to His instructions and to the influences of His light and direction and receive in the beams of His divine light—and thus go about duties—namely, prayer, conference, preaching, reading, etc.—with an eye fixed on Him and with a soul open to Him and free of all sinful preengagement and love to error.

VIII. With singleness of heart, they should give up their souls to Christ as the truth, that He would write the truth in their souls and frame their souls to the truth, and to that truth which is most questioned and by which they are most in hazard to be drawn away. And [they should] urge and press Him by prayer and supplication to do the duty of a head, a husband, guide, and commander, etc., to them, and that He would be a light to them in that day of darkness and not suffer them to dishonor

Him or prove scandalous to others by departing from the
truth and embracing error. A serious singlehearted dealing
with Him on the grounds of the covenant promises and His
relations and engagements might prove steadable in this case,
if accompanied with a lying open to the influences of truth
and to the light of information which He is pleased to send by
the Spirit of truth.

Cautions and Directions
For further clearing of this matter, we will hint at some cautions
and further directions useful here, such as:

I. They should beware of thinking that God should come to
them with light and instruction in an extraordinary manner
and reveal the truth of the question controverted somewhat
immediately—for this were a manifest tempting and limiting
of the Holy One of Israel. We must be satisfied with the means
of instruction which He has provided and run to the law and
to the testimony. We have the Scriptures, which are able to
make the man of God perfect and "thoroughly furnished unto
all good works" (2 Tim. 3:16–17) and to "make thee wise unto
salvation" (v. 15). There must we see light. And there must we
wait for the breathings of His Spirit with life and coming with
light to clear up truth to us—for they are the Scriptures of
truth (Dan. 10:21); and the law of the Lord, which is "perfect,
converting the soul"; and the commandment of the Lord
that is pure, "enlightening the eyes" (Ps. 19:7–8). We have the
ministry which God has also appointed for this end: to make
known to us His mind. There must we wait for Him and His
light. Thus must we wait at the posts of wisdom's doors and wait
for the king of light in His own way in which He has appointed
us to wait for Him. And if He think good to come another way

more immediate, let Him always be welcome. But let not us limit Him nor prescribe ways to Him but follow His directions.

II. When anything is borne in on their spirit as a truth to be received or as an error to be rejected more immediately, they should beware of admitting of every such thing without trial and examination. For we are expressly forbidden to believe every spirit and commanded to try them whether they are of God or not (1 John 4:1). The Lord will not take it ill that even His own immediate motions and revelations be tried and examined by the Word, because the Word is given us for this end: to be our test and standard of truth. The way of immediate revelation is not the ordinary way now of God's manifesting His mind to His people. He has now chosen another way and given us a more sure word of prophesy than was, even a voice from heaven, as Peter says (2 Peter 1:18–19). It is commended in the Bereans (Acts 17:11), who on this account were "more noble than those in Thessalonica, in that they received the word with all readiness of mind, and searched the scriptures daily, whether those things were so." Even Paul's words, though he was an authorized and an infallible apostle of Christ's, are here put to the touchstone of the Word. Many false prophets may go out and deceive many and speak "great swelling words of vanity" (1 John 4:1; 2 Peter 2:18). And the devil can transchange himself into an angel of light (2 Cor. 11:14). And though an angel out of heaven should preach any other thing than what is in the written Word, we ought not to receive his doctrine but to reject it and to account him accursed (Gal. 1:8). So that the written Word must be much studied by us, and by it must we try all motions, all doctrines, all inspirations, all revelations, and all manifestations.

III. Much more, they should beware of thinking that the dictates of their conscience obliges them, so as that always they must of necessity follow the same. Conscience, being God's deputy in the soul, is to be followed no further than it speaks for God and according to truth. An erring conscience, though it bind so far as that he who does contrary to the dictates of it sins against God in that knowing no other than that the dictates of conscience are right and consonant to the mind of God yet dare counteract[s] the same and thus formally rebel[s] against God's authority. Yet it does not oblige us to believe and to do what it asserts to be truth and duty. It will not then be enough for them to say, "My conscience and the light within me speaks so and instructs me so." For that light may be darkness and error and delusion and so no rule for them to walk by. "To the law and to the testimony." And if their conscience, mind, and light within them "speak not according to this word, it is because there is no light in them" (Isa. 8:20). I grant, as I said, they cannot without sin counteract the dictates even of an erring conscience, because they know no better but that these dictates are according to truth. And thus an erring conscience is a most dangerous thing and brings people under a great dilemma—that whether they follow it or not, they sin. And there is no other remedy here but to lay by the erring conscience and get a conscience rightly informed by the Word, putting it in Christ's hand to be better formed and informed that so it may do its office better. This then should be especially guarded against, for if once they lay down this for a principle that whatever their conscience and mind or inward light (as some call it) dictate must be followed, [then] there is no delusion, however false, however abominable it be but they may be at length in hazard to be drawn away with. And so the rule that they will walk by be nothing in effect but the spirit of lies and of delusion and the motions and dictates of him who is the father of lies—that is, the devil.

IV. Such as pretend to walk so much by conscience should take heed that they take not that for the dictate of conscience which really is but the dictates of their own humors, inclinations, preoccupied minds, and biased wills. When conscience speaks, it grounds on the authority of God, whether truly or falsely, and proposes such a thing to be done or to be refrained from merely because God commands that and forbids this, though sometimes it [makes] mistakes. But though the dictates of men's humors, inclinations, preoccupied judgments, and wills may pretend God's authority for what they say, yet really some carnal respect, selfish end, and the like lies at the bottom and is the chief spring of that motion. And also the dictates of humor and biased wills are usually more violent and fierce than the dictates of conscience, for wanting the authority of God to back their assertions and prescriptions, they must make up that with an addition of preternatural force and strength. Hence, such as are purely led by conscience are pliable, humble, and ready to hear and receive information, whereas others are headstrong and pertinacious, unwilling to receive instruction or to hear anything contrary to their minds, lest their conscience, receiving more light, speak with a higher voice against their inclinations and former ways and so create more trouble to them, while as now they enjoy more quiet within, so long as the cry of their self-will and biased judgments is so loud that they cannot well hear the still and low voice of conscience.

V. They should labor for much self-denial and sincerity and to be free from the snares and power of selfish ends, as credit, a name, and applause, or what of that kind that may be like "the fear of man [that] bringeth a snare" (Prov. 29:25). For that will be like a gift that blinds the eyes of the wise (Ex. 23:8). Love to carry on a party or a design to be seen or accounted somebody to maintain their credit and reputation lest they be accounted changelings and the like—[this] will prove very dangerous in this case; for these may forcibly carry the soul away to embrace one error after another and one error to strengthen and confirm another [so] that it is hard to know where or when they will stand. And these, by respects, may so forcibly drive the soul forward that he will neither hear the voice of conscience within nor any instruction from without.

VI. They should study the Word of truth without prejudice and any sinful preengagement, lest they be made by this to wiredraw and wrest the Word to their own destruction, as some of whom Peter speaks (2 Peter 3:16). It is a dangerous thing to study the Word with a prejudicate opinion and to bow or wiredraw the Word and make it speak what we would have it speak for the confirmation of our opinions and sentiments. For this is but to mock God and His law and to say, "Let His law speak what it will, I will maintain this opinion and so make the Word speak as we would have it or else lay it by." This is to walk by some other rule than the Word and to make the Word serve our lusts and confirm our errors, than which a greater indignity cannot be done to the Spirit of truth speaking in the Word.

VII. In reading and studying of the Word, there should be much single dependence on the Spirit for light, waiting for clearness from Him whom Christ has promised to lead us into all truth—an earnest wrestling with Him for His assistance [in] enlightening the mind with divine light to understand the truth and inclining the soul to a ready embracing and receiving of the truth declared in the Word.

VIII. Though one place of Scripture be enough to confirm any point of truth and ground[s] sufficient for us to believe what is there said, there being nothing in Scripture but what is truth, yet, in such a time of abounding errors and when many are going abroad speaking perverse things to lead the simple away, it were spiritual wisdom to be comparing Scripture with Scripture and not be lightly embracing whatever may seem probable and fairly deducible from some one passage or other of Scripture, but to be comparing that with other passages and see what concord there is. For this is certain: whatever point contradicts other clear and manifest testimonies of Scripture cannot be true, however a cunning sophister may make it seem very probably to flow out of such or such a passage of Scripture. The testimony of the Spirit is uniform and free from all contradictions. And therefore we must see if such an assertion that some would draw from such a passage agree with other plain passages and, if not, be sure that is not the meaning of the place. When the devil did wrest and abuse that passage of truth, "He shall give his angels charge over thee, etc." (Ps. 91:11), and from it would infer that Christ might cast Himself down (Matt. 4:6), Christ shows that this inference was bad because it did not agree with other divine testimonies, particularly not with that "ye shalt not tempt the LORD your God" (Deut. 6:16). And by this He teaches us to take this course in times of temptation and so compare spiritual things with spiritual, as Paul speaks (1 Cor. 2:13). Especially they should beware of expounding clear scriptures by such as are more dark and mysterious (see 2 Peter 3:16). It is always safer to explain darker passages by such as are more clear.

IX. Let them guard against a humor of newfangledness, nauseating old and solid truths and seeking after something new, having ears itching after new doctrines, indeed, or new modes and dresses of old truths. For this is provoking to God and proves dangerous, for such turn away their ears from the truth and are turned into fables, as Paul tells us (2 Tim. 4:3–4): "For the time will come," he says, "when they will not endure sound doctrine; but after their own lusts shall they heap to themselves teachers, having itching ears; and they shall turn away their ears from the truth, and shall be turned unto fables." This savors of a spirit of levity and inconstancy, which is dangerous.

X. They should labor to have no prejudice at the truth but receive it in the love of it, lest for that cause God give them up to strong delusions to believe lies and to be led with the deceivableness of unrighteousness, as we see: "And with all deceivableness of unrighteousness in them that perish; because they received not the love of the truth, that they might be saved; and for this cause God shall send them strong delusion, that they should believe a lie: that they all might be damned who believed not the truth, but had pleasure in unrighteousness" (2 Thess. 2:10–12).

XI. So should they beware of stifling the truth, of making it a prisoner and detaining it in unrighteousness, like those spoken of (Rom. 1:18): For which cause God them up to uncleanness and vile affections, and they became vain in their imaginations, and their foolish heart was darkened, yea, professing themselves to be wise, they became fools (v. 21, etc.). They should let truth have free liberty and power in the soul and should yield up themselves to be ruled and guided by it and not torture with it, lay chains on it, or fetter it and keep it as a prisoner that can do nothing.

XII. For this cause they should hold fast the truth which they have learned and have been taught by the Spirit out of the Word. When Paul would guard and fortify Timothy against seducers that crept into houses, leading captive silly women, etc., among other directions, [he] gave him this: "But continue thou in the things which thou hast learned and hast been assured of, knowing of whom thou hast learned them; and that from a child thou hast known the holy scriptures, which are able to make thee wise unto salvation, etc." (2 Tim. 3:14–15). So he would have the Colossians walking in Christ, rooted and built up in Him, and [e]stablished in the faith as they had been taught (Col. 2:6–7).

XIII. Especially they would be holding the groundwork fast— faith in Christ. It were good in such a time of erring from the way of truth to be gripping Christ faster and cleaving to Him by faith and living by faith in Him. This is to hold the foundation fast. And then let the tempest of error blow as it will, they will ride at a sure anchor and be safe because fixed on the Rock of Ages. And further, living near Christ in such a dangerous day would be a noble preservative from the infection of error. The soul that is dwelling in Christ and gripping to Him daily by faith and acting love on Him dwells in light [and] will discover error sooner than another, because living under the rays of the Sun of Righteousness, which discovers error.

XIV. They should labor to learn the truth as it is in Jesus. And the truths which they have heard of Him and have been taught by Him, as the truth is in Him, will abide when other truths that have been learned but of men and heard of men and as it was in the preaching of men and in books will soon vanish in a day of trial. This is to learn Christ, as the apostle speaks: "But ye have not so learned Christ; if so be that ye have heard him, and have been taught by him, as the truth is in Jesus" (Eph. 4:20–21). When we learn the truth as it is in Jesus, it brings us always to Him and has a tendency to fix our hearts on Him and is a piece of the bond that binds us to Him and His way. We receive it then as a piece of His doctrine which we must own and stand to. Oh, if we learned all our divinity thus, we would be more constant and steadfast in it than we are!

XV. When controversies arise, and they know not which side to choose—both seems to them to be alike well founded on the Word—they should exercise their spiritual sagacity and set their gift of discerning a work to see which of the two tends most to promote piety and godliness and the kingdom of Christ and so see which of the two is the truth "which is after godliness," as the apostle speaks (Titus 1:1). They must look which of the two is the doctrine which is according to godliness (1 Tim. 6:3). That is the truth which is Christ's and which should be owned and embraced; namely, [that] which flows from a spirit of godliness and tends to promove godliness and suits with the true principles of godliness, even gospel godliness wrought according to the tenor of the covenant of grace—that is, by the strength of the Spirit of Jesus dwelling and working in us—and not according to the tenor of the covenant of works; that is, wrought by our own strength, etc.

XVI. Yet in addition they should take heed that they mistake not here, for they may look on some ways and doctrines as having a greater tendency to promove godliness than others—which indeed have not but only seem so. They should therefore consider well what is the way of godliness laid down in the noble device of the gospel, which is the way that only glorifies God, Father, Son, and Holy Ghost. And [they should] see what suits most with that according to the Word and not what seems most suitable to godliness in their apprehension. The Word is the best judge and test of true godliness. And in the Word we have the only safest mean[s] of true godliness held forth. Therefore, we should see what doctrine tends most to promote godliness according to the way held forth in the Word, and choose that.

XVII. They should guard against pride and self-conceit, as thinking they are wise enough and understanding enough in those matters and so need not take a lesson of any. This may be of great prejudice, for it is the meek that God guideth in judgment; and to the meek will He teach His way (Ps. 25:9). Therefore, it were good for His people in such a day to be meek and humble, willing and ready to learn of any person, however mean, that can teach the ways of God. The Lord may bless a word spoken by a private person, when He will not bless the word spoken by a minister—for His blessings are free. And it is not good to despise any mean[s]. Apollos, though instructed in the way of the Lord, mighty in the Scriptures, fervent in spirit, and teaching diligently the things of the Lord (Acts 18:24–25), yet was content to learn of Aquila and of his wife, Priscilla, when they expounded to him the way of God more perfectly (v. 26).

XVIII. In such a time, it is not unsafe to look to such as have been eminent in the ways of God and lie near to Him. For it is probable they may know much of the mind of God in those questioned matters. Hence we find the apostle putting Timothy and others to this duty in a time when false teachers were going abroad, saying, "But thou hast fully known my doctrine, manner of life" (2 Tim. 3:10); and, "Wherefore I beseech you, be ye followers of me" (1 Cor. 4:16); and 1 Corinthians 11:1 and again Philippians 3:17: "Brethren, be followers together of me." All which say that though we should call no man "rabbi," as hanging our faith absolutely on him, yet in such a time of prevailing error and of false teachers going abroad, some respect should be had to such as have found grace of the Lord to be faithful in times of trial and have maintained truth and stood for it in times of persecution and have with singleness of heart followed the Lord—it not being ordinary with God to leave such as in sincerity seek Him and desire to follow His way in truth and uprightness and to give the revelation of His mind and the manifestation of His Spirit to others who have not gone through such trials.

XIX. They should also at such a time be much in the sincere practice of uncontroverted duties and in putting uncontroverted and unquestionable and unquestioned truths into practice. And this may prove a notable mean[s] to keep them right, for then are they in God's way, and so the devil has not that advantage of them that he as of others who are out of the way of duty. David understood more than the ancients, because he kept God's precepts (Ps. 119:100).

XX. It were good and suitable at such a time to be much in the fear of God, remembering what a one He is and how hazardous it is to sin against Him by drinking in the least point of error. The promise is made to such (Ps. 25:12): "What man is he that feareth the LORD, him shall he teach in the way that he shall choose."

XXI. Finally, at such a time they should be much in communion with Jesus, lying near Him, much in prayer to Him, studying His relations, offices, furniture, readiness to help with light and counsel. And they should draw near to Him with humility, boldness, faith, confidence, love, tenderness, and sincerity. And then they will not find that He will fail them or disappoint them.

Enough of this. I proceed therefore to another case, which is:

CHAPTER 17

How to Make Use of Christ as the Truth That We May Get Our Case and Condition Cleared Up to Us

The believer is often complaining of darkness concerning his case and condition, so as he cannot tell what to say of himself or what judgment to pass on himself, and he knows not how to win to a distinct and clear discovery of his state and condition. Now, it is truth alone, and the truth, that can satisfy them as to this. The question then is how they will make use of and apply themselves to this truth to the end they may get the truth of their condition discovered to them. But first let us see what this case may be.

The Condition of the Believer

Consider then:

I. That grace may be in the soul and yet not be seen nor observed. This is manifest by daily experience.

II. Not only so, but a gracious soul that is reconciled with God in Christ and has the Spirit of grace dwelling in it may suppose itself a stranger yet to this reconciliation and void of the grace of God and so be still in the state of nature.

III. Indeed, a soul may not only suppose and conclude itself in nature while it is in a state of grace, but further, may be filled with terror and apprehensions of God's wrath and indignation—and that in such a measure as that by this it may be as a distracted person, as we see it was with Heman who said, "While I suffer thy terrors I am distracted" (Ps. 88:15). The wrath of God lay hard on him, and he said that he was afflicted with all God's waves (v. 7). Hence he cried out, "Thy fierce wrath goeth over me; thy terrors have cut me off. They came round about me daily [or, all the day], like water; they compassed me about together" (vv. 16–17). And yet for all this, the first word of his complaint was faith (v. 1). Many such complaints hear we out of Job's mouth, to whom God despite this was that gracious that he never came to question his state before God or to conclude his hypocrisy or his being still in the state of nature. But it is not so with everyone that is so exercised.

IV. Indeed, further, with those inward strokes on the soul, they may have sin and guilt charged on their consciences. And this will make their life yet more bitter and put a sharper edge on the rods. Thus was Job made to possess the sins of his youth (Job 13:26) and made to say, "My transgression is sealed up in a bag, and thou sewest up mine iniquity" (14:17).

V. Moreover, they may be in such a condition a long time and all the while have no light of comfort, as we may see in Job and Heman. They may even walk in darkness and have no light of comfort (Isa. 50:10).

VI. Indeed, and also be without the hope of a delivery or outgate. Hence cries Heman, "I am counted with them that go down into the pit:… free among the dead, like the slain that lie in the grave, whom thou rememberest no more: and they are cut off from thy hand" (Ps. 88:4–5). Indeed, they may be driven to the very border of despair and conclude that there is no hope, as the church did, "Our bones are dried, and our hope is lost: we are cut off for our parts" (Ezek. 37:11), and as Job, "My days are swifter than a weaver's shuttle, and are spent without hope" (7:6), and, "He hath destroyed me on every side, and I am gone: and mine hope hath he removed like a tree" (19:10).

The Grounds for Hope

Now, though sometimes, as we see in Job and in Heman too, a soul may be under such a sad and sharp dispensation and yet not brought to question their state or to conclude themselves children of wrath, lying still in black nature, yet it is not so with all who are so exercised. But many under such a dispensation may at least be in the dark as to their state before God. And if they do not positively assert their state to be bad, yet they do much question if they be in the state of grace and would be comforted under all their pressures and afflictions if they could win to the least well-grounded apprehension of their interest in Christ.

In such a case as this is, there is ground for a poor soul to make use of Christ for outgate. And an outgate may be had in God's time and as He sees fit by a right use-making of and going out to Him who is the truth. So, then, the soul that would have its state and condition cleared up and a discovery of its being reconciled to God through Jesus and in a state of grace and would make use of Christ as the truth for this end would:

I. Look out to Christ as a feeling high priest, faithful and merciful, who, being like us in all things except sin, does sympathize with and succor such as are tempted (Heb. 2:17–18). And [look on Him] as a priest that is "touched with the feeling of our infirmities" (4:15). Even though Christ, in the deepest of His darkness, was never made to question His sonship but avouched God to be His God even when He was forsaken (Ps. 22:1; Matt. 27:46; Mark 15:34), yet He knew what it was to be tempted to question His sonship when the devil said to Him, "If thou be the Son of God" (Matt. 4:3). And He knows what such a distress as He Himself was into, wrestling with an angry God, hiding Himself and forsaking, will work in a poor sinner. And being a merciful and sympathizing high priest, He cannot but pity such as are under such a distemper and, as a gracious head, sympathize with them. Now, the believer would look out to Him as such a one and on this ground go to Him with confidence and boldness and lay out their case before Him that He may help and send relief.

II. They would also eye Christ as able to save out of that condition and to command light to shine out of darkness, and so as one "able also to save them to the uttermost that come unto God by him" (Heb. 7:25).

III. And not only so, but eye Him also as given, sent, and commissioned of the Father to be a light to such as sit in darkness, even to the Gentile[s] (Isa. 42:6; 49:6; Luke 2:32; John 8:12; Acts 13:47; 26:23). And this will encourage the poor souls to go out to Him with their darkness when they see that He is sent as a light and as the truth to clear up poor souls that walk in darkness and have no light. When they see that it is His place and office to help them and consider that He is true to His trust and true and faithful in all that was committed to Him, it not only will embolden them to come forward to Him, but it will strengthen their hope and encourage them to wait on.

IV. They would stay themselves on Him as an all-sufficient helper, renouncing all other[s], crying out that they will have no light but His light and that they will seek nowhere else for light but wait at His door till He who is the Sun of Righteousness will arise in their soul and come with healing light in His wings.

V. They would by faith roll and cast their darkened souls, their confused case, their overwhelmed hearts on Him and leave them there. For He is the only physician, and the blind soul must be put in His hand who can take away the film and cause the scales [to] fall off and make light break into the soul and discover to it its condition.

VI. It would be useful and very steadable in such a time of darkness for the believer to be frequent in acting direct acts of faith on Christ—that is, be frequent in going to Him as an all-sufficient mediator, as the only refuge and shadow for a poor, weary, scorched soul (Isa. 4:6). "And a man shall be as an hiding place from the wind, and a covert from the tempest; as rivers of water in a dry place, as the shadow of a great rock in a weary land" (32:2), [and] as one who is "a strength to the needy in his distress, a refuge from the storm, a shadow from the heat, etc." (25:4). When the soul is thus overwhelmed with clouds and doubts of its interest in Christ, it would then put it out of doubt by flying to Him for refuge from the storm of God's indignation and lay hold on Him as He is freely offered in the gospel and thus renew its grips of Him as the offered all-sufficient mediator. And frequent direct acts of faith will help at length to [make this] a reflex act.[1] The soul that is daily running to Christ according to the covenant with all its necessities and laying hold on Him as only able to help will at length come to see that it has believed on Him and is made

---

1 Here, most likely referring to the reflexive act of faith, in contrast to a physical reflex.

250 Christ the Way, the Truth, and the Life
250   Christ the Way, the Truth, and the Life

welcome by Him and accepted through Him. So that reiterated acts of faith on an offered cautioner and salvation will dispel at length those clouds of darkness that trouble the soul.

VII. Such souls would beware of making their bands stronger and their darkness greater by their folly and unwise carriage. For this cause they would beware:

1. To cry out in despondency of spirit as if there were no hope and to conclude peremptorily that they are cut off and it is vain to wait any longer. For this course will but darken them the more and multiply the clouds over their head.

2. To run away from Christ through unbelief and despair, for that will make their case yet worse.

3. To walk untenderly and not circumspectly, for the more sins appear, the less light will be had. Oh, but souls would be tender in all their conversation at that time and guard against the least sin or appearance of evil!

4. To fret and repine against God because of that dispensation, for that will but entangle the soul more and wreathe the yoke straiter about its neck and put itself further out of case to be relieved and to receive light.

VIII. Such would do well not to limit the Holy One of Israel but to wait with patience till His time come to speak in light to the soul, knowing that such as wait on Him will never be ashamed (Isa. 49:23) because He waits to be gracious. And therefore blessed are all they that wait on Him (30:18).

Question and Encouragement

Question

But what if for all this I get no outgate, but my distress and darkness rather grow on my hand?

Answer. That such a thing may be, I grant, the Lord thinking it fit:

1. To exercise their faith, dependence, patience, hope, and desire more.
2. And to discover more to them their own weakness, faintings, faithfulness.
3. To show His absolute power and sovereignty.
4. To make His grace and mercy more conspicuous and remarkable at length.
5. And to train them up in a way of dependence on Him in the dark and of leaning to Him when walking in darkness, indeed, and in a way of believing when they think they have no faith at all.

Encouragement

And [also] for other holy ends. Yet the soul would not despond, for there are several things that may serve to support and bear up the heart even in that case, as:

I. This is not their case alone. Others have been in the like before, and many have had the like complaints in all ages, as is known to such as have been acquainted with exercised souls.

II. It may yield peace and comfort to know that they are about duty when looking to Him and depending on Him and waiting for His light.

III. The promises made to such as wait for Him may support the soul and yield comfort.

IV. The distinct knowledge and uptaking of their condition, though it be comfortable and refreshing, yet it is not absolutely necessary. A soul may be a saved soul, though those clouds should continue to its dying day, and though as long as they lived they should never get a clear discovery of their gracious state but spend their days in mourning, complaining, and crying out of darkness.

V. Such a soul should think that it is much that he is kept out of hell so long. And sure[ly] the thoughts of what he is and of what he deserves may make him sober and not to think much, though he reach not so high as to see his name written in the Book of Life.

VI. They should know that full assurance of hope and of faith is but rare. And even such as have it do not ordinarily keep it long. So that it should not much trouble them if, after all their pains, they cannot win at it.

VII. If they win to any real ground of hope, however small, they should think much of that—for many dear to Christ live long and never know what so much is.

VIII. It is no small matter that they are not sinking in the gulf of inconsideration and plagued with an indifferency in these matters but are made to value Christ and an interest in Him at such a rate.

IX. Their going to Christ with all their wants, laying all on Him, and their making that their daily exercise may keep up their hearts from fainting, indeed, and fill their souls with joy—for that is really the exercise of faith. And the great and gracious promises are made to such as believe and not to such only as know they do believe. I grant such as know not that they do believe cannot draw comfort from these promises. Yet it is true that one may by reflecting on the actings of his own soul see and know that really he is going out to Christ, forsaking himself, casting his burden on Him, waiting and depending on Him, [even] when yet he will not say that he does believe. And when he sees this working of soul toward Christ, he is obliged to believe that he believes and on this rejoice in hope of the great promises. And however the very sight and knowledge of this acting and motion of soul may give them some comfort, though they will not take it for faith because it is the way of duty and it is the thing the gospel calls for, and because they cannot show an instance of any one soul that did so and perished. But the truth is [that] the right understanding of the nature of faith would clear many doubts and prevent many questions.

I come to speak a little to the last case which I will handle, which is:

CHAPTER 18

How We Will Make Use of Christ as the Truth That We May Win to Right and Suitable Thoughts of God

*T*his is a case that much troubles the people of God: they cannot get right and suitable thoughts of God, which they earnestly desire to have, nor know not how to win at them. And certain it is [that] He only who is the truth and came out of the bosom of the Father can help here.

Things to Remember

Therefore, for our use-making of Him for this end, it would be remembered:

I. That the mind of man through the fall is nothing but a mass of ignorance and blindness—that the understanding is darkened (Eph. 4:17–18); and naturally we are in darkness (1 John 2:9, 11); yea, under the power of darkness (Col. 1:13). And, which is more, our minds are naturally filled with prejudice against God and enmity through wickedness naturally residing there, and which the prince of the power of the air, the spirit which works in the children of disobedience, increases and stirs up.

II. That this evil is not totally taken away even in the godly but helped only in part, for they see and know but in part (1 Cor. 13:13).

III. That hence it comes to pass that through the working of corruption the soul of a believer can sometimes win to no right thought of God at all or at best to some very narrow and unsuitable conceptions of Him and His ways. Indeed, sometimes all the thoughts they can get of God are vain and idle, if not misshapen and blasphemous.

IV. That as we are, we cannot see God—for no man has seen Him (Matt. 11:27; John 6:46), for He is an invisible God (1 Tim. 1:17; Heb. 11:27). He dwelleth in light which no man can approach unto. Him no man hath seen, nor can see (1 Tim. 6:16; 1 John 4:12).

V. That all that knowledge of God which is saving is to be found in Christ, who is the "brightness of his glory, and the express image of his person" (Heb. 1:3) and "the image of the invisible God" (Col. 1:15) and is for this end come out from the bosom of the Father that He might acquaint us with Him and with all His secrets (Matt. 11:27; John 1:18), so far as is needful for us to know. He is God incarnate, that in Him we may see the invisible. Thus "God was manifest in the flesh" (1 Tim. 3:16), and "The Word was made flesh, and dwelt among us" (John 1:14).

VI. That therefore if we would see and know God, we must go to Christ, who is the temple in which God dwells and manifests His glory. And in and through Him must we see and conceive of God. The light that we get of the knowledge of the glory of God must be in the face of Jesus Christ (2 Cor. 4:6)—that is, in the manifestations that Christ has made of Himself in His natures, offices, ordinances, works, dispensations of grace, mediate and immediate, etc. And thus does God, who commanded the light to shine out of darkness, cause this light of the knowledge of his glory shine into our hearts—namely, in the face of Jesus

Christ; that is, in the dispensations of grace in the gospel, which is the glorious gospel of Christ (2 Cor. 4:4), and, as it were, the face of Jesus Christ. For as by the face a man is best known and distinguished from others, so Christ is visibly and discernibly and manifestly seen and known in and by the gospel dispensations. There are all the lineaments and draughts of the glory of God which we would know, lively and clearly to be seen.

Things to Be Considered

So then, if we would make use of Christ for this end that we may win to a right sight of God and suitable conceptions of His glory, we would consider these things:

I. We would live under the sense and thorough conviction of the greatness and incomprehensibleness of God, as being every way past finding out, and also under the conviction of our own darkness and incapacity to conceive aright of Him, even as to what He has revealed of Himself.

II. We would know that what the works of creation and providence declare and preach forth of God, though it be sufficient to make heathens and others that do not improve the same to a right acknowledging of Him inexcusable, as Paul teaches us (Rom. 1:20), yet all that is short of giving to us that saving knowledge of Him which must be had and which is life eternal (John 17:2).

III. We would know that what of God is to be found out by the works of creation and providence is more distinctly seen in Christ and in the gospel. Here is a greater and more glorious discovery of God and of His glorious attributes, His justice, power, wisdom, goodness, holiness, truth, etc., than can be found by the deepest diving naturalist and most wise moral observer of providence that is not taught out of the gospel.

IV. Indeed, there is something of God to be seen in Christ, in the gospel, which can be observed in none of His works of creation or common providence. There is the grace of God that brings salvation that is made to appear only by the gospel (Titus 2:11). And there is a peculiar kindness and love of God toward man which is only discovered by Christ in the gospel (3:4). There is that manifold wisdom of God, that mystery which was hid from the beginning of the world in God, that principalities and powers in heavenly places, the greatest and wisest of naturalists must learn by the church wherein that is preached and proclaimed by the dispensations of the gospel (Eph. 3:9–10). His mercy pardoning poor sinners, justice being satisfied, cannot be cleared by nature. Nature cannot unfold that mystery of justice and mercy concurring to the salvation of a sinner—only the gospel can clear that riddle.

V. We would remember that all the beams of that glory which are necessary and useful for us to know are, to speak so, contracted in Christ and there veiled, to the end that we may more steadily look on them. We may go to our brother who is flesh of our flesh and there through the veil of His flesh see and behold what otherwise was invisible. As we can look to the sun better shining in a pail of water than by looking up immediately, so can we behold God and His glory better in Christ where there is a thin veil (to speak so) drawn over that otherwise blinding, indeed, killing glory, than by looking to God without Christ. For, alas, we could not endure one glance of an immediate ray of divine glory. It would kill us outright.

VI. We must then go to Christ and there see God, for he who sees Him sees the Father also (John 14:9). Particularly, we must go [to] the face of Jesus Christ, that is, that by which He has made Himself known, the noble contrivance of the glorious gospel in which all things are so carried on as that God is glorified in His Son in the salvation of poor sinners. The whole work of salvation is laid on Christ, and the Father is glorified in Him who is His servant and His chosen, whom He upholds and furnishes for the work (Isa. 42:1–2). He is called the covenant itself. He is the undertaker in the covenant of redemption and in the covenant of grace. All is founded on Him. All the good things of it are given out by Him. All the grace by which we close with it and accept of Him according to it is given by Him. Now, in this gospel contrivance are all the lines of the glorious face of Christ to be seen. And in that face must we see and discern the glory of God, all the rays of which are centered in Christ. And there will we get a noble prospect of that glorious object. So that all such as would make use of Christ for this end that they might come to have right and suitable thoughts and apprehensions of God must be well acquainted with the whole draught and frame of the gospel, and so acquainted with it as to see Christ the substance, ground, and all of it, and to see Him in every part of it.

VII. Whatever we know or learn of God by His works of creation and providence in the world or about ourselves, we would bring it in here, that it may receive a new tincture and a deeper impression. That is done when we find and learn something of Christ there and are brought nearer Christ by it and made by it to discover something more of the glory of God in the face of Christ, or are made to understand better something of the revelation that is made of God in the gospel or moved by it to improve it better.

VIII. In all this matter, we must not go without our guide, lest we wander in this wilderness and it prove a labyrinth to us. We must take Christ with us all along. He must teach us to understand His own face and to read the glorious characters of that excellent glory which is to be seen in His face. He must be our interpreter and teach us how to read this book and how to understand what is written in it. He must give the discerning eye and the understanding heart, even the spirit of wisdom and understanding to take up the mysteries of God.

IX. And for this cause we should by faith lay hold on the promises of the Spirit, by which we may be made spiritual and have our understandings enlightened more and more to understand the mysterious characters of divine majesty and glory.

X. In all this exercise, we should walk with fear and carry with us impressions of the dreadful majesty and glory of God that we may tremble and fear and stand in awe and read what we read of this glory of God in the face of Jesus Christ, this glorious Bible, with reverence and godly fear. And thus we may be helped to win to right and suitable thoughts of God.

Cautions

Yet in addition, we should for cautions consider a few things further, as:

I. That we must not think to "find out the Almighty unto perfection" (Job 11:7).

II. Nor must we think to get any one point of God known and understood perfectly. Corruption will mix in itself, [even if we] do our best. And our shortcomings will not easily be reckoned up.

III. We must beware of carnal curiosity and of unlawful diving into this depth, lest we drown.

IV. We should not dream of a state here in which we will not need Christ for this end. Indeed, I suppose, in glory, He will be of use to us as to the seeing of God. For even there, as He is today, so will He forever abide [as] God and man in two distinct natures and one person, and that cannot be for naught. And as God [He] will be still God invisible and unsearchable, so we, though glorified, will remain finite creatures and therefore will stand in need of Christ, that in His glorious face we may see the invisible. He must be our *lumen gloriae*.[1]

V. We should think it no small matter to have the impressions of this sight on our hearts that we cannot see Him and that we, in this state of sin, cannot get right and suitable apprehensions of Him. I say, the impression of this on our spirits, that is, such a sight of impossibility to get Him seen aright, as will keep the heart in awe and cause us [to] walk before Him in fear and reverence and to humble ourselves in the dust, and to tremble whenever we make mention of His name or begin to meditate on Him, knowing how great a one He is and how dangerous it is to think amiss of Him and how difficult to get a right thought of Him.

---

1. *Lumen gloriae*: light of glory.

CHAPTER 19

"And the Life": How Christ Is the Life

This, as the former, being spoken indefinitely, may be universally taken as relating both to such as are yet in the state of nature and to such as are in the state of grace. And so [it] may be considered in reference to both and ground three points of truth, both in reference to the one and in reference to the other; namely,

1. That our case is such as we stand in need of His help, as being the life.

2. That no other way but by Him can we get that supply of life which we stand in need of, for He only is the life, excluding all other.

3. That this help is to be had in Him fully and completely, for not only is He able to quicken, but He is called the life—so that the help which He gives is full, excellent, and complete.

What Men Are by Their Nature

Looking on the words in reference to such as are in nature, they point out these three truths to us:

I. That all of us by nature are dead, standing in need of quickening and of life. For this is presupposed while He is said to be the life, and that both legally and really: *legally*, being under the sentence of death for Adam's transgression (Rom. 5:15) and for that original corruption of heart we have; and *really*, the sentence of the law being in part executed, and that both as to the body and as to the soul. As to the body, it is now subject to death and all the forerunners of it such as weakness, pains, sickness, fears, torment, trouble, weariness, indeed, and in hazard of hellfire and the torments of the second death forever. As to the soul, it also is many ways dead, but first in a way that is purely penal and next in a way that is also sinful— and both ways, as to what is present and as to what is future. For as to that which is penal and present, it is (1) separated from God and His favor (Gen. 3:8, 10, 24); (2) is under His curse and wrath, from which it comes to pass that by nature we are children of wrath (Eph. 2:2, 5), servants of Satan (2 Tim. 2:26)—the consequence of which is sad and heavy, for hence it is that we cannot please God, do what we will. Till we be brought out of that state, our ordinary and civil actions, even ploughing the ground, is sin (Prov. 21:4). Indeed, our religious actions, whether natural or instituted, are abomination—even our sacrifices (15:8; 21:27) and prayers (Ps. 10:7; Prov. 28:9), indeed, and all our thoughts and purposes (15:26) and likewise all our ways (15:9).

As to what is penal and future, it is obnoxious to that everlasting excommunication from the presence of the Lord and from the glory of His power (2 Thess. 1:8–9) and to the torments of hell forever (Mark 9:44, 46, 48; Luke 16). As to what is not only penal but also sinful, the soul here is under the stroke of darkness in the understanding, perverseness, and rebelliousness in the will, irregularity and disorder in the affections, by which the soul is unfit for anything that is good (Rom. 3:10–20; 5:6; 8:7–8; Eph. 2:1–3), from which proceeds all our actual transgressions (James 1:14–15). And moreover, sometimes the soul is given up to a reprobate mind (Rom. 1:28); to strong delusion (2 Thess. 2:2); to hardness of heart (Rom. 2:5); horror of conscience (Isa. 33:14); to vile affections (Rom. 1:26); and the like spiritual plagues, which, though the Lord inflict on some only, yet all are obnoxious to the same by nature and can expect no less if the Lord should enter with them into judgment. And finally, as to what is future of this kind, they are, being fuel for Tophet, obnoxious to that malignant, sinful, blasphemous, and desperate rebellion against God, in hell forevermore!

Oh how lamentable on this consideration must the condition of such be as are yet in the state of nature! Oh, if it were but seen and felt! But, alas, there is this addition to all: that people know not this. They consider it not; they believe it not; they feel it not; they see it not. And hence it comes to pass that (1) they cannot bewail and lament their condition nor be humbled for it; (2) they cannot and will not seek after a remedy, for the whole will not trouble themselves to seek after a physician.

And sure[ly] on this account their case calls for pity and compassion from all that know what a dreadful thing it is to be in such a condition and should stir up all to pray for them and to do all they can to help them out of that state of sin and misery, which is dreadful to think on.

Should not the thoughts and consideration of this put us all to try and search if we be yet translated from death to life and delivered out of that dreadful and terrible state and made partakers of the first resurrection? It not being my purpose to handle this point at large, I will not here insist in giving marks by which this may be known and which are obvious in Paul's Epistles and to be found handled at large in several practical pieces, chiefly in Mr. Guthrie's "[The Christian's] Great Interest." I will only desire everyone to consider and examine:

1. Whether or not the voice of Christ, which quickens the dead, has been heard and welcomed in their soul. This is effectual calling.

2. Whether or not there be a thorough change wrought in their soul, a change in the whole man, so as all things are become new (2 Cor. 5:17).

3. Whether or not there be a principle of life within and they be led by the Spirit.

4. Whether or not there be a living to the glory of the Lord Redeemer.

And when by an impartial trial a discovery is made of the badness of our condition, should we not be alarmed to look about us and to labor by all means for an outgate?—considering:

1. How doleful and lamentable this condition is.

2. How sad and dreadful the consequences of it are.

3. How happy a thing it is to be delivered from this miserable and sinful condition.

4. And how there is a possibility of outgate.

Finally, it may break a heart of stone to think how people that are in such a condition are so unwilling to come out of it, for:

1. How unwilling are they once to suspect their condition or to suppose that it may be bad and that they may be yet unconverted?

2. How unwilling are they to sit down seriously to try and examine the matter and to lay their case to the touchstone of the Word?

3. Indeed, how unwilling are they to hear anything that may tend to awaken them or to discover to them the deadness of their condition?

4. How ready to stifle challenges of conscience or any common motion of the Spirit which tends to alarm their soul?

5. How great enemies are they to such ordinances as serve to awaken sleeping consciences?

6. And how do they hate such ministers as preach such doctrine as may serve to rouse them up and set them a-work about their own salvation?

II. We learn hence that without Christ there is no imaginary way of delivery out of this natural state of death. No other name is given under heaven by which we can be saved (Acts 4:12). And angels can make no help here, nor can one of us deliver another. The redemption of the soul is more precious than so (Ps. 49:7–8). Nor is there anything we can do for ourselves that will avail here. All our prayers, tears, whippings, fastings, vows, alms-deeds, purposes, promises, resolutions, abstinence from some evils, outward amendments, good morality and civility, outward religiousness, indeed, and if it were possible, our keeping of the whole law—[all] will not help us out of this pit. And we may weary ourselves in such exercises in vain, for they will prove but bodily exercises that profit little. And when in this way we have spent all our time, parts, spirits, and labor, we will at length see and say that we have spent our money for that which is not bread.

This should put all of us to try what it is which we lean to for life. And what it is, the consideration of which gives us peace and quietness when the thoughts of death, judgment, hell, and the wrath of God come on us and trouble us. For if it be anything beside[s] Christ that our soul leans to and that we are comforted by and found all our hopes on, we will meet with a lamentable (Oh! Forever lamentable!) disappointment. Be sure then that our hearts renounce all other ways and means of outgate out of this death besides Jesus, the resurrection and the life, else it will not be well with us.

III. We see here that delivery out of this natural state of death is only had by Christ. For He alone is the life, and the life that is in Him is suitable and excellent. Hence He is called the "bread of life" (John 6:35, 48); "the resurrection; and the life" (11:25); "the water of life" (Rev. 21:6; 22:17); "the tree of life" (Rev. 22:2, 14); "the Prince of life" (Acts 3:15); "our life" (Col. 3:4); "the Word of life," and life itself (1 John 1:1–2).

And as He is a suitable and excellent life, so is He an all-sufficient and perfect life, able every way to help us and to deliver us from all the parts of our death—for:

1. He delivers from the sentence of the law (Rom. 5:17–18), undergoing the curse of the law and becoming a curse for us (2 Cor. 5:21).

2. He takes away the curse and sting of all temporal plagues, indeed, and of death itself, causing all to work together for good to such as love Him (Rom. 8:28). He has killed him that had the power of death—that is, the devil (Heb. 2:14). And through Him the sting of death, which is sin, is taken away (1 Cor. 15:56–57).

3. He reconciles to God, taking away that distance and enmity (2 Cor. 5:20). And so He is our peace and peacemaker, purchasing access to us to the Father (Eph. 2:14, 16; 3:12, 24).

4. He also delivers from the power of sin and corruption (Romans 7).

1. And from all those spiritual strokes, such as blindness, hardness of heart, etc.—for He is our light and has procured a new heart for us, even a heart of flesh.

2. So delivers He from hellfire, having satisfied justice and having brought life and immortality to light. And He gives life eternal, as we see (Rev. 2:3).

Oh! It is sad that Christ is so little made use of and that so many will forsake the fountain of living waters and dig to themselves broken cisterns that can hold no water and slight, despise, and undervalue the gospel of Christ, which brings life and immortality to light.

Oh! If the consideration of this could move such as never found any change in themselves to run to and make use of Jesus Christ for life, and [that they] would for this end:

1. Cry to Him that He would make them sensible of their deadness and waken them out of their deep sleep.

2. Cry to Him to set them to work to renounce all other help beside[s] His as being utterly unable to quicken and put life in them.

3. Cry to Him that He would draw and determine their souls to a closing with Him by faith alone, to a hearing of His voice, to an obeying of His call, to a following of His direction, to a giving up of themselves to Him, leaning to Him and waiting for all from Him alone—in a word, to take Him for their life in all points and to lean to Him for life and to expect it from Him through faith in the promises of the gospel.

The Use of Christ as the Life
Next, this being spoken to the disciples, whom we suppose to have been believers, it will give us ground to speak of it in reference to believers and so yield three points of truth, which we will briefly touch and then come to speak of use-making of Christ as the life in some particular cases:

I. It is here clearly presupposed that even believers have need of Christ to be life to them and so have their fits of deadness. If it were not so, why would Christ have said to believers that He was life? And daily experience does abundantly confirm it, for:

1. They are often so weak and unable to resist temptation or to go about any commanded duty, as if they were quite dead.

2. They are often so borne down with discouragement because of the strength of opposition which they meet with on all hands and because of the manifold disappointments which they meet with that they have neither heart nor hand. And they faint and set up in the ways of the Lord and cannot go through difficulties but oftentimes lie by.

3. Through daily fighting and seeing no victory, they become weary and fainthearted, so that they lie by as dead (Isa. 40:29).

4. They often fall sick and decay and have need of restoration and quickening.

5. The want of the sense of God's favor and of the comforts of the Holy Ghost makes them to dwine[1] and droop and look out as dead.

6. While under soul desertions on one account or other, they look on themselves as free among the dead, that is, as dead men, of the society of the dead, with Heman (Psalm 88).

7. Indeed, many times they are as dead men, led captive in chains of unbelief and corruptions, as we see David was when his heart panted, and his strength failed

---

1. *Dwine*: to waste away.

him, and the light of his eyes were gone from him
(Ps. 38:10).

8. Many times the frequent changes and ups and downs
they meet with take all courage and heart from them
[so] that they become like men tossed at sea, so as they
have no more strength.

And many such things befall them which make them look
as dead and to stand in need of quickening, reviving, and
strengthening cordials from Him who is the life. And thus the
Lord thinks good to dispense with His own people:

1. That they may be kept humble and know themselves to
be indigent creatures, needing influences of life daily.

2. That they may have many errands to Him who is the
life and have much to do with Him and depend on
Him continually.

3. That He may show Himself wonderful in and about
them, giving proof of His skill in quickening the dead
and in bringing such through to everlasting life who
were daily, as it were, giving up the ghost and at the
point of death.

4. That heaven may be heaven—that is, a place where
"the weary be at rest" (Job 3:17) and the troubled rest
(2 Thess. 1:7) and where the inhabitants will not say
they are sick (Isa. 33:24).

5. That they may be taught more the life of faith and of
dependence on Him and trained up in that way.

6. That He may be owned, acknowledged, and submitted
to as a sovereign God, doing what He will in heaven
and in earth.

For all this, there is no cause that any should take up any prejudice at Christianity—for, for all this their life is sure, and the outgate is sure and safe. Nor would they think it strange to see believers often mourning and drooping, seeing their case will often fall for new supplies of life. Their fits are not known to everyone, nor does everyone know what lies sometimes at their heart, nor would they think it such an easy matter to win to heaven as they imagine, and so deceive themselves. The righteous are saved through many deaths.

And as for believers, they would not think it strange to meet with such fits of deadness nor thence conclude that all their former work was but delusion and that they are still in the state of nature. But rather [they would] observe the wisdom, faithfulness, and power of God in bringing their broken ship through so much broken water, indeed, and ship-wrecks, and His goodness in ordering matters so as they will be kept humble, watchful, diligent, and constant in dependence on Him who is and must be their life, first and last. And hence [they would] learn a necessity of living always near to Christ and depending constantly on Him by faith. For He being their life, they cannot be without Him, but they must die and decay.

II. We hence learn that under all these fits of deadness to which His people are subject, nothing without Christ will help—not:

1. All their pains in and about ordinary means, prayer, reading, hearing, meditation, conference, etc. They will all cry out that help is not in them—for He is the life.

2. Nor extraordinary duties such as fasting and prayer and vows. These will never revive and quicken a drooping or fainting, sickly soul—for they are not Christ, nor the life.

3. Nor will a stout, courageous spirit and resolution of heart avail. If He who is the life breathe not, all that will melt away and vanish.

4. Nor will the stock of habitual grace which remains in the soul be sufficient to quicken and revive the sick soul if the life breathe not on these habits. And if new influences of life and strength flow not in on the soul and new rays come not down from this Sun of Righteousness to warm the frozen soul, the habits will lie by as dead.

5. Far less will their great gifts and endowments help them out of that dead condition. All their light and knowledge without the influences of this life will prove weak and insufficient for this end and purpose.

6. Nor will sound, pure and lively-like ordinances work out this effect. For till He look down, all these ordinances may prove dead and deadening to them.

It were good if believers were living under the conviction of this daily and by their practice and carriage declaring if they believe that Christ only is the life and that they must live in Him and be quickened and revived through Him alone.

III. We see hence that Christ is the life—that is, one that sufficiently, indeed, and abundantly can help the believer while under those fits of deadness which have been mentioned, and the like. There is in Him a rich supply of things that tend to revive, encourage, strengthen, and enliven a soul under spiritual deadness and fainting. Therefore is He called the life, as having in Him all that which is necessary for and answerable to souls under spiritual sicknesses, distempers, desertions, fainting, and swooning fits, etc.—for with Him "is the fountain of life" (Ps. 36:9) and He it is that upholdeth the soul in life (66:9) and can command "the blessing, even life for ever-more" (133:3).

Further Considerations

For further clearing of this, we would consider these things:

I. That He is God, equal with the Father in power and glory, and by this "hath life in himself" (John 5:26) and "quickeneth whom he will" (v. 21). By this He proves His own Godhead and equality with the Father, so (John 1:4) it is said that "in him was life," and that life was the light of men, by which also His Godhead is confirmed. This should be firmly believed and rooted in our hearts as being the ground of all our hope, comfort, and life—for, were it not so that our mediator were the true God, all our hopes were gone, our comforts could not be long lived, and our life were extinct.

II. As mediator God-man, He is fully and thoroughly furnished to quicken and enliven His members and followers, first and last. And all along their life must be hid with Christ in God, "for in him dwelleth all the fulness of the Godhead bodily" (Col. 2:9). As mediator, He is called "a tree of life" (Prov. 3:18), quickening and enlivening all that feed on Him, and "the bread of life" (John 6:35, 48). Indeed, because of power and authority to command life to the dead soul, He is called "the Prince of life" (Acts 3:15). And as a living, quickening stone, He gives life to all that are built on Him (1 Peter 2:4). Indeed, as being fully fitted and furnished for this work, He calls Himself "the resurrection, and the life" (John 11:25). This should be riveted in our hearts as a comfortable and encouraging truth.

III. Of this stock of life and quickening and reviving grace which He has got and is furnished with as mediator and redeemer of His people, He is communicative—"of his fulness have all we received, and grace for grace" (John 1:16). He got it that He might give it out and that from Him as a head it might flow to His members. And therefore He is the bread that came down from heaven and gives life to the world (6:35). Indeed, He gives eternal life to all His sheep (10:28). And He is come for this end: that His sheep might have life (v. 10). Therefore has He taken on such relations as may give ground of confirmation of this, as of a head, of a stock or root, and the like. This consideration is strengthening and reviving.

IV. He communicates of this stock of life and of reviving strength, which He has most sweetly and on most easy terms, so that:

1. Such as seek Him will find life by Him (Ps. 69:32).

2. Indeed, such as know Him will not miss life (John 17:3; 1 John 5:20).

3. If we will believe on Him and rest on Him, we have life first and last (John 3:15, 16, 36; 6:40, 47; 1 Tim. 1:16).

4. If we will come to Him (John 5:40) and cast our dead soul on Him, we will live.

5. If we will hear His voice (Isa. 55:3) and receive His instructions, we will live, for they are the instructions of life.

6. Indeed, if the soul be so dead that it can neither walk nor hear, if it can but look to Him, He will give life (Isa. 45:22).

7. And if the soul be so weak that it cannot look nor lift up its eyes, yet if it be willing, He will come with life (Rev. 22:17). Oh, if this were believed!

V. As He is communicative of that life which He has gotten as head, and that on easy terms, so He gives out of that life liberally, largely, abundantly, indeed, more abundantly (John 10:10). The water of life which He gives is "a well of water springing up to everlasting life" (4:14). Therefore, He allows His friends to drink abundantly (Cant. 5:1).

VI. Yet it would be remembered that He is Lord and master of it and prince of this life and so may dispense it and give it out in what measure He sees fit. And He is wise to measure out best for His own glory and to their advantage.

VII. All this life is sure in Him—none of His will be disappointed of it. His offices, which He has taken on, and His commission, which He has of the Father, abundantly clear this. And love to His will not suffer Him to keep up anything that is for their advantage. He is faithful in His house as a son and will do all that was committed to Him to do. The whole transaction of the covenant of redemption and suretyship and all the promises of the new covenant of grace confirm this to be a sure truth—so that they that have Him have life (Prov. 8:35; 1 John 5:2).

VIII. Indeed, all that is in Christ contributes to this life and quickening. His words and doctrine are the words of eternal life (John 6:63, 68; Phil. 2:16). His works and ways are the ways of life (Acts 2:28). His natures, offices, sufferings, actings, [and] all He did as mediator concur to the quickening and enlivening of a poor, dead soul.

IX. This fullness of life which He has is fully suited to the believer's condition in all points, as we will hear.

X. This life is eminently and transcendently in Him and exclusively of all others. It is in Him and in Him alone. And it is in Him in a most excellent manner. So that He is the life in the abstract—not only a living head and an enlivening head, but life itself, the life, the "resurrection and the life."

CHAPTER 20

Some General Uses

*B*efore we come to speak of some particular cases of deadness in which believers are to make use of Christ as the life, we will first propose some useful consequences and deductions from what has been spoken of this life, and:

Faith in These Truths Are of Great Use
The faith of those things which have been mentioned would be of great use and advantage to believers. And therefore they should study to have the faith of this truth fixed on their hearts and a deep impression of it on their spirits, to the end that:

I. Be their case and condition what it will, they might be kept from despair and despondency of spirit, from giving over their case as hopeless, and from looking on themselves as irremediably gone. The faith of Christ being life, and the life, would keep up the soul in hope and cause it say, "However dead my case be, yet life can help me. And He who is the resurrection and the life can recover me."

II. Indeed, be their case and condition what it will, they would have here some ground of encouragement to go to Him with their dead soul and to look to Him for help, seeing He is the life, as mediator, to the end He might enliven and quicken His dead, fainting, swooning members and to recover them from their deadness.

III. They might be freed from many scruples and objections that scar and discourage them. This one truth believed would clear up the way so as that such things as would have been impediments and objections before will vanish and be rolled out of the way now—such as the objections taken from their own worthlessness, their long continuance in that dead condition, and the like.

IV. They might by this likewise be freed from that dreadful plague and evil of jealousy by which the soul is often kept back from coming to Christ. For they fear He will not make them welcome. They doubt of His love and tenderness and question His pity and compassion. Indeed, their jealousy makes them to doubt of His faithfulness, so that the faith of this truth would cure this jealousy and deliver the soul from it and open a way for the soul to come forward with boldness and confidence.

V. They might also be by this helped to wait with patience and to be still and quiet under the Lord's various dispensations, so as they would not fret nor repine against Him, knowing that He would prove Himself to be life, even the life, in His own good time. So that the soul would patiently wait at His door till He were pleased to look out and with His look convey life into their dead soul.

VI. They might be preserved by this from looking out to or expecting any help from any other quarter, knowing that He alone is the life, and so that help can nowhere else be had. The faith of this truth would guard from any sinistrous[1] ways which the soul in a time of strait is ready to run to for relief—for by this would it see that neither instruments nor means nor outward administrations nor anything of that kind can quicken their dead soul, and that He and He alone must breathe in life into them, as at first, so now again.

Admiration of the Goodness of God

May we not see and observe here great matter of admiration at the goodness and rich bounty of God toward His people, who has found out and condescended on such a sure, safe, and satisfying way by which He becomes all things to His people which they stand in need of, and that despite:

1. That we are most unworthy of any such dispensation of grace at His hands.

2. That we too often are too desirous of other guests in our hearts beside[s] Him. Oh how much corruption, sin, and death lodge within our souls! And how more desirous are we oftentimes of death than of life!

3. That we little improve the noble advantages for life which we have granted to us. Indeed, many a time we abuse them. And this He did foresee, and yet despite this would condescend to us.

4. That we do little express our thankfulness for such mercies.

But not for our sakes has He done this but for His own name's sake. For noble and holy ends has He resolved on this course, as:

---

1. *Sinistrous*: sinister.

1. That He might be all in all (Col. 3:11), and they nothing. That He alone might fill all in all (Eph. 1:23), and they be empty and nothing without Him.

2. That He might wear the glory of all—"for of him, and through him, and to him, are all things" (Rom. 11:36), and that no man might share in it.

3. That man might be His everlasting debtor and cast down in testimony of it his crown at His feet who sitteth on the throne, as those did (Rev. 4:10), and might cry out with these same elders, "Thou art worthy, O Lord, to receive glory and honour and power, etc." (v. 11), and with those, "Worthy is the Lamb that was slain to receive power, and riches, and wisdom, and strength, and honour, and glory, and blessing" (5:12).

4. That man's mouth might be stopped forever and all boasting excluded, for man is a proud creature and ready to boast of that which is nothing and vanity. Now God has chosen this noble way of the covenant of grace that no man might boast any more. Where is boasting then? It is excluded. By what law? By the law of works? No, but by the law of faith, says the apostle (Rom. 3:24).

5. That all might be sure to the poor chosen believer. The Lord will not have the stock of life any longer to be in a man's own hand, for even Adam in the state of innocency could not use it well but made shipwreck of it and turned a bankrupt. Much more would man now do so in this state of sin in which he lies at present. Therefore has God, out of love and tenderness to His chosen ones, put all their stock in the hand of Christ who is better able to manage it, to God's glory and man's advantage, being faithful in all things and

a trusty servant, having the fullness of the Godhead dwelling in Him bodily. "Therefore," the apostle says, "it is of faith, that it might be by grace; to the end the promise might be sure to all the seed" (Rom. 4:16).

6. That believers might have strong consolation, despite all the opposition of enemies without and within, when they see that now their "life is hid with Christ in God" (Col. 3:3), and that their life is in their head. They will not fear so much devils and men without nor their own dead and corrupt hearts within.

Those without Excuse

How inexcusable must all such be:

1. Who will not lay hold on this life, on Jesus who is the life, sure life, indeed, everlasting life.

2. Who seek life any other way than by and through Him who is the life.

3. Who oppose this way of life and not only reject the offers of it but prove enemies to it and to all that carry it or preach it.

Encouragement for Those in the Way of Life

Here is strong encouragement to all that would be at heaven to enter into this gospel, which is a way of life. Such need not fear that their salvation will not be advanced. Let Satan and all their adversaries do what they can, all that enter into this way will live. For the way itself is life, and nothing but life. So that here all objections are obviated. Life can answer all. If the believer fear that he will never win through difficulties, he will die by the way, or, by fainting, succumbing, and swooning, dishonor the profession and at length fall off and apostatize, or despair and give over all hope—here is that which may answer and obviate all: "I am the life." And who can perish in the way which is the way of life, an enlivening way, indeed, the way which is life itself—indeed, the life in a singular and eminent manner?

Reproof for Those Not Living as They Should

Here is ground of reproof even of believers who, though they have come to Christ, yet do not live in Him as they ought, do not walk in Him with that liveliness and activity which is called for, but:

I. Lean too much to their own understanding, gifts, or grace, and think by this to ride out storms and to wade through all difficulties, while as, if He who is the life do not breathe on us, all that will fail us in the day of trial. Our understanding and parts or gifts may dry up, and our graces may wither and decay and go backward.

II. Rest too much on duties, when they should in them go to Him who is the life. For only in Him is life to be had, and Him should they seek to in the ordinances that they might have life from Him in those outward duties. And this appears in their way of going about duties without that dependence on Him and single eyeing of Him which is called for. As also by their fretting and repining when duties do not their business, as if life lay all in duties, and concluding all will be right because they get duties somewhat tolerably performed, and, on the contrary, desponding when duties fall heavy on them and they find themselves indisposed for duty. All which clearly evinces that they lay too much weight on duties, while as it would be otherwise with them if they were purely depending on Christ and looking for all from Him.

III. Despond too soon because they get not help and relief instantly, or because they are not preserved from every degree of fainting.

IV. Neglect to make use of Him and to come to Him with all their wants, failings, and necessities as they ought, or come not with that freedom and boldness which the gospel grounds allow.

The Misery of Those Outside of Christ
This preaches out the woeful misery of such as are strangers to Christ. For being strangers to the life, they have no life. They are dead, and death is engraven on all they do, even though:

I. They should be very diligent in external duties, indeed, and outstrip many true believers—as the Pharisees had their fasts twice a week (Luke 18).

II. They should be eminently gifted, able to instruct others and to speak of the mysteries of the gospel to purpose and to edification. For such gifts of knowledge and utterance may be where the lively operations of the grace of Christ are not and, consequently, where Christ is not as the life.

III. They should seem eminent in all their outward carriage and seem to carry most Christianly in all their walk and appear most devout in the matter of worship.

IV. And they should have something more than ordinary, even taste of the heavenly gift and be made partakers of extraordinary gifts of the Holy Ghost—indeed, and taste the good word of God and the powers of the world to come (Heb. 6:4–5).

The Blessed Condition of Those in Christ

This discovers the noble advantage of such as have accepted of Christ for their life. Their condition is happy, sure, desirable, and thriving; for Christ is theirs, and life is theirs—because Christ, who is the life, is theirs.

Objections and Answers

No Blessed Condition?

But some wicked persons may say, "We see not that happy and advantageous condition of such as go for believers, for we observe them to be as little lively oftentimes as others and as unfit for duties, indeed, and sometimes as much subject to sin and corruption as others."*Answer:*

I. However it be with them either in your eyes or possibly in their own sometimes, yet you may hold your peace. For in their worst condition, they would not exchange with you for a world. In their deadest-like condition, they are not void of all life as you are, despite all your motions and seeming activeness in duty—because all your motion in and about duty is but like the moving of children's puppets, caused by external motives such as a name, applause, peace from a natural conscience, or the like, and not from any inward principle of grace and life.

II. Even though they sometimes seem to be dead, yet they are not always so. Life does really work sometimes in them, whereas there was never any true or kindly motion of life in you.

III. There may be more life in them, indeed, life in motion, when they seem to be overcome with some lusts or corruption, indeed, when really they are overcome, than beholders that are strangers to the heart can observe. For when temptation is violent, as having the advantage of the time and place, of the constitution of the body, and the like, it argues no small degree of life and of life in motion to make some resistance and opposition to it, though at length he should be overcome by it. And this opposition and resistance, flowing from a principle of grace, speaks out life, though corruption, having the advantage, should at that time overpower the motion of life and carry the man away.

IV. If it be not otherwise with believers than is objected, they may blame themselves for not improving Christ better for life.

No Confirmation?
But some who are true believers will object the same and cry out of themselves as dead and say they find not that liveliness and activity in their souls that will evidence Christ, the life, dwelling and working in them. *Answer.* It may be they prejudge themselves of that lively frame they might enjoy and so wrong themselves:

I. In not exercising faith on Christ and drawing life from Him and through Him. The life which they live should be by faith (Gal. 2:20). How then can such as do not eat become fat? By faith we feed on Christ.

II. In not watching but giving way to security and by this encouraging and strengthening the adversary, as we see in David. When they stand not on their watchtower, they invite Satan to set on. And he is vigilant enough and knows how to take his advantage and to improve his opportunity.

III. In giving way to laziness and not stirring up themselves, as we see in the bride (Cant. 3:1; 5:3). When they stir not up the grace of God which is in them, how can they be lively? If grace be laid by, it will contract rust. The best way to keep grace lively is to keep it in exercise, however little it be.

IV. By their rashness, walking without fear, as is to be observed in Peter when he slipped so foully. When through their want of circumspection, they precipitate themselves into danger and cast themselves among their enemies' hands, is it any wonder that it go not with them as they would, and that they provoke God to leave them to themselves that they may know what they are and learn afterward not to tempt the Lord and to walk more circumspectly?

V. By leaning too much to their attainments and not looking out for new influences of grace and life. By this they provoke God to let them know to their expense that, for as great a length as they are come, they must live by faith and be quickened by new influences from the Spirit of life.

VI. So they may wrong themselves through their ignorance of Christ and of the way of making use of Him. And if they through unacquaintedness with Christ and the right way of improving the fullness that is in Him miss the fruit and advantage which otherwise they might have, they can only blame themselves.

VII. They may also prejudge themselves by their self-love, self-esteem, self-seeking, self-pleasing, etc., which piece and piece[2] will draw them off Christ and cause them forget the way of sucking life from Him who is the fountain of life.

VIII. When they give way to small sins, they open a door to greater. And they lose by this their tenderness and so provoke

---

2. *Piece and piece:* piece by piece.

the Lord to withdraw. And this is another way by which they prejudge themselves of that benefit of liveliness which they might otherwise have.

IX. So also by worldly-mindedness, which alienates their mind from God.

X. And by their impatience and fretting and repining against God and His wise dispensations, they also prejudge and wrong themselves. For while they are in that mood, they cannot with due composedness of spirit go to Christ and draw life from Him through faith.

Complaints?
But is there not even some of those who are most tender that complain of their deadness and shortcomings? *Answer:*

I. It may be that they complain without cause and that they have more cause of rejoicing and of blessing the Lord for what He has done to them than of complaining.

II. Their complaining will not prove the want of life but rather the contrary. For when they complain most, they must be most sensible if their complaints be real and not merely for a fashion. And sense is a manifest evidence of life.

III. It would be remembered that the Lord can make their failings and shortcomings contribute to the furthering of their life, as we see it did in Peter.

IV. It would also be remembered that Christ does not distribute and give out of this life to all His members and followers in a like measure, but to some more and to others less, according as He sees it meet and convenient, both for His own glory and their good. He has more service for some than for others. And some He will employ in greater and more difficult work, which will call for more life. And others He will employ in common work, which will not call for such an eminent degree of life.

V. And on the same account, He may think it good to give to the same person a larger measure of grace at one time than at another.

VI. And that for wise reasons and noble ends, as:

1. That all may see how absolute He is in His dispensations—a sovereign that does with His own what He will and will not give an account of any of His ways or communications to us.

2. That we may learn submission and quietly to stoop before Him, whatever measure He be pleased to dispense toward us.

3. That we may learn to depend on Him more closely all along—in all our ways to acknowledge Him.

4. That we may learn to exercise patience, which must have its perfect work in waiting on Him as a great king. This is His glory, and it is the testifying of our homage to Him.

5. He will train us up so as to be well contented and satisfied if He bring us home at length, though not with such a convoy of the graces of His Spirit as we would wish.

6. That we may see and read our daily obligation to Christ our life and the daily need we have of Him keeping our life in by fresh gales of His Spirit and new heavenly influences.

7. And that getting new proofs of His kindness and faithfulness, we may give Him new songs of praise daily and

so express our thankfulness to Him, which will tend to set forth His glory.

Duties

This may point out to believers several duties to which they are called. We will name some few of many, as:

I. That they should rejoice and be comforted in the thoughts of this: that they have such a complete mediator, one that is thoroughly furnished and made all things for them—not only the way, and the truth, but the life also.

II. The thoughts of this should also stir up the wondering at the wisdom, graciousness, and goodness of God and to thankfulness for providing such an all-sufficient way for them.

III. This should also encourage them under all temptations, faintings, backsets, and fits of deadness that they fall into that there is one who is the life, and that He whom their soul has chosen is the life and so fully able to quicken and enliven them.

IV. This should teach them humility and not to be proud of anything they have or do—for it is He who is the life who keeps them in life and helps them to any duty. Indeed, it is life that works all in them.

V. And likewise it should teach them to acknowledge Him to whom they are obliged for anything they do, for any life they have, or any acts or fruits of life that appear in them, and to be thankful to Him therefore.

VI. And mainly, they should here read their obligation and duty to improve this advantage and to draw life out of this fountain and so live by this life, act and do all in and through this life, and so be quickened by this life in all their fits of deadness. And for this cause [they] would keep these things in mind:

1. That they should live in a constant conviction of their own weakness, deadness, and inability to do any acts of life of themselves, and far less to recover themselves out of any distemper and fit of deadness which they fall into.

2. That they should live in the faith of this: that there is life enough in Him who is the life to do their business. They should be persuaded of His all-sufficiency.

3. That He is not only an all-sufficient deliverer, able to deliver a soul that is, as it were, rotting in the grave and to cause the dead to hear His voice and live, but also most willing and ready to answer them in all their necessities according to wisdom and as He sees it for His glory and their soul's advantage. The faith of this is necessary and will be very encouraging.

4. That they should go to Him however dead-like their condition be and by faith roll their dead case on Him who is the life.

5. That they should pray on the promises of grace and influence, even out of the belly of hell or of the grave, with Jonah (2:2)—for He is faithful and true and tenderhearted and will hear and give a good answer at length.

6. That in the exercise of faith and prayer they should wait with patience till He be pleased to come and breathe on the dry bones and till the Sun of Righteousness arise on their souls with healing in His wings.

But of this more particularly in the following cases, which now we come to speak a little to, of purpose to clear more fully how the believer is to make use of Christ as the life when he is under some one distemper or other that calls for life and quickening from Christ the life. We cannot handle distinctly all the particular cases which may be brought under this head. It will suffice for clearing of this great duty to speak to some few.

CHAPTER 21

How to Make Use of Christ as the Life When the Believer Is So Sitten-Up in the Ways of God That He Can Do Nothing

*S*ometimes the believer is under such a distemper of weakness and deadness that there is almost no commanded duty that he can go about. His heart and all is so dead that he cannot so much as groan under that deadness. Indeed, he may be under such a decay that little or no difference will be observed between him and others that are yet in nature. And [he may] be not only unable to go actively and lively about commanded duties, indeed, or to wrestle from under that deadness but also be so dead that he will scarce have any effectual desire or longing to be out of that condition. Now, in speaking to the use-making of Christ for quickening in this dead case, we will do these things:

1. For clearing of the case, we will show how probably it is brought on.

2. How Christ is life to the soul in such a case as this.

3. How the believer is to make use of Christ for the life in this case.

4. And further clear the matter by answering a question or two.

The Causes of Weakness and Deadness

As to the first, such a distemper as this may be brought on the soul:

I. Through some strong and violent temptation from without meeting with some evil disposition of the heart within and so surprising and overpowering the poor soul, as we see in David and Peter.

II. Through the cunning and sleight of Satan stealing the believer that is not watchful enough insensibly off his feet and singing him asleep by degrees.

III. Through carelessness in not adverting at first to the beginnings and first degrees of this deadness and upsitting, when the heart begins to grow formal and superficial in duties and to be satisfied with a perfunctorious performance without life and sense.

IV. Through torturing of conscience in light and smaller matters, for this may provoke God to let conscience fall asleep and so the soul become more untender and scruple little, at length, at great matters. And thus deadness may come to a height, God ordering it so, for a further punishment to them for their untenderness and uncircumspectness.

V. Through them not stirring up themselves and shaking off that spirit of laziness and drowsiness when it first seizes on them, but, with the sluggard, yet another slumber and another sleep and a folding of the hands to sleep.

VI. Continuing in some known sin and not repenting of it may bring on this distemper, as may be observed in David.

How Christ Is the Life of the Soul

As to the second particular, Christ is life to the soul in this case, in that:

I. He keeps possession of the soul, for the seed remains. The root abides fast in the ground. There is life still at the heart, though the man make no motion, like one in a deep sleep or in a swoon—yet life is not away.

II. He in due time awakens and rouses up the soul and so recovers it out of that condition by some means or other, either by some alarm of judgment and terror, as He did David, or dispensation of mercy and tenderness, as He did Peter. And usually He recovers the soul:

1. By discovering something of this condition by giving so much sense and knowledge and sending so much light as will let the soul see that it is not well and that it is under that distemper of lifelessness.

2. By the discovering the dreadfulness of such a condition and how hazardous it is to continue in it.

3. By putting the soul in mind that He is the life and the resurrection, and through the stirring up of grace, causing the soul to look to Him for quickening and outgate.

4. By raising up the soul at length out of that drowsiness and sluggish folding of the hands to sleep and out of that deep security, and putting it into a more lively, vigilant, and active frame.

How to Make Use of Christ

As to the third, the believer that would make use of Christ for a recovery out of this condition would mind these duties:

I. He would look to Christ as the light of men and the enlightener of the blind, to the end [that] he may get a better and a more thorough discovery of his condition. For it is half health here to be sensible of this disease. The soul that is once brought to sense is half recovered of this fever and lethargy.

II. He would eye Christ as God, able to cause the dead and dry bones to live (as Ezekiel 27). And this will keep from despondency and despair. Indeed, it will make the poor believer conceive hope when he sees that his physician is God, to whom nothing is impossible.

III. He would look to Him also as head and husband and life to the poor soul that adheres to Him. And this will strengthen his hope and expectation, for he will see that Christ is engaged (to speak so) in point of honor to quicken a poor, dead, and lifeless member—for the life in the head is for the good of the whole body and of every member of the body that is not quite cut off. And the good that is in the husband is forthcoming for the relief of the poor wife that has not yet got a bill of divorce. And Christ being life, and the life, He must be appointed for the relief, the quickening and recovering from death of such as are given to Him, that they may be finally raised up at the last day. He must present all His members lively in that day.

IV. He would by faith wrap himself up in the promises and lie before this Sun of Righteousness till the heat of His beams thaw his frozen heart and bring warmth into his cold and dead soul and thus renew his grips of Him, accepting of Him as the life and as his life. Christ Himself tells us (John 11:40) that this is the Father's will that has sent Him: that everyone that sees the Son and believes on Him might have everlasting life, and He will raise him up at the last day. Faith closing with Him—as it was the mean[s] of life at first, so it will be the mean[s] of recovery out of a dead distemper afterward.

V. He would mourn for such sins and provocations as he discovers in himself to have caused and brought on this distemper. Repentance and godly sorrow for such evils as have sinned Christ and life away is a way to bring life back again.

VI. He would be sure to harbor no known sin in his soul but to set himself against every known evil as an enemy to the life and recovery which he is seeking.

VII. He must wait on Christ his life in the appointed means, for that is the will of the Lord that He should be waited on there and sought for there. There is little hopes of recovery for such as lay aside the ordinances. Though the ordinances without Him cannot revive or quicken a poor soul, yet He has condescended so far as to come with life to His people in and through the ordinances and has appointed us to wait for Him there. We must be willing to accept of all His condescensions of love and seek and wait for Him there where He has said He will be found.

VIII. In going about those ordinances of life, he would beware of putting them in Christ's room—that is, he would beware of thinking that ordinances will do his business, as some ignorantly do who think that by praying so often a-day and reading so much and hearing so much [that] they will recover their lost lively frame, when, alas, all the ordinances, without Him, signify nothing. They, without Him, are cold and lifeless and can never bring heat and warmth to a cold soul. It is He in the ordinances whom we are to seek and from whom alone life is to be expected, and none else.

IX. Though life lies not in the ordinances as separated from Christ, and life is to be expected from Him alone, yet he would beware of going about the ordinances in a careless, superficial, and indifferent manner—for this will argue little desire after life and will bring on more deadness. The ordinances then should be gone about seriously, diligently, and with great carefulness, indeed, with such earnestness as if life were not about the ordinances at all. This is the right way of going about the ordinances.

X. He must in all this wait with patience without fretting or quarrelling with Him for Him delaying to come. He must wait with much humility. It becomes not him who has through his folly sinned life away to quarrel now with God because He restores him not again to life at the first asking. He may be glad if at length after long seeking, waiting, and much diligence He come and restore to him the joy of salvation, and if he be not made to lie as bedrid[den] all his days for a monument of folly in sinning away his life, strength, and legs as he did.

XI. He must beware of giving way to anything that may increase or continue this deadness—such as untenderness in his walk, unwatchfulness, negligence, and carelessness. And especially he must beware not to provoke God by sinning against light.

XII. He would also beware of limiting the Lord to any set measure of life and strength. For it becomes not beggars to be carvers,[1] far less such beggars as through folly have sinned away a good portion. It was not for the prodigal to seek a new patrimony after he had dilapidated the former. It might suffice him to be made as a servant.

---

1. *Beggars to be carvers*: beggars to be choosers.

XIII. He would use well any small measure of life he gets for God and His glory. Gets he but one talent, he should use it that he may gain by it. We say, use limbs and have limbs; use strength and have it. This will be the way to get more.

XIV. He would be taking on the vows of the Lord, and that in the Lord to walk more watchful in time coming, charging all within and without not to stir or provoke the Lord to depart further or to scare Him from coming to the soul.

Further Questions
As to the last particular, if it be inquired:

I. What can that soul do that is not sensible of this deadness and weakness?

Answer. Though there be not any real sense and feeling of this condition, yet there may be a suspicion that all is not right. And if this be, the soul must look out to Christ for the life of sense and for a sight of the provocations that have brought on that condition. He that is the life must recover the very beginnings of life. And when the soul wins to any real apprehension and sense of this deadness, it must follow the course formerly prescribed for a recovery.

II. But it will be asked, How can a soul act faith in such a case? And if it cannot act faith, how can it come to Christ and make use of Him?

Answer. It is true; while the soul is in that case, it cannot act a strong and lively faith. Yet it can act a weak and a sickly faith. And a weak faith and a sickly faith can lay hold on an enlivening Christ and so bring in more strength and life to the soul. If the soul be so weak as that it cannot grip, yet it can look to Him that can quicken the dead and has helped many a poor soul before out of a dead condition. Or if it cannot do so much as look, yet it may give a half look and lie before Him who waits to be gracious and sustain itself if it can get no more with a maybe He will come.

III. But further, it may be asked, What can the soul do when, after all this, it finds no help or supply but deadness remaining—indeed, and it may be growing?

Answer. The soul in that case must lie at His door, waiting for His salvation and resolving if no better may be to die at His door, and leave no approved means or commanded duty unessayed that it may recover its former vigor, activity, and strength. And while the believer is waiting sure that he will never be ashamed (Ps. 25:3; 69:6; Isa. 50:18).

CHAPTER 22

How Christ Is to Be Made Use of as Our Life in Case of Heartlessness and Fainting through Discouragements

There is another evil and distemper which believers are subject to, and that is a case of fainting through manifold discouragements, which make them so heartless that they can do nothing, indeed, and to sit up, as if they were dead. The question then is how such a soul will make use of Christ as in the end it may be freed from that fit of fainting and win over those discouragements. For satisfaction to which we will:

1. Name some of those discouragements which occasion this.

2. Show what Christ has done to remove all those discouragements.

3. Show how the soul should make use of Christ for life in this case.

4. And add a few words of caution.

Some Discouragements Which Cause This

As to the first, there are several things which may give occasion to this distemper. We will name these few:

I. The sense of a strong, active, lively, and continually stirring body of death, and that despite means used to bear it down and kill it. This is very discouraging, for it made Paul cry out, "Woe is me, miserable man. Who will deliver me from this body of death?" (cf. Rom. 7:24). It is a most discouraging thing to be still fighting and yet getting no ease, let be victory—to have to do with an enemy that abides always alike strong, fight and oppose as we will, indeed, not only is not weakened, far less overcome, but that grows in power and prevails. And this many times affects the hearts of God's children and causes them to faint.

II. It may be the case of some that they are assaulted with strange temptations and buffetings of Satan that are not usual. This made Paul cry out thrice (2 Corinthians 12). And if the Lord had not told him that His grace was sufficient for him, what would he have done? Hence some of His cry out in their complaint, "Was there ever any so tempted, so assaulted with the devil, as I am?" Sure[ly] this dispensation cannot but be much afflicting, saddening, and discouraging.

III. The sense of the real weakness of grace under lively means and despite their serious and earnest desires and endeavors after growth in grace cannot but disquiet and discourage them. For they may readily conclude that all their pains and labor will be in vain for anything they can observe.

IV. The want of sensible incomes of joy and comfort is another fainting and discouraging dispensation—as the feeling of these is a heart-strengthening and most encouraging thing, which made David so earnestly cry for it (Ps. 51:8, 12). When a poor soul that has the testimony of his own conscience that it has been in some measure of singleness of heart and honestly seeking the face of God for a good many years and yet cannot say that ever it knew what those incomes of joy and comfort meant which some have tasted largely of, it cannot choose but be discouraged and much cast down, as not knowing what to say of itself or how to judge of its own case.

V. The want of access in their addresses to God is another heart-discouraging thing. They go about the duty of prayer with that measure of earnestness and uprightness of heart that they can win at—at least this is their aim and endeavor. And yet they meet with a fast closed door, when they cry and shout. He shuts out their prayer, as the church complains (Lam. 3:8). This sure[ly] will affect them deeply and cause their hearts sometimes to faint.

VI. The want of freedom and liberty in their addresses to God is another thing which causes sorrow and fainting. They go to pray, but their tongue cleaves to the roof of their mouth. They are straitened and cannot get their hearts vented.

VII. Outward persecution that attends the way of godliness and afflictions that accompany such as live godly is another discouraging thing, both to themselves who are under afflictions and to others who hear it and see it. Wherefore the apostle desires earnestly that the Ephesians should not faint at his tribulation (Eph. 3:13).

VIII. The Lord's sharp and sore dispensations for sin, as toward David (Psalm 51), or out of His sovereignty for trial and other ends, as toward Job, is likewise a discouraging, heartbreaking thing, and that which will make strong giants to roar and faint and look on themselves as dead men, as we see in these two eminent men of God.

How Christ Removes These Discouragements

As to the second thing, Christ is life to the believer in this case: in having done that which in reason may support under all these discouragements and having done so much for removing or weakening of these, indeed, and for carrying them over all, which may be in a word cleared as to each.

I. As for the body of death, let it stir in the believer as fast as it will or can, it is already killed. And all that struggling is but like the struggling of a man in the pangs of death—for our "old man is crucified with Christ" (Rom. 6:6). And the believer is dead to sin and risen legally with Him (Col. 2:11–12; 3:3). But of this I spoke abundantly above.

II. As to Satan troubling the poor believer, through Christ also he is a vanquished enemy. He hath overcome "him that had the power of death, that is, the devil" (Heb. 2:14).

III. As for that felt weakness of grace, that is no ground of discouragement, so long as He lives who can make the lame to leap as a hart and can make waters break out in the wilderness and streams in the desert (Isa. 35:6–7), and "giveth power to the faint; and to them that have no might he increaseth strength." So that such as "wait upon the LORD shall renew their strength; and they shall mount up with wings as eagles; they shall run and not be weary; and they shall walk, and not faint" (40:29, 31). For in Him are all the promises yea and amen (2 Cor. 1:20). So that they need not faint on this account nor be discouraged—for the work He has begun, He will finish it, and He will quicken in the way (Ps. 119:37).

IV. As for the want of sensible incomes of joy and comfort, He has promised to send the Comforter in His own good time (John 14:26; 15:26). As one whom "his mother comforteth," so will He comfort His (Isa. 66:13). Joy and gladness is promised in the covenant (Jer. 31:13). But further, though He keep up these influences of joy and comfort, He supports another way. The lively hope of heaven may bear up the heart under all this want, for there will the soul have fullness of joy and pleasures forevermore—no tears, no sorrow there (Ps. 16:11; Isa. 35:10).

V. As for the want of access in their prayers, they may possibly blame themselves, for He has by His merits opened the door and is become (to speak so) master usher to the poor soul to lead him to the Father, so that by Him we have access (Eph. 2:18), indeed, boldness and access through faith in Him (3:12). And He is our advocate (1 John 2:1) and, as our attorney, is gone to heaven before us, and there lives forever to make intercession (Heb. 6:28; 7:25). And what is there more to be done to procure us access or to move and encourage us to "come boldly unto the throne of grace, that we may obtain mercy, and find grace to help in time of need" (4:14, 16)?

VI. As to that want of freedom and liberty in prayer, He helps that also. For He makes the dumb to sing (Isa. 35:6) and makes the tongue of the stammerer to speak elegantly (32:4). He can enlarge the heart and help the soul to pour out his heart before God.

VII. As to outward persecution, He can easily take that discouragement away by giving the hundredfold with it, by supporting under it and bringing safe through it. When His presence is with them through fire and water (43:2), what can trouble them? And when He makes their consolations abound (2 Cor. 1:5), what can discourage them? Have not His sung in the very fires and rejoiced in all their afflictions? The resting of the

Spirit of God and of glory, which Peter speaks of (1 Peter 4:14), is comfortable enough.

VIII. As for all those sharp dispensations mentioned in the last place, He having taken the sting of all, even of death, away by taking away sin and purchas[ing] the blessing and love of the Father, having made reconciliation through His blood— all those dispensations flow from love, even such as seem sharpest, being inflicted for sin, as we see (Heb. 12:6). So that there is no cause here of fainting or of being so discouraged as to give over the matter. But for help in this case, there should be a use-making of Jesus as the life.

How to Make Use of Christ
And that is the third thing which we will speak a little to— namely, how the soul should make use of Christ as the life to the end it may be delivered from this fainting occasioned through manifold discouragements.

I. The believer in this case would mind the covenant of redemption in which Christ has promised and so stands obliged and engaged to carry on His own through all discouragements to the end. So that if any one believer miscarry, Christ loses more than they lose—for the believer can but lose his soul, but Christ will lose His glory, and this is more worth than all the souls that ever were created. And, further, not only will Christ lose His glory as redeemer, but the Father will lose His glory in not making good His promise to Christ His Son. For by the same covenant He stands engaged to carry through the seed that Christ had died for. And His appointing Christ to be His servant for this end and choosing Him from among all the folk and His upholding of Him, concurring with Him, delighting in Him, and promising that He will bring forth

judgment to the Gentiles, and that to victory, or to truth—
[all these] speak out His engagement to see all true believers
brought home (see Ps. 89:19–21, 28–29, 35–37; Isa. 42:1–4;
Matt. 12:17–21). Sure[ly] the faith of this would support the
poor believer under all those discouragements.

II. They would mind likewise the covenant of grace in which all
things are contrived and laid down, so far as that the believer
may have abundant consolation and comfort in all cases, and
in which there is enough to take away all cause of fainting and
discouragement, as might fully be made to appear, if any did
question it.

III. They would remember how richly Christ is furnished with
all qualifications, suiting even that case in which they are like
to be overwhelmed with discouragements. And could the
believer but think on and believe these three things, he might
be kept up under all discouragements:

1. That Christ is a compassionate, tenderhearted mediator, having bowels more tender than the bowels of any
mother, so that He will not break the bruised reed, nor
quench the smoking flax (Isa. 40:2). He had compassion on the very bodies of the multitude that followed
Him and would not let them go away fasting, lest
they should faint in the way (Matt. 15:32; Mark 8:3).
And will He not have compassion on the souls of His
followers, when [they] like to faint through spiritual
discouragements?

2. That He has power and authority to command all
things that can serve to carry on a poor believer, for
all power in heaven and in earth is given to Him. All
things are made subject to Him.

3. That He has a great readiness and willingness on many accounts to help His followers in their necessities.

Sure[ly], were these three firmly believed, the believer could not faint, having Christ, who is tender and loving and willing to help and in addition able to do what He will to look to and to run to for supply.

IV. They would take up Christ under all His heart-strengthening and soul-comforting relations as a tender brother, a careful shepherd, a fellow-feeling high priest, a loving husband, a sympathizing head, a life-communicating root, an all-sufficient king, etc.—any of which is enough to bear up the head and comfort the heart of a drooping, discouraged, and fainting soul. Much more may all of them yield strong consolation to support and revive a soul staggering and fainting through discouragement. Oh! If you would but rightly improve and dwell on the thoughts of the comforting and heart-quickening relations! Our hearts would not fail us so much as they do.

V. They would eye Him as now in glory who, as head and captain of salvation, has wrestled through and overcome all difficulties and discouragements that were in His way, and in name and behalf of all believers that are His followers and members of His body, is now possessed of glory. And from this [they should] draw a heart-comforting and soul-strengthening conclusion, thus: Is He entered into glory as head? Then such a poor, fainthearted, discouraged worm as I am may at length come there as a little bit of His body—especially since He said that, seeing He lives, all His will live also (John 14:19).

VI. They would remember how Christ, who was always heard of His Father (John 11:41), did supplicate for this as mediator and intercessor for His people (17:24), saying, "Father, I will that they also, whom thou hast given me, be with me where I am, etc." May not the poor, fainthearted believer that is looking to Jesus draw a heart-reviving and soul-encouraging conclusion out of this and say, "Though my prayers be shut out, and when I cry for relief under my discouragements, I get no hearing, but, on the contrary, my discouragements grow and my heart faints the more—yet Christ always was heard, and the Father will not say Him nay.[1] Why then may not I lift up my head in hope and sing in the hope of the glory of God in the midst of all my discouragements?"

VII. By faith, they would cast all their discouragements, entanglements, and difficulties as burdens too heavy for their back on Christ and leave them there with Him who only can remove them. And in addition, [they would] resolve never to give over but to go forward in His strength and thus become daily stronger and stronger in resolutions, purposes, desires, and endeavors, when they can do no more.

VIII. They would look to Jesus, the author and finisher of faith, and set Him before them as a copy of courage, "who for the joy that was set before him endured the cross, despising the shame" and endures contradiction of sinners against Himself (Heb. 12:2–3). And this may prove a mean[s] to keep us from wearying and fainting in our minds, as the apostle hints there.

IX. They would remember that Christ going before as the captain of their salvation has broken the ice to them and the force and strength of all those discouragements, as we did

---

1. *Say Him nay:* tell Him no.

lately show. So that now they should be looked on as broken and powerless discouragements.

X. They would fix their eye by faith on Jesus as only able to do their business, to bear up their head, to carry them through discouragements, to apply cordials to their fainting hearts. And [they would] remain fixed in that posture and resolution, looking for strengthening and encouraging life from Him and from Him alone, and thus declare that:

1. They are unable of themselves to stand out such storms of discouragements and to wrestle through such difficulties.

2. They believe He is only able to bear them up and carry them through and make them despise all those discouragements which the devil and their own evil hearts muster up against them.

3. That, come what will come, they will not quit the bargain. They will never recall or take back their subscription and consent to the covenant of grace and to Christ, as theirs, offered in it, though they should die and die again by the way.

4. That they would fain be kept on in the way and helped forward without failing and fainting by the way.

5. That they cannot run through hard walls. They cannot do impossibilities. They cannot break through such mighty discouragements.

6. That yet through Him they can do all things.

7. That He must help, or they are gone and will never win through all these difficulties and discouragements but will one day or other die by the hand of Saul.

8. That they will wait, earnestly seeking help from Him, crying for it, and looking for it, and resolve never to give over—and if they be disappointed they are disappointed.

Words of Caution

Now for the last particular, the word of caution—take these:

I. They would not think to be altogether free of fainting, for there is no perfection here, and there is much flesh and corruption remaining, and that will occasion fainting.

II. Nor would they think to be free of all the causes and occasions of this fainting—namely, the discouragements formerly mentioned or the like, for if the devil can do anything, he will work discouragements both within and without. So that they would lay their resolution to meet with discouragements, for few or none ever went to heaven but they had many a storm in their face. And they must not think to have a way paved for themselves alone.

III. They would not pore too much or dwell too long and too much on the thoughts of those discouragements, for that is Satan's advantage and tends to weaken themselves. But it were better to be looking beyond them, as Christ did (Heb. 12:2). When He had the cross and the shame to wrestle with, He looked to the joy that was set before Him. And that made Him endure the cross and despise the shame. And as Moses did (11:25–27) when he had afflictions and the wrath of the king to wrestle against. He had respect to the recompense of the reward, and so he endured as seeing Him who is invisible.

IV. They would remember that as Christ has tender bowels and is full of compassion and is both ready and able to help them, so is He wise and knows how to let out His mercies best. He is not like a foolish, affectionate mother that would hazard the life of the child before she put the child to any pain. He sees what is best for His own glory and for their good here and hereafter. And that He will do with much tenderness and readiness.

V. They would look on it as no mean mercy if, despite all the discouragements and storms that blow in their face, they are helped to keep their face up the hill and are fixed in their resolution, never willingly to turn their back on the way of God but to continue creeping forward as they may, whatever storms they meet with. Indeed, on this account ought they heartily to bless His name and to rejoice, for their hearts shall live that seek Him (Ps. 22:26).

VI. They would remember for their encouragement that, as many have been helped through all discouragements and have been brought home at length, so may they be brought through all those storms which now they wrestle with. It is the glory of the mediator to bring His broken, torn, and sinking vessel safe to shore.

Now, I come to a third case, and that is:

CHAPTER 23

_____

How to Make Use of Christ as the Life When the Soul Is Dead as to Duty

$\mathcal{S}$ ometimes the believer will be under such a distemper as that he will be as unfit and unable for discharging of any commanded duty as dead men or one in a swoon is to work or go a journey. And it were good to know how Christ should be made use of as the life to the end the diseased soul may be delivered from this. For this cause we will consider these four things:

1. See what are the several steps and degrees of this distemper.

2. Consider from where it comes or what are the causes or occasions of it.

3. Consider how Christ is life to the soul in such a dead case.

4. And point out the way of the soul's use-making of Christ that would be delivered from it.

The Steps and Degrees of This

As to the first, this distemper comes on by several steps and degrees. It will be sufficient to mention some of the main and most remarkable steps, such as:

312   CHRIST THE WAY, THE TRUTH, AND THE LIFE

I. There is a falling from our watchfulness and tenderness. And when we leave our watchtower, we invite and encourage Satan to set on us, as was said before.

II. There is going about duty but in a lazy way, when we love and seek after carnal ease and seek out ways of doing the duty so as may be least troublesome to the flesh, as the spouse did (Cant. 3:1) when she sought her beloved on her bed.

III. There is a lying by and not stirring up ourselves to an active way of going about duty, of which the prophet complains (Isa. 54:7) when he says [that] there is none that stirs up himself to take hold of [the Lord].

IV. There is a giving way to spiritual drowsiness and upsitting in duties and in the way of God. "I sleep," said the spouse (Cant. 5:2–3), and "I have put off my coat, etc." She knew she was not right but was drowsy, and yet she did not shake it off but composed herself for it, took off her coat, and washed her feet, and so lay down to sleep.

V. There is a satisfaction and contentment with his condition, as thinking we are pretty well, at least for that time. And thus was the spouse in that forementioned place led away. She was so far from being dissatisfied with her condition that she rather expressed contentment with it.

VI. There may be such a love to such a condition and such a satisfaction in it as that they may shift everything that has a tendency to rouse them up out of that sluggish laziness, as not loving to be awakened out of their sleep. So we see the bride shifts and puts off Christ's call and invitation to her to arise and open to Him.

VII. Indeed, there is a defending of that condition as at least tolerable and none of the worst—a justifying of it or at least a pleading for themselves and excusing the matter and covering over their neglect of duty with fair pretexts, as the spouse did when she answered Christ's call with this: that she had washed her feet and might not defile them again.

VIII. Indeed, further, there is a pleading for this case by alleging an impossibility to get it helped as matters now stand. Or, at least, they will muster up insuperable-like difficulties in their own way of doing duty, as the sluggard will say that there is a lion in the way and the spouse alleged she could not put on her coat again.

IX. Indeed, it may come yet higher—even to a peremptory refusing to set about the duty. For what else can be read out of the bride's carriage than that she would not rise and open to her beloved?

X. There is also a desperate laying the duty aside as supposing it impossible to be got done. And so [there is] a resolute laying of it by as hopeless and as a business they need not trouble themselves with because they will not get through it.

XI. And hence flows an utter indisposition and unfitness for duty.

XII. Indeed, and in some it may come to this height: that the thoughts of going about any commanded duty, especially of worship, either in public or private, or their minting and attempting to set about it will fill them with terror and affrightment that they will be constrained to forbear—indeed, to lay aside all thoughts of going about any such duty.

The Causes of This

This is a very dead-like condition. What can be the causes or occasions of it?

I answer (and this is the second particular): Some or all of these things may be considered as having a hand in this:

I. No care to keep up a tender frame of heart but growing slack, loose, and careless in going about Christian duties may bring on such a distemper.

II. Slighting of challenges for omission of duties or leaving duties over the belly of conscience may make way for such an evil.

III. Giving way to carnality and formality in duties is a ready mean[s] to usher in this evil. For when the soul turns carnal or formal in the discharge of duties, duties have not that spiritual luster which they had. And the soul becomes the sooner wearied of them, as seeing no such desirableness in them nor advantage by them.

IV. When people drown themselves in cares of the world, they occasion this deadness to themselves. For then duties not only are not gone about heartily, but they are looked on as a burden, and the man becomes weary of them. And from that he comes to neglect them. And by continuing in the neglect of them, he contracts an aversion of heart for them. And then an utter unfitness and indisposition for discharging of them follows.

V. Satan has an active hand here, driving on with his crafts and wiles from one step to another.

VI. The hand also of a sovereign God is to be observed here, giving way to this, indeed, and ordering matters in His justice and wisdom so as such persons will come under such an indisposition, and that for wise and holy ends—as:

1. That by such a dispensation He may humble them who possibly were puffed up before, as thinking themselves fit enough to go about any duty, however difficult or hazardous, as Peter, who boasted so of his own strength as he thought nothing to lay down his life for Christ and to die with Him. And yet at length [he] came to that, that he could not, or durst not speak the truth to a damsel.

2. That he may punish one spiritual sin with another.

3. To give warning to all to watch and pray and to work out their salvation with fear and trembling and not to be high-minded but fear.

4. That by this, in His just and righteous judgment, He may lay a stumbling block before some to the breaking of their neck when they will, for this cause, reject and mock at all religion.

5. That He may give proof at length of His admirable skill in recovering from such a distemper, that no flesh might have ground to despair in the most dead condition they can fall into.

6. And to show, sometimes, what a sovereign dispensator of life He is and how free He is in all His favors.

How Is Christ the Life?

As to the third particular, how Christ is life in this case, we answer:

I. By keeping possession of the believer, even when he seems to be most dead, and keeping life at the root when there is neither fruit appearing nor flourish[ing] and hardly many green leaves to evidence life.

II. By blowing at the coal of grace in the soul in His own time and way and putting an end to the winter and sending the time of the singing of the birds—a springtime of life.

III. By loosing the bands with which he was held fast formerly, enlarging the heart with desires to go about the duty, so that now he willingly rises up out of his bed of security and cheerfully shakes off his drowsiness and sluggishness and former unwillingness. And now with willingness and cheerfulness he sets about the duty.

IV. By sending influences of life and strength into the soul, by which the wheels of the soul are made to run with ease, being oiled with those divine influences.

V. And this He does by touching the heart and wakening it by His Spirit—as He raised the spouse out of her bed of security and laziness by putting in His hand at the hole of the door. Then were her bowels moved for Him (Cant. 5:4). And thus He sets faith on work again, having the key of David to open the heart (Rev. 3:7).

VI. By giving a discovery of the evil of their former ways and courses, He works up the heart to godly sorrow and remorse for what is done, making their bowels move for grief and sorrow that they should so have dishonored and grieved Him.

VII. By setting the soul thus on work to do what formerly it neither could nor would do. And thus He makes the soul strong in the Lord and in the power of His might (Eph. 6:10) and able to run and not be weary and to walk and not be faint (Isaiah 40).

VIII. By discovering the great recompense of reward that is coming and the great help they have at hand in the covenant and promises of it and in Christ their head and Lord. He makes the burden light and the duty easy.

How to Make Use of Christ
Duties
As to the last particular—namely, how a believer in such a case should make use of Christ as the life that he may be delivered from [such deadness]—when the poor believer is any way sensible of this decay and earnestly desiring to be from under that power of death and in case to go about commanded duties, he should:

I. Look to Christ for enlightened eyes that he may get a more thorough discovery of the hazard and wretchedness of such a condition, that by this, being awakened and alarmed, he may more willingly use the means of recovery and be more willing to be at some pains to be delivered.

II. He should run to the blood of Jesus to get the guilt of his bygone sinful ways washed away and blotted out, to the end he may obtain the favor of God and get His reconciled face shining on him again.

III. He should eye Christ as a prince exalted to give repentance that so his sorrow for his former sinful courses may be kindly, spiritual, thorough, and affecting the heart. He would cry to Christ that He would put in his hand by the hole of the door that his bowels may become moved for Him.

IV. He should also look to Him as that good shepherd who will strengthen that which is sick (Ezek. 34:16). And take notice also of his other relations and of his obligations by it and by the covenant of redemption. And this will strengthen his hope.

V. He should lay hold on Christ as his strength by which his feet may be made like hinds' feet, and he may be made to walk on His high places (Hab. 3:19). And he would grip to that promise, "I will strengthen thee" (Isa. 41:10), and lay hold on Christ in it.

VI. Having done thus, he should set about every commanded duty in the strength of Jesus, looking to Him for help and supply from whom comes all his strength. And though he should not find that help and assistance which he expected, yet he should not be discouraged but continue and, when he can do no more, offer himself as ready and willing to go about the duty, as if he had strength.

VII. He should lie open to and be ready to receive the influences of strength which He who is the head will think good to give in His own time, manner, and measure. And this takes in these duties:

1. That they should carefully guard against the evils formerly mentioned which brought on this distemper— such as carelessness, untenderness, unwatchfulness, laziness, carnal security, formality, and want of seriousness, etc.

2. That they should beware of giving way to despondency or concluding the matter hopeless and irremediable— for that is both discouraging to the soul and a tempting provocation of God.

3. That they should be exercising the grace of patient waiting.

4. That they should be waiting in the use of the appointed means and by this, as it were, rubbing the dead and cold member before the fire till it gather warmth.

5. That they should be keeping all their sails up, waiting for the gale of the Spirit that should make their ship sail.

6. That they should be looking to Him alone who has promised that quickening Spirit and patiently waiting His leisure, not limiting Him to any definite time.

7. That they should be cherishing and stirring up any small beginnings that are.

8. That they should be welcoming most cheerfully every motion of the Spirit and improving every advantage of that kind and striking the iron when it is hot and hold the wheels of the soul a-going, when they are once put in motion. And so [they should] be loath to grieve the good and Holy Spirit of God (Eph. 4:30) or to quench His motions (1 Thess. 5:19).

If these duties were honestly minded and gone about in Him and in His strength, none can tell how soon there may be a change wrought in the soul.

Question

But if it be asked what such can do to whom the very thoughts of the duty and aiming at it is matter of terror.

Answer. It may be something, if not much, of that may flow from a bodily distemper, as occasions the alteration of the body on the thorough apprehension of anything that is weighty and of moment, so as they cannot endure to be much affected with anything. But leaving this to others, I would advise such a soul to these duties:

I. To be frequently setting to the duty, as, for example, of prayer, though that should raise the distemper of their body. For through time that may wear away or at least grow less. Whileas, their giving way to it will still make the duty the more and more terrible and so render themselves the more unfit for it. And thus they will gratify Satan, who, it may be, may have a hand in that bodily distemper too. When the poor soul is thus accustomed or habituated to the attempting of the duty, it will at length appear not so terrible as it did. And so the body may become not so soon altered by it as it was.

II. When such a one can do no more, he should keep his love to the duty and his desires after it fresh and lively and should not suffer these quite to die out.

III. He should be much in the use of frequent ejaculations and of short supplications darted up to God. For these will not make such an impression on the body and so will not so occasion the raising and wakening the bodily distemper, as more solemn addresses to God in prayer would possibly do.

IV. If he cannot go to Christ with confidence to draw out of Him life and strength according to his need, yet he may give a look to Him, though it were from afar. And he may think of Him and speak of Him frequently and would narrowly observe everything that points Him out or brings anything of Him to remembrance.

V. Such souls should not give way to despairing thoughts, as if their case were wholly helpless and hopeless. For that is a reflecting on the power and skill of Christ and therefore is provoking and dishonorable to Him.

VI. Let Christ and all that is His be precious always and lovely to them. And thus they should keep some room in their heart open for Him till He should be pleased to come to them with salvation. And who can tell how soon He may come?

But enough of this. There is a fourth case of deadness to be spoken to, and that is:

CHAPTER 24

How Will the Soul Make Use of Christ as the Life Which Is under the Prevailing Power of Unbelief and Infidelity

*T*hat we may help to give some clearing to a poor soul in this case, we will:

1. See what are the several steps and degrees of this distemper.

2. Consider what the causes of it are.

3. Show how Christ is life to a soul in such a case.

4. And give some directions how a soul in that case should make use of Christ as the life to the end it may be delivered from it.

The Steps and Degrees of This

And, first, there are many several steps to and degrees of this distemper. We will mention a few, as:

I. When they cannot come with confidence and draw out of Him by faith what their soul's case calls for. They cannot with joy draw waters out of the wells of salvation (Isa. 12:3) but keep at a distance and entertain jealous thoughts of Him. This is a degree of unbelief making way for more.

II. When they cannot confidently assert and avow their interest in Him, as the church did, saying, "Behold, God is my salvation; I will trust, and not be afraid: for the LORD JEHOVAH is my strength and my song; he also is become my salvation" (Isa. 12:2).

III. When they much question if ever they have indeed laid hold on Christ, and so cannot go to Him for the supplies of their wants and necessities.

IV. When, moreover, they question if they be allowed of God and warranted to come to Him and lay hold on Him— indeed, and they think they have many arguments by which to maintain this their unbelief and justify their keeping a-back from Christ.

V. Or, when, if they look to Him at all, it is with much mixture of faithless fears that they will not be the better, or at least doubting whether it will be to their advantage or not.

VI. This unbelief will advance further, and they may come to that, not only to conclude that they have no part or portion in Him but also to conclude that their case is desperate and irredeemable. And so [they] say there is no more hope. They are cut off for their part (as Ezek. 37:11) and so lie by as dead and forlorn.

VII. Indeed, they may come higher and vent some desperate thoughts and expressions of God to the great scandal of the godly and the dishonor of God.

VIII. And yet more, they may come at length to question all the promises and to cry out with David in his haste (Ps. 116:11) that "all men are liars."

IX. Indeed, they may come to this: to scout the whole gospel to be nothing but a heap of delusions and a cunningly devised fable or but mere notions and fancies.

X. And at length come to question if there be a God that rules in the earth.

These are dreadful degrees and steps of this horrible distemper and enough to make all flesh tremble.

The Causes of This

Let us see next from where this comes. The causes of it we may reduce to three heads:

I. The holy Lord has a holy hand in this and has noble ends and designs before Him in this matter, as:

1. The Lord may think good to order matters thus that He may magnify His power and grace in rescuing such as were returned to the very brink of hell and seemed to many to be lost and irrecoverably gone.

2. That in punishing them thus for giving way to the first motions of unbelief, He might warn all to guard against such an evil and not to foster and give way to groundless complaints nor entertain objections moved against their condition by the devil.

3. To warn all to walk circumspectly and to work out their salvation with fear and trembling, not knowing what may befall them before they die.

4. To teach all to walk humbly, not knowing what advantage Satan may get of them before all be done, and to see their daily need of Christ to strengthen their faith and to keep their grips of Him fast.

5. So the Lord may think good to dispense so with some that He may give a full proof of His wonderfully great patience and longsuffering in bearing with such, and that so long.

6. As also to demonstrate His sovereignty in measuring out His dispensations to His own as He sees will most glorify Himself.

II. Next, Satan has an active hand in this, for:

1. He raises up clouds and mists in the believer so that he cannot see the work of God within himself and so is made to cry out that he has no grace and that all was but delusions and imaginations which he looked on as grace before.

2. He raises up in them jealousies of God and of all His ways and puts a false gloss and construction on all which God does, to the end he may confirm them in their jealousies, which they have drunk in of God.

3. Having gained this ground, he works then on their corruption with very great advantage and thus drives them from evil to worse and not only to question their perfect interest in Christ but also to quit all hope for the time to come.

4. This being done, he drives the soul yet farther and fills it with prejudices against God and His glorious truths. And from this he can easily bring them to call all in question.

5. Indeed, he will represent God as an enemy to them. And when this is done, how easy it is with him to put them on desperate courses and cause them to speak wickedly and desperately of God.

6. And when this is done, he can easily darken the under-standing that the poor soul will not see the glory of the gospel and of the covenant of grace nor the luster and beauty of holiness—indeed, and raise prejudices against the same because there is no hope of partaking of the benefit of it. And so [he may] bring them on to a plain questioning of all as mere delusions.

7. And when he has gotten them brought this length, he has fair advantage to make them question if there be a God and so drive them forward to atheism. And thus deceitfully he can carry the soul from one step to another.

III. But, third, there are many sinful causes of this within the man's self, as:

1. Pride and haughtiness of mind, as thinking their mountain stands so strong that it cannot be moved. And this provokes God to hide His face (as Psalm 30).

2. Self-confidence, a concomitant of pride, supposing themselves to be so well rooted that they cannot be shaken, whereas it were better for them to walk in fear.

3. Want of watchfulness over a deceitful heart and an evil heart of unbelief that is still departing from the living God (Heb. 3:12). It is good to be jealous here.

4. Giving way to doubtings and questionings too readily at first. It is not good to tempt the Lord by parleying too much and too readily with Satan. Eve's practice might be a warning sufficient to us.

5. Not living in the sight of their wants and of their daily necessity of Christ nor acting faith on Him daily for the supplying of their wants. And when faith is not

used, it may contract rust and be weakened and come at length not to be discerned.

6. Entertaining of jealous thoughts of God and hearkening too readily to anything that may foster and increase or confirm these.

7. Not delighting themselves in and with pleasure dwelling on the thoughts of Christ, of His offices, of the gospel and promises—so that these come at length to lose their beauty and glory in the soul and have not the luster that once they had. And this does open a door to much mischief.

8. In a word, not walking with God according to the gospel, provoking the Lord to give them up to themselves for a time.

How Is Christ the Life?

We come now to the third particular, which is to show how Christ is life to the poor soul in this case. And for the clearing of this, consider:

I. That Christ is "the author and finisher of our faith" (Heb. 12:2). And so, as He did rebuke unbelief at the first, He can rebuke it again.

II. That He is the great prophet clearing up the gospel and everything that is necessary for us to know, bringing life and immortality to light by the gospel (2 Tim. 1:10) and so manifesting the luster and beauty of the gospel.

III. He brings the promises home to the soul in their reality, excellency, and truth, being the faithful witness and the amen (Rev. 3:14) and the confirmer of the promises, so that they are all yea and amen in Him (2 Cor. 1:20). And this serves to establish the soul in the faith and to shoot out thoughts of unbelief.

IV. So does He by His Spirit dispel the mists and clouds which Satan through unbelief had raised in the soul.

V. And by this [He] also rebukes those mistakes of God and prejudices at Him and His ways, which Satan has wrought there through corruption.

VI. He discovers Himself to be a ready help in time of trouble and the hope and anchor of salvation (Heb. 6:19) and a priest living forever to make intercession for poor sinners (7:25).

VII. And by this He clears up to the poor soul a possibility of help and relief and thus rebukes despair or prevents it.

VIII. He manifests Himself to be the marrow and substance of the gospel. And this makes every line of it pleasant and beautiful to the soul and so frees them from the prejudices that they had at it.

IX. So in manifesting Himself in the gospel, He reveals the Father that the soul comes to "the knowledge of the glory of God in the face of Jesus Christ" (2 Cor. 4:6). And this saves the soul from atheism.

X. When the soul cannot grip Him nor look to Him, yet He can look to the soul and by His love quicken and revive the soul and warm the heart with love to Him and at length move and incline it sweetly to open to Him and thus grip and hold fast a lost sheep, indeed, and bring it home again.

How to Make Use of Christ

But what should a soul do in such a case? To this (which is the fourth particular to be spoken to), I answer:

I. That they should strive against those evils formerly mentioned, which procured or occasioned this distemper. A stop should be put to those malignant humors.

II. They should be careful to lay again the foundation of solid knowledge of God and of His glorious truths revealed in the gospel and labor for the faith of God's truth and veracity—for till this be, nothing can be right in the soul.

III. They should be thoroughly convinced of the treachery, deceitfulness, and wickedness of their hearts that they may see it is not worthy to be trusted and that they may be jealous of it and not hearken so readily to it as they have done, especially seeing Satan can prompt it to speak for his advantage.

IV. They should remember also that it is divine help that can recover them and cause them [to] grip to the promises and lay hold on them of new again as well as at first, and that of themselves they can do nothing.

V. In using of the means for the recovery of life, they should eye Christ. And because this eyeing of Christ is faith, and their disease lies most there, they should do as the Israelites did who were stung in the eye with the serpents—they looked to the brazen serpent with the wounded and stung eye. So should they do with a sickly and almost dead faith grip Him and with an eye almost put out and made blind look to Him, knowing how ready He is to help and what a tender heart He has.

VI. And to confirm them in this resolution, they should take a new view of all the notable encouragements to believe with which the whole gospel abounds.

VII. And in addition fix on Him as the only author and finisher of [the] faith.

VIII. And, in a word, they should cast a wonderfully unbelieving and atheistical soul on Him who is wonderful in counsel and excellent in working and is wonderful in mercy and grace and in all His ways. And thus may He at length in His own time and in the way that will most glorify Himself raise up that poor soul out of the grave of infidelity in which it was stinking and so prove Himself to be indeed the resurrection and the life, to the praise of the glory of His grace.

We come now to speak to another case, which is:

CHAPTER 25

How Christ Is Made Use of as the Life by One That Is So Dead and Senseless as He Cannot Know What to Judge of Himself or His Own Case, Except What Is Naught

We spoke something to this very case on the matter when we spoke of Christ as the truth. Yet we will speak a little to it here but will not enlarge particulars formerly mentioned. And therefore we will speak a little to these five particulars, and so:

1. Show what this distemper is.
2. Show from where it proceeds, and how the soul comes to fall into it.
3. Show how Christ as the life brings about a recovery of it.
4. Show how the soul is to be exercised that it may obtain a recovery.
5. And answer some questions or objections.

What This Is

As to the first, believers many times may be so dead as not only not to see and know that they have an interest in Christ and to be uncertain what to judge of themselves but also be so carried away with prejudices and mistakes as that they will judge no otherwise of themselves than that their case is naught. Indeed, and [they] not only will deny or miscall the good that God has wrought in them by His Spirit but also reason themselves to be out of the state of grace and a stranger to faith and to the workings of the Spirit. And on this [they] will come to call all delusions which sometime[s] they had felt and seen in themselves, which is a sad distemper, and which grace in life would free the soul from.

From Where It Comes

This proceeds (which is the second particular) partly from God hiding of His face and changing His dispensations about them and compassing them with clouds, and partly from themselves and their own mistakes, as:

I. Judging their state not by the unchangeable rule of truth but by the outward dispensations of God, which change on the best.

II. Judging their state by the observable measure of grace within them and so concluding their state bad because they observe corruption prevailing now and then and grace decaying, and they perceive no victory over temptations nor growth in grace, etc.

III. Judging also their state by others. And so they suppose that they cannot be believers because they are so unlike to others whom they judge true believers. This is also to judge by a wrong rule.

IV. Judging themselves by themselves—that is, because they look so unlike to what sometimes they were themselves, they conclude that their state cannot be good, which is also a wrong rule to judge their state by.

V. Beginning to try and examine their case and state and coming to no close or issue, so that when they have done, they are as unclear and uncertain what to judge of themselves as when they began.

VI. Or taking little or no pains to try themselves seriously as in the sight of God, but resting satisfied with a superficial trial, which can come to no good issue.

VII. Trying and examining, but through the sleight of Satan, and, because pitching on wrong marks, coming to no good issue but condemning themselves without ground.

VIII. There is another thing which occasions this misjudging— namely, the want of distinctness and clearness in covenanting with Christ and the ignorance of the nature of true saving faith.

How Christ Is the Life
As to the third particular, how Christ is life to the believer in this case, I answer [that] Christ manifests Himself to be life to the soul in this case (1) by sending the Spirit of life that enlightens, informs, persuades, and seals; (2) by actuating grace so in the soul that it manifests itself and evidences itself to be there—as the heat and burning of a fire will discover itself without other tokens.

How to Make Use of Christ
The fourth particular—namely, how the soul should be exercised or how it should employ Christ for an outgate from this—has been abundantly cleared above, where we showed that believers in this case should:

1. Be frequent in gripping Christ and closing with Him as their all-sufficient mediator. And faith thus frequently acting on Him may discover itself at length.

2. Look to Christ that has eye salve and is given for a witness.

3. Keep grips fast of Him, though they be in the dark, and walk on gripping to Him.

4. Keep love toward Him and His working and in exercise.

5. Beg of Him to clear up their state, by His Spirit explaining the true marks of grace and discovering the working of grace in the soul.

Objections

I. But it will be said—and so I come to the last particular—"What, if after all this, I remain as formerly as unable to judge aright of my state as ever?"

Answer. Yet you should continue gripping Christ, loving Him, looking to Him, casting a lost, dead soul with all your wants on Him, and mind this as your constant work. Indeed, you should labor to be growing in these direct acts of faith and learn to submit to God in it, knowing that those reflect acts are not absolutely necessary and that you should think it much if He bring you to heaven at length, though covered with a cloud all your days.

II. But others get much more clearness.

Answer. I grant that. Yet know that everyone gets not clearness, and such as have it, have it not in the same measure. And must God give you as much as He gives to another? What if you could not make that use of it that others do but wax proud by it and forget yourself? Therefore, it will be best to give God liberty to dispense His favors as He will, and that you be about your commanded duty, the exercise of faith, love, fear, patience, etc.

III. But if at any time I got a sight of my case, it would be some peace and satisfaction to me.

Answer: I grant that. And what know you but you may also get that favor before you die. Why then will you not wait His leisure?

IV. But the want of it in the meantime makes me go heartlessly and discouragedly about commanded duties and makes that I cannot apply things distinctly to myself.

Answer: Yet the word of command is the same; the offer is the same; and the encouragement is the same. Why then should you not be going on, leaning to Christ in the wilderness, even though you want that comfortable sight?

V. But it is one thing to want a clear sight of my state. It is another thing to judge myself to be yet in the state of nature. And this is my case.

Answer: I grant [that] this is the wors[e] of the two. Yet, what if you misjudge yourself without ground. Should you not suffer for your own folly, and whom can you blame but yourself? And if you judge so, you cannot but know that it is your duty to do the thing that you suppose is not yet done—that is, run away to Christ for life and salvation and rest on Him and abide there. And if this were frequently renewed, the grounds of your former mistake might be easily removed.

Yet further, I would add these few things:

1. Take no pleasure in debating against your own soul, for that is but to serve Satan's design.

2. Be not too rash or ready to drink in prejudices against the work of God in your own souls, for that is to conclude with Satan against yourselves.

3. Make much of any little light He is pleased to give, were it but of one mark, and be not ill to please. For one scriptural mark, as love to the brethren, may sufficiently evidence the thing.

4. See how your soul would like the condition of such as are carnal, profane, careless in the matters of God. And if your soul does really abhor that, and you would not on any account choose to be in such a case, you may gather something from that to your comfort. But enough of this case here.

CHAPTER 26

How Is Christ as the Life to Be Applied by a Soul That Misses God's Favor and Countenance

The sixth case that we will speak a little to is a deadness occasioned by the Lord hiding of Himself, who is their life and "the fountain of life" (Ps. 36:9) and whose "loving-kindness is better than life" (63:3) and in whose favor is their life (30:5)—a case which the frequent complaints of the saints manifest to be rife enough, concerning which we will:

1. Show some of the consequences of the Lord hiding His face, by which the soul's case will appear.

2. Show the reasons of this dispensation.

3. Show how Christ is life to the soul in this case.

4. And point out the soul's duty, or how he is to make use of Christ for a recovery.

The Consequences of God Hiding His Face

As to the first, we may take notice of these particulars:

I. They complain of God hiding of Himself and forsaking them: "My God, my God, why hast thou forsaken me?" (Ps. 22:1) and, "How long wilt thou forsake me?" (13:1).

II. They cry out for a blink of His face and get it not, for He has withdrawn Himself (Ps. 13:1): "How long wilt thou hide thy face from me?" Heman (Psalm 88) cried out night and day, but yet God's face was hid (vv. 1, 9, 14). The spouse seeks long (Canticles 5; see Ps. 22:1–2).

III. They are looking for an outgate but get none. And "hope deferred" makes their "heart sick" (Prov. 13:12).

IV. They are in the dark and cannot tell why the Lord dispenses so toward them. "Why," said Heman (Ps. 88:14), "castest thou off my soul? why hidest thou thy face from me?" They cannot understand wherefore it is. So Job cried out, "Shew me wherefore thou contendest with me?" (10:2).

V. They may also be walking in the meanwhile without light or counsel, so as they will not know what to do. "How long shall I take counsel in my soul?" (Ps. 13:2).

VI. Moreover, they may have their heart filled with sorrow, as we see (Ps. 13:2). "Having sorrow in my heart," said David. He also says that his sorrow was continually before him (38:17) and, "I found trouble and sorrow" (116:3).

VII. They may be so, as the sweet experience of others may yield them no supply of comfort at present (Ps. 22:4–6). "Our fathers trusted in thee," said David, "and thou didst deliver them. They cried unto thee, and were delivered; they trusted in thee, and were not confounded." But that gave him no present ease or comfort, for immediately he adds, "But I am a worm, and no man; a reproach of men, etc." (v. 6).

VIII. Indeed, all their own former experiences may yield them little solace, as we see in the same place (Ps. 22:9–10; cf. vv. 14–15): "Thou art he," says he (v. 9), "that took me out of the womb, etc." And yet he complains (v. 14) that he was "poured out like water," and his bones out of joint, that his heart was melted in the midst of his bowels, etc.

IX. They may be brought near to a giving over all in despondency and be brought, in their sense, to the very dust of death (Ps. 22:15).

The Reasons for This

If it be inquired, Why the Lord dispenses so with His own people? We answer—and this is the second particular—that He does it for holy and wise reasons, of which we may name a few, as:

1. To punish their carelessness and negligence, as we see He did with the spouse (Canticles 5).

2. To chastise them for their ill-improving of His favor and kindness when they had it, as the same passage evidences.

3. To check them for their security and carnal confidence, as He did David (Ps. 30:6–7) when he said his mountain stood strong and he should never be moved. Then did the Lord hide His face, and he was troubled.

4. To try if their obedience to His commands be pure and conscientious and not in a sort mercenary, because of His lifting up on them the light of His countenance. And to see if conscience to a command drives them to duty when they are in the dark and have no encouragement.

5. To put the graces of the Spirit to trial and to exercise— as their faith, patience, hope, love, etc. (Ps. 13:5–6, 22, 24).

6. To awaken them from their security and to set them to a more diligent following of duty, as we see in the spouse (Canticles 5).

7. To sharpen their desire and hunger after Him, as this instance clears.

How Christ Is the Life

Even in such a case as this, Christ is life to the soul, which is the third particular:

1. By taking away the sinful causes of such a distance, having laid down His life and shed His blood for the remission of their sins so that such a dispensation is not flowing from pure wrath but is rather an act of mercy and love.

2. By advocating the poor man's cause in heaven, where He is making intercession for His own and by this obtaining a delivery from that condition in God's own time, even the shining again of His countenance on them.

3. By keeping life in, as to habitual grace, and by breathing on it so that it becomes lively and operative even in such a winter day.

4. By supporting the soul under that dispensation and keeping it from fainting through the secret influences of grace, which He conveys into the soul—as He did to the poor woman of Canaan (Matthew 15).

5. By setting the soul a-work to use such means as God has appointed for a recovery, as to cry, to plead, to long, to wait, etc. "Their heart shall live that seek him."

6. By teaching the soul to submit to and acquiesce in what God does, acknowledging His righteousness,

greatness, and sovereignty. And this quietness of heart is its life.

7. By keeping the heart fast to the covenant of grace so that, whatever come, they will never quit that bargain, but they will trust in Him though He should kill them. And they will adhere to the covenant of grace, though they should be dragged through hell.

8. At length when He sees it fit and convenient, He quickens by drawing back the veil and filling the soul with joy in the light of God's countenance and causing it to sing, as having the heart lifted up in the ways of the Lord.

The Duties of the Soul

As to the last particular, concerning the duty of a soul in such a case, we say:

I. He should humble himself under this dispensation, knowing that it is the great God with whom he has to do, and that there is no contending with Him, and that all flesh should stoop before Him.

II. He should justify God in all that He does and say with David, "But thou art holy, O thou that inhabitest the praises of Israel" (Ps. 22:3).

III. He should look on himself as unworthy of the least of that kind. "I am a worm," said David (Ps. 22:6), "and no man."

IV. He should search out his provocations and run away to the fountain, the blood of Christ, that these may be purged away and his conscience sprinkled from dead works and his soul washed in the fountain opened to the house of David for sin and for uncleanness.

V. He must also employ Christ to discover to him more and more of his guiltiness by which he has grieved the Spirit of God. And as sins are discovered to him, he would repent of them and run away with them to the blood that cleanses from all sin. This was Elihu's advice to Job: "Surely it is meet to be said unto God, I have borne chastisement, I will not offend any more: that which I see not teach thou me: if I have done iniquity, I will do no more" (34:31–32).

VI. He should grip to Christ in the covenant and rest there with joy and satisfaction. He should hold that fast that he may ride out the storm in a dark night. "Though he make not mine house to grow," said David (2 Sam. 23:5), yet this was all his salvation and all his desire: that He had made with him "an everlasting covenant, ordered in all things, and sure." The spouse took this course when she could not get a sight of him whom her soul loved (Cant. 6:3) and asserted her interest in him: "I am my beloved's, and my beloved is mine."

VII. He should be entertaining high and loving thoughts of God, commending Him highly, let His dispensations be what they will. So did the spouse (Cant. 5:10, 16).

VIII. He should earnestly seek after Him. The spouse did so (Cant. 5:6). The discouragement she met with at the hands of the watchmen did not put her off her pursuit (v. 7), but she continued, indeed, was "sick of love" (v. 8). And her looks had a prevailing power with him, as we see (6:5), where the bridegroom uttered that most astonishing word: "Turn away thine eyes from me, for they have overcome me."

IX. This new manifestation which he is seeking for must be expected in and through Christ, who is the true tabernacle and He who was represented by the mercy seat. He is the only trusting place. In Him alone will the Father be seen.

X. He should also look to Him for strength and support in the meantime, and for grace that he may be kept from fainting and may be helped to wait till He come, who knows the fittest season in which to appear.

Questions

But it will be said: What if, after all this, we get no outgate, but He hides His face still from us? I answer:

I. Such should know that life is one thing, and comfort is another thing. Grace is one thing, and warm blinks of God's face is another. The one is necessary to the very being of a Christian; the other, not, but only necessary to his comfortable being. And therefore they should be content if God give them grace, though they miss comfort for a time.

II. They should learn to commit that matter to Christ who knows how to give that which is good and best for them.

III. They should be hanging on Him for strength and for duty and in His strength setting about every commanded duty and be exercising faith, love, patience, hope, desire, etc.

IV. Let the well-ordered covenant be all their salvation and all their desire. And though they should not get a comfortable blink of God's face so long as they were here, yet holding fast this covenant, they should at length be saved souls—and what would they have more? And when they get this, what will they miss?

How Will One Make Use of Christ as the Life When Wrestling with an Angry God because of Sin

That we may give some satisfaction to this question, we will:

1. Show what are the ingredients in this case, or what uses to concur in this distemper.

2. Show some reasons why the Lord is pleased to dispense thus with His people.

3. Show how Christ is life to the soul in this case.

4. Show the believer's duty for a recovery.

5. And add a word or two of caution.

The Ingredients of This

As to the first, there may be these parts of or ingredients in this distemper:

I. God's presenting their sins to their view, so as they will cry out, "Our sin is ever before us" (Ps. 51:3), and say, as it is, "Thou hast set our iniquities before thee, our secret sins in the light of thy countenance" (90:8). And so [this will] cause them [to] see the Lord contending for sin, as the church did (Isaiah 59): We roar all like bears and mourn sore like doves. We look for judgment but there is none, for salvation but it is far off from us; for our transgressions are multiplied before Thee, and our sins testify against us; for our transgressions are with us. And as for our iniquities, we know them, etc.

II. Indeed, God may bring on them the iniquities of their youth, as Job speaks (13:26), and so bring on them or suffer conscience to charge them with their old sins formerly repented of and pardoned. And this is more terrible. David is made to remember his original sin (Psalm 51).

III. And, as Job speaks (15:17), God may seem to be sealing up all their sins in a bag that none of them may be lost or fall by without being taken notice of. And [He may], as it were, be gathering them together in a heap.

IV. He may pursue sore with signs of wrath and displeasure because of those sins, as we see in David (Psalms 4; 38:51) and in several others of His people, chastened of the Lord because of their transgressions—of which there are many instances in Scripture.

V. Indeed, and that for a considerable time together, and cause them [to] cry out with David, "But thou, O Lord, how long!" (Ps. 6:3).

VI. And that not only with outward but also with inward plagues and strokes, as David's case clears in the forecited psalms.

VII. Indeed, and not even themselves but even their posterity, as David's child was smitten with death, and the posterity of Manasses, who found mercy himself (2 Chron. 33:13), was carried into captivity for his sin (2 Kings 23:26–27).

VIII. Further, the Lord may deprive them of all their former joy and comfort, which made David cry out, "Restore unto me the joy of thy salvation; and uphold me with thy free Spirit" (Ps. 51:12).

IX. And, which is yet more terrible, write their sin on their judgment, as when He caused the sword and whoredom [to] follow David's house.

X. And, finally, He may cause them [to] fear utter off-casting (as Ps. 51:11): "Cast me not away," said he, "from thy presence."

The Reasons for This
And this the Lord thinks good to do (that we may speak a word to the second particular) for these and the like reasons:

1. To discover to them and to all the world how just, holy, and righteous a God He is that cannot approve of or bear with sin, even in His own children.

2. To make all fear and tremble before this great and holy God, who is terrible in His judgments, even when they come from a Father's hand that is not pursuing in pure anger and wrath but chastening in love. Sure[ly] all must think that His dispensations with the wicked will be much more fearful and horrible, seeing they are not yet reconciled to Him through the blood of Jesus.

3. To press believers more earnestly into Christ that they may get a new extract of their pardon and their souls washed in the blood of Jesus.

4. To teach them to walk more circumspectly afterward and to guard more watchfully against Satan's temptations and to employ Christ more as their strength, light, and guide.

5. To cause them [to] see their great obligation to Jesus Christ for delivering them from that state of wrath in which they were by nature, as well as others, and would have lain in to all eternity, had He not redeemed them.

6. To exercise their faith, patience, and hope to see if in hope they will believe against hope and lay hold on the strength of the Lord, that they make peace with Him (Isa. 27:5).

7. To give a fresh proof of His wonderful mercy, grace, love, and compassion, upholding the soul in the meantime and at length pardoning them and speaking peace to their souls through the blood of Jesus.

How Christ Is the Life

But as to the third particular, we may look on Christ as the life to the soul in this case on these accounts:

I. He has satisfied justice and so has borne the pure wrath of God due for their sins. He hath trodden the wine press alone (Isa. 63:5). He was wounded for our transgressions and bruised for our sins (53:5, 10). And therefore they drink not of this cup which would make them drunk and to stagger and fall and never rise again.

II. Indeed, He has procured that mercy and love will accompany all those sharp dispensations and that they will flow from mercy—indeed, and that they will be as a covenanted blessing promised in the covenant (Ps. 89:30, etc.).

III. And sometimes He is pleased to let them see this clear difference between the strokes they lie under and the judgments of pure wrath which attend the wicked. And this supports the soul, for then he sees that those dispensations, however sharp they be, will work together for good to him and come from the hand of a gracious, loving Father, reconciled in the blood of Christ.

IV. He is a prince, exalted to give repentance and remission of sins to Israel (Acts 5:31). Indeed, He has procured such a clause in the covenant, which is well ordered in all things and sure, that on their renewing of faith and repentance, their after sins will be pardoned. And besides the promises of faith and repentance in the covenant, His being a prince exalted to give both gives assurance of their receiving of both.

V. He clears to them their interest in the covenant and their right to the promises of the covenant. And through them closing with Christ by faith, He raises up their heart in hope and causes them to expect an outgate, even remission of their sins and turning away the displeasure in due time through Him. And this is a great part of their life.

VI. Being the author and finisher of faith and a prince to give repentance, He by His Spirit, works up the soul to a renewing of its grips of Himself by faith and to a running to the death and blood of Christ for pardon and washing. And [this] works godly sorrow in the heart, on which follows pardon, according to the gospel constitution, though the believer as yet perceives it not. And sin being pardoned before God, conform[ing] to the tenor of the covenant of grace, the man is a living man, whatever fears of death he may be kept under for a time.

VII. He helps also to a justifying of God and to a holy, submissive frame of spirit under that dispensation. So that they are willing to bear the indignation of the Lord because they have sinned against Him (Mic. 7:9) and to wait for an outgate in God's own time and to kiss the rod and to accept of the punishment of their sin.

VIII. When He sees it fit for His own glory and their advantage, He speaks peace at length to the soul and says, "Son (or daughter), be of good cheer. Your sins are forgiven you." And then is the soul restored to life.

The Duties of the Soul

As to the fourth particular, the soul that is wrestling with an angry God for sin and would make use of Christ as the life should do these things:

I. He should look to Christ as standing under God's curse in our room and as satisfying justice for all the elect and for all their sins.

II. He should eye the covenant in which new pardon is promised upon the renewing of faith and repentance.

III. He should eye Christ as the great Lord dispensator of both faith and repentance and hang on Him for both and thus believe that he may believe and repent or lay his soul open to Him that He may work in him both repentance and faith.

IV. He should flee to the blood of sprinkling that speaks better things than the blood of Abel, that he may be washed and sprinkled with hyssop, as David did (Ps. 51:7).

V. He should eye Christ as a prince to give pardon and remission of sins and as exalted for this end and should fix his eye on Him as now exalted in glory for this end.

VI. He should close with Christ of new as his only all-sufficient mediator. And having done this and repented of his sins by which God has been provoked, he should conclude through faith that a pardon is passed in the court of heaven, conform[ing] to the tenor of the gospel, and wait on Christ until the intimation come.

Cautions
As for the cautions which I promised to speak to, in the last place, take these few:

I. Do not conclude there is no pardon because there is no intimation of it made to your soul as yet. According to the dispensation of grace condescended on in the gospel, pardon is had immediately upon a soul's believing and repenting. But the intimation, sense, and feeling of pardon is a distinct thing and may, for several ends, be long kept up from the soul. Sure[ly] they go not always together.

II. Do not conclude there is no pardon because the rod that was inflicted for sin is not as yet taken off. God pardoned David's sin and did intimate the same to him by Nathan, and yet the sword did not depart from his house till he died. God can forgive and yet take vengeance on their inventions (Ps. 99:8).

III. Do not on this ground question God's faithfulness or conclude that God's covenant does not stand fast. He is the same, and the covenant abides fast and firm. But the change is in you.

IV. Do not think that because you have once received Christ that, therefore, without any new act of faith on Him or of repentance toward God, you should immediately be pardoned of your sins as soon as they are committed. For the gospel method must be followed, and it should satisfy us.

CHAPTER 28

No Man Comes to the Father but by Me

*T*his being added for further confirmation of what was formerly said will point out to us several necessary truths, as:

I. That it is most necessary to be sound and clear in this fundamental point of coming to God only in and through Christ, for:

1. It is the whole marrow of the gospel.

2. It is the hinge of our salvation. Christ is the chief cornerstone (Isa. 38:16; 1 Peter 1:5–6).

3. [And He is] the only ground of all our solid and true peace and comfort.

4. An error or a mistake here is most dangerous, hazarding, if not ruining all.

5. Satan endeavors mainly against this, raises up heresies, errors, and false opinions, and prompts some to vent perplexing doubts and objections—and all to darken this cardinal point. So does he muster up all his temptations for this end: at length to keep poor souls from acquaintance with this way and from making use of it or entering into it.

6. Our corrupt hearts are most averse from it and will close with any way, however troublesome, however expensive and costly it may seem to be, rather than with this.

7. There are a multitude of false ways, as we did show above.

All which do clear up this necessity and should teach us to be very diligent to win to acquaintance with it and to make sure that we are in it and to hold it fast and to keep it pure in our practice, without mixing anything with it or corrupting of it.

II. That it is no small difficulty to get this truth believed and practiced that through Christ alone we come to the Father. Therefore is the same thing asserted and inculcated again on the same matter, for:

1. Nature will not teach this way. It is far above nature.

2. Indeed, our natural inclinations are much against it, opposing it, and fighting against it.

3. This way is altogether contrary to that high esteem which naturally all of us have of ourselves.

4. And [it] is opposite to that pride of heart which naturally we are subject to.

5. Indeed, there is nothing in us by nature that will willingly comply with this way, but, on the contrary, all is opposite to it.

6. And therefore it is the Christian's first lesson to deny himself.

The consideration of which should humble us and make us very jealous of our own hearts and inclinations and of all those courses which they are inclinable to and bent on. And it should put us to try if ever we have overcome this difficulty and have now all our hopes and comforts founded on Him and on nothing else and are up and down in our peace and joy according as we win in to Him or are shut out from Him. And in all our approaches to God, on whatever account, [whether we] are leaning to Him and resting on Him alone, expecting access, acceptance, and a hearing only in Him, and are quieted under all our fears and temptations with this: that Christ is our way to the Father.

III. That even believers have need to have this truth inculcated often, for:

1. Satan is busy pulling them off this ground by all the wiles and temptations he can.

2. Their own corruption within and the evil heart of unbelief is always opposing this way and drawing them off it.

3. Through the sleight of Satan and the power of corruption, they are oftentimes declining from this pure gospel way.

4. The experience of believers can tell that, when they are at their best, it is a great work and exercise to them to keep their hearts right in this matter.

5. Is it not too often seen that they are the spiritual plague of formality, which steals them off their feet here?

6. And is it not found oftentimes that they are too ready to lean to something beside[s] Christ?

How ought all to be convinced of this and humbled under the sense of it! And see also how necessary it is to be often preaching on this subject and to be often thinking on and studying this fundamental truth.

IV. It should be a strong motive and incitement to us to make use of Christ as the way to the Father, that no man comes to the Father but by Him. For this may be looked on as an argument enforcing their use-making of Him as the way.

V. It discovers the ground of that truth that there are but few that are saved, for none comes to the Father but by Him. Few, in respect of the whole world, once hear of Him. And of such as hear of Him, few have the true way of employing and applying Him as the way to the Father clears up to them. And again, of such as have the truth, as it is in Jesus preached to them, oh how few go to Him and make use of Him according to the truth and believe and practice the truth!

VI. That in and through Christ alone we must come:

1. To the knowledge of the Father—"for no man knoweth the Father but the Son." And He alone who came out of the bosom of the Father reveals Him.

2. To the favor and friendship of the Father, for He alone is our peace, and in Him alone is the Father well pleased.

3. To the kingdom of the Father here, for here only is the door (John 10), and by His Spirit are we effectually called.

4. To the kingdom of the Father above, for He alone has opened that door and is entered into the holiest of all as our forerunner and is gone to prepare a place for us.

5. Through Him alone must we address ourselves to the Father in our supplications (John 16:23; Rev. 8:3), in our thanksgiving (Rom. 1:8; Col. 3:17), and praise (Eph. 3:21; Heb. 13:15).

6. Through Him alone have we access and an open door to the Father (Eph. 2:18; 3:21; Heb. 4:16).

I will only speak to one case here; namely:

CHAPTER 29

How Should We Make Use of Christ in Going to the Father in Prayer and Other Acts of Worship

*I*n short, for answering of this question, I will lay down these particulars:

I. There should be a lively sense of the infinite distance that is between the great God and us finite creatures, and yet more between the Holy Ghost and us sinful wretches.

II. There should be an eyeing of Christ as the great peacemaker, through His death and merits having satisfied justice and reconciled sinners to God, that so we may look on God now no more as an enemy but as reconciled in Jesus.

III. There should be, sometimes at least, a more formal and explicit actual closing with Christ as ours, when we are going about such duties, and always an implicit and virtual embracing of Him as our mediator or a habitual hanging on Him and leaning to Him as our mediator and peacemaker.

IV. There should be an eyeing of Him as our Great High Priest now living forever to make intercession for us and to keep the door of heaven open to us—on which account the apostle presses the Hebrews to come boldly to the throne of grace (Heb. 4:14, 16; see also 5:24–25).

V. There should be a gripping to Him even in reference to that particular act of worship and a laying hold on Him, to speak so, as our master usher to bring us by the hand into the Father, conscious of our own unworthiness.

VI. There should be a confident leaning to Him in our approaching, and so we should approach Him without fear and diffidence—and that despite that we find not our souls in such a good frame as we would wish, indeed, and guilt looking us in the face.

VII. Thus should we roll all the difficulties that come in our way and all the discouragements which we meet with on Him [so] that He may take away the one and the other and help us over the one and the other.

VIII. As we should take an answer to all objections from Him alone and put Him to remove all scruples and difficulties and strengthen ourselves against all impediments and discouragements alone in and through Him, so there should be the bringing of all our positive encouragements from Him alone and all our hopes of coming speed with the Father should be grounded on Him.

IX. We should expect all our welcome and acceptance with the Father only in and through Christ and expect nothing for anything in ourselves nor for our graces, good frame, preparation, or anything of that kind. So we should not found our acceptance nor our peace and satisfaction on ourselves nor on anything we have or do. Nor should we conclude our exclusion or want of acceptance because we do not apprehend our frame so good as it ought to be. So we should not found our acceptance on our right performance of duties, for that is not Christ.

X. We should quiet ourselves on Him alone in all our approaches, whatever liveliness we find or miss in duty. We are too much tickled and fain when duties go well with us and troubled on the other hand when it is not so. And the ground of all this is because we lean too much to our own duties and do not quiet ourselves on Him alone. And hence it is that we are often quieted when we get the duty done and put by, though we have not met with Him there nor gotten use made of Him as was necessary. All our comfort, peace, and quiet should be founded on Him alone.

XI. We should look to Him for the removal of all the discouragements that Satan casts in our way while we are about this or that piece of worship to put us back or cause us to advance slowly and faintingly. And casting them all on Him, [we should] go forward in our duty.

XII. We should look for all our returns and answers only in and through Him and lay all the weight of our hopes and expectations of a good answer only on Him (1 John 5:13–15).

Cautions
For caution I would add a word or two:

I. I do not think that the believer can explicitly and distinctly act all these things whenever he is going to God or can distinctly perceive all these several acts. Nor have I specified and particularly mentioned them thus for this end but to show at some length how Christ is to be employed in those acts of worship which we are called to perform, and that because we oftentimes think the simple naming of Him and asking of things for His sake is sufficient, though our hearts lean more to some other thing than to Him. And the conscientious

Christian will find his soul when he is rightly going about the duties of worship looking toward Christ thus, sometimes more distinctly and explicitly as to one particular, and sometimes more as to another.

II. Though the believer cannot distinctly act faith on Christ all these ways when he is going about commanded duties of worship, yet he should be sure to have his heart going out after Christ as the only ground of him approaching to and acceptance with and of being heard by the Father. And [he should strive] to have his heart in such a habitual frame of resting on Christ that really there may be a relying on Him all these ways, though not distinctly discerned.

III. Sometimes the believer will be called to be more distinct and explicit in looking to and resting on Christ, as to one particular, and sometimes more as to another. When Satan is dissuading him to go to God because He is an infinitely holy one, and he himself is but a sinner, then he is called to act faith on Christ as the mediator, making reconciliation between God and sinners. And when Satan is dissuading from approaching to God because of their want of an interest in God, then should they act faith on Christ and embrace Him according to the gospel and rest there and so approach. And when Satan casts up his unworthiness and former sins to keep him a-back or to discourage him, then he is called to lay hold on Christ as the Great High Priest and advocate and, casting that discouragement on Him, to go forward. So likewise, when Satan is discouraging him in his duty by bringing before him his sins, he should take this course. And when because of his sinful way of worshipping God and calling on Him and other things he is made to fear that all is in vain and that neither God regards him nor his services, and that he will not come speed—then should he cast all the burden of his acceptance and of obtaining what he asks and desires on Christ and quiet himself there, and so as to the rest. And hence appears the usefulness of our branching out of this matter.

IV. In all this, there must be an acting in the strength of Jesus, a looking to Christ and resting on Christ, according to the present case and necessity in Christ—that is, by His strength and grace communicated to us by His Spirit. Then do we worship God in the Spirit and in the newness of the Spirit when all is done, in the matter of worship, in and through Jesus.

THE END